Foreign Aid in South Asia, edited by one of South Asia's most distinguished economists, Saman Kelegama, brings together a number of scholars from across the region to explore the state of the aid debate as it applies to the region. The volume highlights the country/context specific role of aid, differentiating between countries such as Pakistan and Afghanistan where aid is increasingly linked to security concerns, with those relating to its role in post-conflict economies such as Sri Lanka and Nepal. These problem-driven dynamics are then compared to the contrasting role of aid in an emerging economy of the size of India with its role changing from an aid recipient to a donor, and least developed countries such as Bangladesh, Bhutan and Maldives experiencing a transformation in aid receipts. The work is informative and analytical which should be of service to academic researchers and policymakers in South Asia as well as for aid donors to the region. The volume should also be of interest to general readers who have been, for years, exposed to debates on the political economy of aid. They would be particularly benefitted by Saman Kelegama's excellent overview of the discussion which provides a succinct update on the evolution of South Asia, from being highly dependent on aid, and being seen as the poster region for aid donors, to a stage of development where migrant remittances far exceed aid as a source of external financing.

Rehman Sobhan
Chairman, Centre for Policy Dialogue
Dhaka, Bangladesh

Foreign Aid in South Asia

Thank you for choosing a SAGE product! If you have any comment, observation or feedback, I would like to personally hear from you. Please write to me at <u>contactceo@sagepub.in</u>

—Vivek Mehra, Managing Director and CEO,
SAGE Publications India Pvt Ltd, New Delhi

Bulk Sales

SAGE India offers special discounts for purchase of books in bulk. We also make available special imprints and excerpts from our books on demand.

For orders and enquiries, write to us at

Marketing Department
SAGE Publications India Pvt Ltd
B1/I-1, Mohan Cooperative Industrial Area
Mathura Road, Post Bag 7
New Delhi 110044, India
E-mail us at <u>marketing@sagepub.in</u>

Get to know more about SAGE, be invited to SAGE events, get on our mailing list. Write today to <u>marketing@sagepub.in</u>

This book is also available as an e-book.

Foreign Aid in South Asia

The Emerging Scenario

Edited by
Saman Kelegama

⑤SAGE www.sagepublications.com
Los Angeles • London • New Delhi • Singapore • Washington DC

First published in 2012 by

SAGE Publications India Pvt Ltd
B1/I-1 Mohan Cooperative Industrial Area
Mathura Road, New Delhi 110 044, India
www.sagepub.in

**Institute of Policy
Studies of Sri Lanka**

SAGE Publications Inc
2455 Teller Road
Thousand Oaks, California 91320, USA

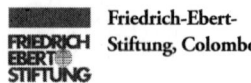

Friedrich-Ebert-
Stiftung, Colombo

SAGE Publications Ltd
1 Oliver's Yard
55 City Road
London EC1Y 1SP, United Kingdom

SAGE Publications Asia-Pacific Pte Ltd
33 Pekin Street
#02-01 Far East Square
Singapore 048763

Published by Vivek Mehra for SAGE Publications India Pvt Ltd, typeset in 10/12 Aldine 410 by Tantla Composition Pvt Ltd, Chandigarh, and printed at Chaman Enterprises, New Delhi.

Library of Congress Cataloging-in-Publication Data

Foreign aid in South Asia : the emerging scenario / edited by Saman Kelegama.
    p. cm.
    Includes bibliographical references and index.
    1. Economic assistance—South Asia. 2. Economic development—South Asia.
3. South Asia—Foreign economic relations. I. Kelegama, Saman.

HC430.6.F67   338.910954—dc23   2012   2012013628

ISBN: 978-81-321-0874-0 (HB)

The SAGE Team: Sharel Simon, Shreya Chakraborti, and Nand Kumar Jha

Contents

Aid Debate and Emerging Donors

Nexus between Aid and Security

Policy Priorities and Role of Aid in Post-conflict Economies

Policy Priorities and Role of Aid in Least Developed Countries

Role of Aid in Small and Vulnerable Economy

List of Tables

List of Figures

List of Abbreviations

AAA	Accra Agenda for Action
ABSD	Accelerating Bhutan's Socio-Economic Development
ACP	African, Caribbean and Pacific
ADB	Asian Development Bank
ADP	Annual Development Programme
AJK	Azad Jammu and Kashmir
AKRSP	Aga Khan Rural Support Programme
ANDS	Afghanistan National Development Strategy
ARTF	Afghanistan Reconstruction Trust Fund
BoP	Balance of Payments
CAS	Country Assistance Strategy
cCAP	Common Country Action Plan
CGE	Computable General Equilibrium
CIS	Commonwealth of Independent States
CNTF	Counter Narcotics Trust Fund
CPIA	Country Policy and Institutional Analysis
CRS	Creditor Reporting System
CSO	Civil Society Organization
DAC	Development Assistance Committee
DAD	Development Assistance Database
DFI	Direct Foreign Investment
DFID	Department For International Development
DFR	Donor Financial Review
EAD	Economic Affairs Division
EC	European Commission
ERCC	External Resources Coordinating Committee
ERD	External Resources Department
ESAP	Enhanced Structural Adjustment Programme

ESDP	Education Sector Development Programme
EU	European Union
FAP	Foreign Aid Policy
FATA	Federally Administered Tribal Area
FDI	Foreign Direct Investment
FES	Friedrich Ebert Stiftung
FoDP	Friends of Democratic Pakistan
GDP	Gross Domestic Product
GNH	Gross National Happiness
GNI	Gross National Income
GNP	Gross National Product
GSP+	Generalized System of Preferences Plus
GUM	General Unrestricted Model
HIPC	Heavily Indebted Poor Country
HLF	High Level Forum
IAP	Immediate Action Plan
IBRD	International Bank for Reconstruction and Development
IDA	International Development Association
IDB	Islamic Development Bank
IDP	Internally Displaced Person
IFI	International Financial Institution
IMF	International Monetary Fund
INGO	International Non-governmental Organization
IPS	Institute of Policy Studies
ISFD	Islamic Solidarity Fund for Development
JCMB	Joint Coordination Monitoring Board
LDC	Least Developed Country
LIC	Low Income Country
LOTFA	Law and Order Trust Fund for Afghanistan
LTTE	Liberation Tigers of Tamil Eelam
MDGs	Millennium Development Goals
MDP	Mahaweli Development Project
MFA	Multi Fibre Arrangement
MfDR	Managing for Development Results
MoU	Memorandum of Understanding
MRRD	Ministry of Rural Reconstruction and Development

MTEF	Medium Term Expenditure Framework
MYRB	Multi Year Rolling Budget
NAP	National Action Plan
NCED	National Council for Economic Development
NDCM	Nepal Donor Consultation Meeting
NDF	Nepal Development Forum
NE	North and East
NGO	Non-governmental Organization
NRSP	National Rural Support Program
NSP	National Solidarity Programme
ODA	Overseas Development Assistance
OECD	Organisation for Economic Co-operation and Development
OFF	Other Financial Flows
PD	Paris Declaration
PDF	Pakistan Development Forum
PEMS	Public Expenditure Management System
PFM	Public Financial Management
PFU	Performance Facilitation Unit
PIU	Parallel Implementation Unit
PLaMS	Planning and Monitoring System
PPAF	Pakistan Poverty Alleviation Fund
PRGF	Poverty Reduction and Growth Facility
PRS	Poverty Reduction Strategy
PRSP	Poverty Reduction Strategy Paper
PRT	Provincial Reconstruction Team
PSDP	Public Sector Development Programme
RBM	Results Based Management
REAP	Rural Economy Advancement Programme
REER	Real Effective Exchange Rate
RER	Real Exchange Rate
ROZ	Reconstruction Opportunity Zone
RSP	Rural Support Programme
RTM	Round Table Meeting
SAM	Social Accounting Matrix
SAL	Structural Adjustment Loan
SAP	Structural Adjustment Programme

SATP	South Asia Terrorism Portal
SBA	Stand By Arrangement
SIDS	Small Island Developing State
SME	Small and Medium Enterprises
SSC	South–South Cooperation
SWAP	Sector Wide Approach
TA	Technical Assistance
UNAMA	United Nations Assistance Mission in Afghanistan
UNCDF	United Nations Capital Development Fund
UNDAF	United Nations Development Assistance Framework
UNDP	United Nations Development Programme
UNFPA	United Nations Population Fund
UNICEF	United Nations Children's Fund
USAID	United States Agency for International Development
VAR	Variance
VAT	Value Added Tax
VECM	Vector Error Correction Model
WFP	World Food Programme

Foreword

The South Asian countries discussed in this book went through changing priorities for foreign assistance programmes set by Western donors since the 1950s. Newly independent countries sought assistance to meet their development needs and aspirations. The bilateral and multilateral initiatives for assistance led to the establishment of Aid Consortiums or Groups under the chair of the World Bank, first for India (1958) and then followed by Pakistan (1960), Sri Lanka (1965) and Bangladesh (1972) after its independence in 1971. These were the initial efforts by the Western donor community, Japan and the multilateral agencies, principally the World Bank and Asian Development Bank (ADB), at setting priorities for the foreign assistance needs of South Asian countries in a coordinated manner. Many issues remain even half a century after the first Aid Consortium was set up.

Several international initiatives were undertaken in the new millennium to assist developing countries to meet the Millennium Development Goals (MDGs) which were adopted by the international community in 2000. The first was the Monterrey Consensus of 2002, which led to the Rome High Level Forum (HLF) (2003), the Paris Declaration (PD) on Aid Effectiveness (2005) and the Accra Agenda for Action (AAA) (2008). The meetings focussed on the modalities for increasing development assistance and enhancing the predictability of aid; harmonization of assistance; ownership, management of projects and programmes for results and mutual accountability; use of country systems for aid delivery, untying aid and increased transparency in reviewing aid.[1] These efforts continued at the HLF in Korea in 2011.

Donors made commitments at the G8 Summit in 2005 and other meetings to increase development assistance.[2] Fifteen members of the European Union (EU) who are also members of the Development Assistance Committee (DAC) of the Organisation for Economic Cooperation and Development committed to reach a minimum ODA/GNI[3] target of 0.51 per cent by 2010. Eight of them met the target. The US did not commit to this target but agreed to double its aid to sub-Saharan Africa between 2004 and 2010 and did so by 2009. Its ODA/GNI ratio was 0.21 per cent in 2010, while that of Japan was 0.20 per cent. The other large donors were France, Germany and the UK, while Denmark, Luxembourg, the Netherlands, Norway and Sweden exceeded the UN ODA/GNI target of 0.70 per cent in 2010.

Since 2008, the global financial crisis is having an impact on the capacity and willingness of donors to continue meeting longer term commitments to increase development assistance that were made earlier. Natural disasters such as those in Japan in the early part of 2011 will also have a bearing. Some donors are directing requests for assistance from countries undergoing political change in the Middle East to multilateral institutions.

It has been a challenge for countries to coordinate foreign assistance from different sources following multiple objectives. Donor consortiums or aid groups were expected to assist but the recipients face difficulties due to capacity problems within government administrations. Initially, countries dealt with bilateral and multilateral lenders and multiple agencies for technical assistance. Bilateral assistance was often tied. Countries also had to develop the capacity to manage commercial borrowings from banking institutions, export credit agencies and suppliers. An expanding role was given to non-governmental organizations (NGOs), as bilateral donors began to diversify their delivery mechanisms.

These actions exacerbated the capacity problems for recipients. Government agencies have limited ability to monitor activities of NGOs, particularly during humanitarian crises. Examples abound. After the Asian tsunami of December 2004, many NGOs competed for the 'same turf'. As donor governments began to utilize NGOs for aid delivery more extensively, they were reluctant to provide full details of their activities to recipients. The basic requirement of providing the recipient countries with information on aid flows, particularly of grant funds, became another challenge, particularly when the recipient did not have the capacity to follow up the work undertaken by NGOs effectively.

A recent study on aid agencies[4] that measured best practices based on aid transparency, specialization, selectivity, ineffective aid channels and overhead costs found that among the bilateral agencies, the UK did well while the performance of the US was below the average. Among the multilateral agencies, the UN agencies are in the bottom half. The study admits that disaggregated data on the impact of aid on beneficiaries is not available to measure the quality of aid.

Out of the eight South Asian countries, Afghanistan, Bangladesh and Nepal remain in the low income country category with per capita Gross National Income (GNI) below US$995, while the others are in the lower middle income category with per capita GNI in the range of US$996 to US$3945. Afghanistan and Nepal were eligible to seek assistance from the Highly Indebted Poor Countries Initiative which provided debt relief. The latter did not participate in the programme. Afghanistan completed the programme and received full assistance under the Initiative.

As countries move up the income ladder, they will receive reduced amounts of concessional assistance. India and Pakistan are blend countries receiving a mix of concessional and non-concessional assistance from the World Bank, while the others continue to receive all assistance from the International Development Association, though some are in transition to blend status. Similarly, Bangladesh, Pakistan and Sri Lanka receive a blend of resources from the ADB while the others, with the exception of India, continue to receive concessional assistance from the Asian Development Fund.

Grants and concessional loans will decline and will be replaced by loans on harder terms when low income countries move to higher income levels. There will be non-concessional borrowings from export credit agencies, foreign financial and multilateral institutions and international capital markets. Greater efforts will be made to mobilize resources from the domestic capital market, depending on its state of development. The countries will need to develop the capacity not only for coordinating foreign assistance programmes, but also for managing external and domestic public debt, leading to the formulation of a borrowing policy and strategy. This has implications for capacity building within the agencies responsible for this function. There should also be simultaneous and effective coordination of policy formulation among the agencies and staff responsible for foreign assistance programmes, public debt management as well as fiscal, monetary and exchange rate policies of the government.

The authors of the country chapters following this volume are to be congratulated for their contributions to the first comprehensive study of this subject in the region. It would be a pity, however, if these efforts are to remain only at the level of chapters prepared and submitted. South Asian governments would benefit from reviewing the conclusions reached and, where appropriate, using them in the policy-making process.

Nihal Kappagoda
Sovereign Debt
Management Consultant
Ottawa, Canada

NOTES

1. Overview of Global Reforms in Foreign Aid, Indrajith Coomaraswamy, Chapter 2.
2. Development aid reaches a historic high in 2010, OECD, www.oecd.org.
3. Overseas Development Assistance/Gross National Income.
4. Easterly, William and Claudia Williamson, 'Reality vs. Rhetoric: The Best and Worst of Aid Agency Practices', http://williameasterly.files.wordpress.com/2010/08/61_easterly_williamson_rhetoricvsreality_prp.pdf.

Acknowledgements

The topic of Foreign Aid in South Asia came up for discussion at the Institute of Policy Studies of Sri Lanka (IPS) after the institute got involved in preparing the Sri Lankan country paper on foreign aid for a conference on aid organized by the North-South Institute in Ottawa at Wilton Park in May 2007. Thereafter, it was decided to have a detailed look at aid in the South Asian region from the perspective of the individual country situation. The IPS prepared a detailed concept paper on the subject and submitted it to Friedrich Ebert Stiftung (FES), Colombo, for possible funding. The application was successful and the institute then proceeded to mobilize regional experts to prepare country papers to be presented at a Conference in Colombo in July 2010.

The IPS is most grateful to Joachin Schluetter, Resident Director, FES, Colombo, for readily providing financial support for the Conference. Rohini Peiris of FES provided organizational support to which we are very thankful. We are also grateful to all contributors for submitting their papers on time. Thanks go to all chairpersons/discussants of various sessions: Dushni Weerakoon, Darini Rajasingham, W. D. Lakshman, Sridhar Khatri, Sirimal Abeyratne, Vickram Misri, Narhari Rao, Neha Mallik, Shekhar Shah, Zaidi Sattar, Amal Jayawardena, Rohan Gunaratne, Edward Bell and Koshy Mathai. The contributors revised their papers in the light of the comments made by the discussants, members of the audience and the chairpersons. It is these revised papers that have been included as chapters in this volume.

Deshal De Mel, Research Economist, IPS, played a key role in preparing the concept paper and organizing the conference, while Anneka De Silva played a valuable supporting role. I am most grateful to both these researchers from the IPS for their valuable inputs. I am also grateful to Nihal Kappagoda for writing the Foreword to this volume and D. D. M. Waidyasekera for editing the final manuscript.

Last but not least, my thanks go to Sharmini De Silva for taking a lead role in organizing the conference and preparing the manuscript for publication.

Saman Kelegama
IPS, Colombo
July 2011

I

Introduction

Foreign Aid and South Asia

SAMAN KELEGAMA

BACKGROUND

The efficacy of foreign aid as a developmental tool over the last few decades has been mixed. It is no different in South Asia, with foreign assistance having a long history in the postcolonial era but with mixed successes in terms of developmental outcomes.[1]

The literature suggests several factors that influence the efficacy of aid, including the quality of domestic policies (Burnside and Dollar, 2000), types of conditionalities (Devarajan, Dollar and Holmgren, 2001), quality of domestic institutions (Addison and Baliamoune-Lutz, 2006) and rent seeking (Alesina and Weder, 2002). Whilst some studies have found evidence for enhancing aid under certain conditions, such as good economic policies (Burnside and Dollar, 2000; Collier and Dollar, 2002), others have found evidence to the contrary (Easterly, Levine and Roodman, 2004; Rajan and Subramanian, 2005). A recent survey by McGillivary et al. (2006) shows that on average, foreign aid is effective at spurring economic growth in recipient countries. Overall, the message that emerges for policymakers is that aid is necessary, particularly in the context of achieving the Millennium Development Goals (MDGs), but that there is a need for reform in the practice of aid delivery.

Accordingly, since the MDGs were announced in 2000, there have been several multilateral initiatives that have focused on the issue of both increasing the magnitude and quality of aid. In 2002, global leaders met in Monterrey, Mexico, to discuss the modalities of enhancing finance for development. To quote from the Monterrey Consensus (United Nations, 2003):

> We recognize that a substantial increase in ODA [Overseas Development Assistance] and other resources will be required if developing countries are to achieve the internationally agreed development goals and objectives, including those contained in the Millennium Declaration. To build support for ODA, we will cooperate to further improve policies and development strategies, both nationally and internationally, to enhance aid effectiveness.

The Monterrey meeting was followed by the Rome High Level Forum (HLF) in 2003 where heads of donor agencies, both multilateral and bilateral, met with donor and partner countries to discuss measures to enhance harmonization of aid, particularly by working within partner country systems. The Rome HLF was followed up by the HLF in Paris in 2005 which culminated in the Paris Declaration (PD) on Aid Effectiveness. The PD was signed by 91 countries, 26 international organizations (mainly donor agencies) and 14 civil society organizations. The formulation of the PD of Aid Effectiveness in 2005 grew out of the need to understand why aid was not producing the expected results and to step up efforts to meet the ambitious targets set by the MDGs. The PD offers a blueprint for effective aid that maximizes impact from investments, synchronizes donor efforts and integrates the full spectrum of development challenges. Today, it is the rallying point for international consensus on aid effectiveness and many countries adhere to it.

The PD is founded on five core principles, born out of decades of experience on what works for development and what does not. These principles have gained support across the development community, changing aid practices for the better. It is now the norm for aid recipients to forge their own national development strategies with their parliament and electorates (ownership); for donors to support these strategies (alignment) and work to streamline their efforts in-country (harmonization); for development policies to be directed to achieving clear goals and the progress towards these goals to be monitored (managing for development results); and for donors and recipients to be jointly responsible for achieving these goals (mutual accountability). These are the five tenants of donor and partner commitments.

Progress on putting the PD into practice is being closely monitored through three rounds of monitoring surveys (2006, 2008 and 2011). How effective this monitoring is in regard to holding developed and developing countries accountable for their aid remains questionable.

In 2008, to step up implementation of the PD and build countries' capacity to manage their own future, an unprecedented alliance of developing countries, the Development Assistance Committee (DAC) donors, civil society organizations, emerging economies, the UN and multilateral institutions, and global funds agreed on the Accra Agenda for Action (AAA). The AAA proposes improvement in three main areas: *(a)* ownership: developing countries participate in policy formulation, take the lead in aid coordination and have aid delivered through their own country systems; *(b)* inclusive partnerships: all partners—DAC donors and developing countries as well as other donors, foundations and civil society—participate as full partners and *(c)* delivering results: aid is squarely focused on producing real and measurable impact on people's lives.

In other words, the key principles agreed upon in Accra relate to enhancing predictability of aid, ownership (partner countries engaging more with parliaments and civil society), use of country systems in aid delivery, untying aid, country-led division of labour among donors to avoid aid fragmentation, enhanced use of PD principles including South–South partnerships and increased transparency in reviewing aid.

A recent study by the Brookings Institution of the PD and development outcomes shows that ownership, alignment, and predictability and capacity development are key development outcomes. In particular, countries must show strong leadership over their development programmes and be able to count on long-term support from their major partners. A well-thought out exit strategy from aid also emerges as an important feature of successful development (Kharas, Makino and Jung, 2011).

The PD has been criticized for not been able to address development goals of human rights, social justice and equity, and the ROA (2008) argues,

> PD springs from a technocratic depoliticized vision of development, with no accountability for intended beneficiaries. The power in aid relationships is still heavily weighted on the side of donors, and the Declaration does nothing to check this imbalance. The aid effectiveness being promoted remains essentially donor centered.

Although the AAA is an improvement on PD, the AAA too has been criticized for not addressing tied aid, donor conditionality and institutional framework to monitor its implementation (Tandon, 2009).

There is a critical debate ongoing on aid and its relevance in the aftermath of the global economic crisis of 2008/09. Most donors have still not been able to meet the long-standing pledge to provide 0.7 per cent of GDP to ODA although ODA has increased from US$106 billion in 2005 to US$121 billion by 2008 (ROA, 2010). Moyo (2009) and Tandon (2009) are calling for aid exit rather than aid reforms, rejecting the current aid system as a vehicle of promotion of development in the South. They argue for a radical and fundamental restructuring of the aid architecture at the global level.

SOUTH ASIAN CONTEXT

In the midst of these criticisms, the PD has dominated the agenda for aid reform in recent years. Although the PD has arisen out of multi-stakeholder dialogue, the actual priorities of partner countries may not necessarily be in line with the requirements of the PD. Many developing countries have been passive in terms of the ODA receipts and lack a clear policy on foreign assistance, in terms of prioritizing the sectors where foreign assistance is essential and weighing the benefits and costs of foreign assistance compared to other sources of finance (domestic mobilization, commercial borrowing and private donors). Aid is often perceived as a transfer (repayments are usually well beyond the lifespan of individual governments) and, thus, insufficient emphasis is placed on evaluating the necessity of aid. Given the long history of foreign aid in South Asian countries, it would be pertinent to conduct some ex-post analysis to assess the impact of this aid. This would help guide future aid practices and provide lessons as to what has worked and what has not.

In most South Asian countries foreign aid is seen as a long-term option. They rely on foreign assistance for the finance of capital expenditure while fully exhausting domestic financial resources to meet the recurrent expenditures. As per capita incomes rise in South Asia, the availability of external finance from multilateral lenders will decline. With the declining flows of the ODA to South Asian countries, domestic policy would have to be adjusted accordingly—particularly in terms of identifying alternative sources of finance and managing domestic resources more effectively to ensure less reliance on external finance in the longer run. The management of this transition from high levels of foreign assistance to lower levels would be of crucial relevance for the medium-term economic development of South Asian countries.

South Asia is a unique region in that whilst each of the countries is a developing nation or a Least Developed Country (LDC), the role of foreign assistance in each economy stands on its own footing. Sri Lanka and Nepal are countries emerging from long lasting conflicts and Pakistan and Afghanistan are countries still in the midst of conflict and the nexus between security and the ODA is very strong in these cases. The region is also home to the LDCs, Bhutan, Maldives and Bangladesh, which have their own unique circumstances such as Bhutan being landlocked and the Maldives being a Small Island economy with a high per capita income but various developmental challenges, each of which has a unique role for the ODA. Finally, India is a key emerging economy that is a donor in its own right but still has several hundred million people below the poverty line. India is a good example to test aid effectiveness in a large developing economy. Given the diversity in the developmental circumstances of the countries in the region, a deeper understanding of the role of the ODA in South Asian countries will provide important policy lessons both within the region (regarding the different countries' policy approaches to the ODA) and will also resonate beyond the region.

KEY ISSUES

The recent trends in foreign aid have seen a shift from traditional practices. Emerging economies such as China, the Middle East and to a lesser extent India have begun to play an increasingly important role in the ODA. This is accompanied by different donor practices and while these have been welcomed by recipients, there are also different challenges that have to be met by recipient countries, such as new forms of tied aid and longer term geopolitical implications. At the same time, multilateral aid has also fluctuated and in some cases declined in South Asia, until, of course, the global economic crisis of 2008/09 and accompanying economic turbulence resulted in the International Monetary Fund (IMF) bail outs for Pakistan and Sri Lanka.

Developing countries should necessarily make an assessment of the role that foreign assistance plays in the development process. This entails the assessment of the extent to which foreign assistance has been donor driven as opposed to being defined by the developmental priorities in partner countries. This should also take into account the fact that the bulk of the ODA must be repaid with interest and usually accompanied by some currency depreciation, resulting in higher repayment obligations. Alternative sources of financing, particularly the importance of domestic resource mobilization, must be weighed up against the option of the ODA and the costs of the ODA (conditionalities and tied aid, burden on state capacity and macroeconomic implications) need to be taken into account as well.

The circumstances of South Asian countries have changed with time, and the ability to mobilize domestic resources and to engage in commercial financial markets has been enhanced. However, whilst circumstances have changed, the role of the ODA has in many cases not been reassessed in this context. Therefore, an exhaustive analysis of this nature will give a better idea as to the required role of the ODA in development from the perspective of the partner country.

Once the role for ODA is identified, the ODA received must necessarily be utilized in the most efficient manner. Therefore, countries need to identify their own priorities for reform of aid delivery practices, both in terms of obligations of the donor and obligations of the partner country. This could initially be guided by the principles of the PD, but should not be limited by the scope of the PD. The needs of individual countries will not be identical across the spectrum. At the same time, the bottlenecks in domestic governance and economic policy which hinder the efficacy of aid delivery and impact have also to be identified. All this entail that foreign aid policy has to be mainstreamed into national development strategies in an inclusive policymaking process to ensure a broad stakeholder buy in to the process.

In sum, the following issues will need to be addressed:

1. Recent Trends in Foreign Assistance Receipts
   - Key donors and changes in recent years?
   - Has the role of multilateral donors changed?
   - Have new donors emerged?
2. The Role Played by Foreign Assistance in Development
   - Which sectors have foreign assistance been financing?
   - Are these in line with development priorities in the country?

- To what extent has foreign assistance contributed to developmental goals?
3. What Is the Contemporary Role of Foreign Assistance in the Country?
    - Is foreign assistance necessary for medium- and long-term development? If so, why? (Why could these not be financed by domestic resources or alternative sources instead?)
    - What are the key opportunity costs of foreign aid? (Examples include conditionalities, burden on domestic capacity, impacts on inflation/exchange rates and any others.)
    - To what extent is the role for and modalities of foreign assistance articulated in national development strategies or Poverty Reductions Strategy Papers (PRSPs), as opposed to aid being donor driven?
4. Effectiveness of Aid
    - What are the priorities for aid policy reform from the recipient's end and from the donor's end?
    - To what extent are the priorities in the aid reform agenda as articulated in the PD and the AAA in line with priorities of the country, i.e., alignment, harmonization, and managing for results? Are there more pressing needs in the aid reform agenda in the country?
    - What has been the role of domestic governance in promoting or hindering aid effectiveness?
    - To what extent have macroeconomic policies supported or hindered aid absorption? Conversely, how has aid affected macroeconomic stability?
5. Future Policy Priorities
    - Given the fact that aid has opportunity costs and benefits, how should the country perceive the future role of aid?
    - If there has been a decline in recent receipts of foreign aid, how should domestic policy (particularly with regard to domestic resource mobilization and fiscal management) adapt to this trend in the future?
    - How should countries approach 'new donors' such as China and the Middle East countries?
    - Does the country have a longer term exit strategy for aid? Should it?

As mentioned earlier, each South Asian country has unique circumstances that shape the role of the ODA in its developmental process.

Therefore, the above issues, where applicable, are approached from the perspective of a country that is post-conflict, or landlocked or an emerging donor in its own right in this book.

OVERVIEW OF THE CHAPTERS

Chapter 2 provides an overview of the aid reform debate covering areas such as key features of the aid system, emergence of new donors, systemic issues, principles of aid effectiveness and moving beyond aid dependence. It is authored by Indrajit Coomaraswamy who played a key role in the Commonwealth Secretariat as its director general when the aid reform debate started in 2002 until his retirement in 2008.

Chapter 3 is based on South–South Cooperation (SSC), aid effectiveness and India. It shows that in recent times SSC between developing countries, has become a growing and dynamic phenomenon in aid flows as opposed to the customary pattern of aid from developed countries to developing countries ('North–South'). Such South–South aid flows are gradually changing the direction of aid flows and providing a platform to face the new global challenges.

The chapter argues that while there is sufficient recognition of the weaknesses in the present dominant paradigm of North–South aid, steps have not been taken for better integration of the role of the SSC and achieving aid effectiveness. The chapter attempts to provide an underlying foundation for moving in this direction of a greater role for the SSC and demonstrates that the SSC has the potential to contribute significantly to making aid more effective. It ventures into the issues that are critical to promoting the role of the SSC in addressing these challenges, bringing up the benefits and drawbacks of the SSC.

Following a literature review, the chapter identifies reasons for improving aid effectiveness including two central reasons: sustainable development and capacity building. While emphasizing the need for Trilateral Cooperation that brings together donors from advanced and emerging economies to work jointly on projects in developing countries, the chapter states that India is and will continue to shift from a recipient of aid to a donor. It concludes with an emphasis on the importance of making the SSC and trilateral cooperation a core component of global aid flows and better integration of emerging donors in the framework of global aid flows.

Chapter 4 focuses on the impact of aid on growth in India by using a new approach in the aid-effectiveness literature related to the composition of foreign aid. The chapter presents a model of the impact of aid on growth in an aid-recipient economy to derive a reduced-form growth equation, which is subsequently estimated by using time-series data for India over the period 1970–92. The chapter improves upon earlier work in the area of aid effectiveness by focusing on a neglected, though important, issue namely the aid disaggregation and the way it affects the empirics of aid effectiveness. Disaggregated aid data has been constructed by the OECD to test the relevance of the aid-disaggregation hypothesis to aid effectiveness for India. Furthermore, the chapter employs time-series econometric analysis based on general-to-specific modelling and cointegration to shed more light on a highly debatable topic. The empirical results obtained seem to suggest that the composition of aid matters for deriving robust conclusions on aid effectiveness in the case of India; at the same time, they seem to call for further work in this promising area within the context of more individual country studies.

Chapter 5 is based on the nexus between aid and security in the case of Pakistan. Being a frontier nation against violent terrorism, it has remained one of the highest recipients of foreign aid. Nevertheless, despite a domestic energy crisis, terrorism and environmental disasters, Pakistan's economy experienced a decline in foreign aid, in the wake of global food, fuel and financial crises.

Following a literature review, the chapter examines foreign assistance in the context of Pakistan through four main facets: the link between aid, security and growth; impact of foreign aid on economic growth and poverty; aid effectiveness; and policy priorities in the country. The chapter is entirely dependent on the secondary data gathered from national sources.

Aid flows in Pakistan have shown fluctuations which made foreign financing an unreliable option for sustainable growth. The devastating acts of terrorism and environmental hazards have collectively resulted in a massive economic loss and insecurity. In terms of the aid composition, majority accounts for multilateral and non-concessional flows. The sectors that have received highest foreign assistance include power, water, transport and communication, and rural development.

Using a linked Computable General Equilibrium (CGE), the chapter examines the macro–micro impact of foreign resources which indicates that significant increase in foreign savings leads to a very small increase in real private consumption. The security concerns of donors and aid volatility have hampered the aid effectiveness and future aid flows to Pakistan. In terms of policy priorities, Pakistan is in line with the principles outlined in the PD and interacts with various development partners, such as Consortium of Friends of Democratic Pakistan and US.

The chapter points out that the empirical literature on the impact of aid on economic development in Pakistan is inconclusive due to aid being fragmented and volatile. It also concludes that having a national policy is all the more important for Pakistan in the process of seeking foreign assistance.

Chapter 6 is based on the nexus between aid and security in the case of Afghanistan. It is argued that given the fragile nature of the state and the highly reactive character of the insurgents to the changes in the government behaviour, ensuring the stability of the government is imperative. With the country's shaky security environment and low levels of domestic revenue, foreign aid plays a pivotal role in future development plans and sustaining economic growth in Afghanistan. In fact, the country's development expenditure is entirely funded by aid. The US is by far the largest donor to Afghanistan whilst it has been receiving aid from 47 different development partners since 2002. However, the disbursements of aid have continuously been lower than that of commitments. The chapter identifies a number of reasons for this, including lack of absorptive capacity, high levels of corruption and undesirable operating conditions.

Unlike in most South Asian countries wherein multilateral aid is dominant, in Afghanistan, a large proportion of aid comes from the United Sates Agency for International Development (USAID) followed by bilateral aid. In the aftermath of the conflict in 2001, Afghanistan is critically in need of humanitarian assistance and reconstruction of both physical and social infrastructure. The revenue collection has been notoriously poor in the country, and the chapter shows that percentage growth of revenue has a declining trend. The chapter highlights the fact that Afghanistan is responsible for 90 per cent of the world's opium production that is the largest economic activity in the country, which in turn fuels corruption, terrorism and stifles development.

Aid allocation for the security sector has been considerably reduced with greater emphasis on infrastructure, education, economic governance and the rule of law. The chapter also identifies the challenges of external assistance in fiscal management, institutional capacity building, and reducing geographical disparities. In terms of aid effectiveness, as most South Asian countries, Afghanistan follows the principles of the PD. The chapter examines domestic reform priorities in terms of supporting development of domestic institutional capacity, increasing predictability of aid, domestic revenue mobilization and coordination of development activities.

In conclusion, the chapter states that there is an unavoidable reliance on aid in Afghanistan at present and suggests that the dependence on aid for recurrent expenditures must be curbed. The chapter also highlights the limited outreach of the government to rural areas and the subsequent need for the government to develop strong sub-national level institutions. It further states that creating a direct channel of communication between the government and rural communities is essential for improving policy impact, reducing regional disparities, etc.

Chapter 7 is based on policy priorities for foreign aid reform in Sri Lanka. Foreign aid has played a major role in Sri Lanka's development process. Since Sri Lanka has persistently recorded budget deficits, aid has been vital to the island in terms of financing capital intensive government expenditure such as large scale infrastructural projects as well as social projects.

The post-war situation saw a substantial spike in foreign inflows due to the remittances and emergency relief measures. However, with Sri Lanka being classified as a lower-middle income country in the late 1990s, access to concessional finance has declined. Thus, the government has resorted to external commercial borrowing to finance existing debt and development activities. Whilst addressing the unstable macroeconomic environment and the post-conflict concerns, the chapter identifies the contemporary role of aid in Sri Lanka. It further investigates into the potential costs of foreign aid, macroeconomic imbalance, and volatility caused by fiscal indiscipline.

The chapter also discusses the benefits and drawbacks of donor dominance in the development projects while emphasizing the implications for domestic institutions and for private sector capacity. In terms of priorities for enhancing aid effectiveness, Sri Lanka is certainly in line with the areas highlighted in the PD. Whilst addressing the other priorities for reform, the chapter argues that improved targeting of aid is imperative for increasing the effectiveness.

In conclusion, the chapter argues that in the long run it is important for Sri Lanka to reduce reliance on concessional aid despite the fact that foreign aid plays a vital role in financing the country's development objectives. It highlights the importance of enhancing domestic resource mobilization through rationalization of the fiscal position. A number of issues relating to the enhancement of aid effectiveness from the perspective of both donors and recipient government are also highlighted taking into account the post-conflict situation.

Chapter 8 is based on policy priorities for foreign aid reform in Nepal. The chapter attempts to recommend policy changes in both the recipient and donor countries for making the aid programmes as effective as possible. The chapter is dependent on secondary data and statistics from Nepal and other sources where necessary.

Given the severe macroeconomic difficulties, including a high saving–investment gap, continuous high fiscal deficits, political instability, etc., the role of foreign aid has been crucial for Nepal. It has undoubtedly contributed to development in Nepal, but the chapter raises the question whether the foreign aid received has been used effectively and productively. In the early years, foreign aid in Nepal was mostly dominated by bilateral assistance as grants for development projects, but in recent years multilateral assistance has been momentous in financing development activities. Overall, the grant component has been at a rising trend over the years. The sectoral allocation of foreign aid in Nepal is led by the social services sector followed by transport, power and communication sector.

The chapter identifies a few key issues such as opportunity costs, debt burden and conditionality which are shown as major factors hindering foreign aid. It is argued that the inability to utilize aid effectively is the main concern. In regard to foreign aid effectiveness, the chapter reveals that the relationship between aid and per capita real GDP is negative in the short run. The policy priorities in the national plans in Nepal have moved from being infrastructure and production oriented towards sustainable development, poverty reduction and social development by the end of 2009. The chapter also suggests that Nepal's foreign aid policy needs to be revisited particularly after the country was declared a federal republic.

Chapter 9 discusses policy priorities for foreign aid reform in Bangladesh. The chapter shows that the regime of foreign aid in Bangladesh has undergone important changes over the last decades. With gradual decline in aid dependence, it appears that Bangladesh has now evolved from an aid to trade dependent economy. However, the chapter argues that there is a diminishing but significant role of aid in government finances. With this backdrop, the chapter provides an analysis of the importance, focus, composition and effectiveness of aid in Bangladesh.

Until about 1980, Bangladesh was almost entirely dependent on aid but since then, with the increase in exports and remittances, Bangladesh has turned into being trade dependent than aid. This has been further supported by the government's relative success in the mobilization of domestic resources and the increasing dynamism of the private sector. In terms of aid commitment and disbursement, the chapter shows that the ratio of disbursement to commitment has persistently remained low.

Bangladesh's aid basket is comprised of both grants and loans, and it is shown that the country has become loan dependent over time. As loans always come with stringent conditionalities compared to grants, compliance has become costly to the country. The chapter shows that outstanding debt is ever increasing for Bangladesh and, hence, a significant amount of the national budget goes for debt repayments.

The composition of aid to Bangladesh can be divided into food aid, commodity aid and project aid. Project aid can be seen as the largest contributor for the implementation of development programmes. The economy is becoming near self-sufficient and the importance of food aid lessening because of improvement in productivity in the agriculture sector. The gross aid bundle for Bangladesh was dominated by bilateral sources in the early years, but now it is dominated by multilateral sources such as the Asian Development Bank (ADB) and the International Development Association (IDA). Development perspectives in Bangladesh are outlined in a plan covering 2010 to 2021 aimed at implementing vision 2021. In terms of sectoral share, service and infrastructure have always got the priority followed by agriculture and industry. In terms of effectiveness of aid, Bangladesh has not been successful, and the chapter has emphasized this fact by referring to some statistical and econometric analyses.

In conclusion, the chapter argues that the dependence on aid will continue to meet some of the critical human development objectives and infrastructural development goals which are vital for economic growth in the country. It further highlights the need for aid reform within the country whilst arguing that government should not consider aid as a means of solving the fiscal deficits but as a source for enhancing investments.

Chapter 10 discusses the role of foreign aid in the LDC, Bhutan. The chapter examines the role of development assistance, aid effectiveness and policy priorities, highlighting the recent aid trends in Bhutan. Together with its healthy macroeconomic environment, Bhutan has made significant progress in the socio-economic development efforts. However, one fourth of the population is below the national poverty line; thus the chapter highlights the need for foreign assistance in poverty alleviation and development.

Depending on the statistics obtained from secondary sources, the chapter shows that majority of total outlay is financed through domestic revenue followed by foreign aid, in which the grant component is dominant. The education sector receives the largest share of the external grant followed by the agriculture, transport and communication sectors. A noteworthy point is that if Bhutan is able to use the full potential of its hydropower capacity, it can continue to drive the economy towards being self-reliant and less dependent on aid.

India is the oldest and the largest development partner to Bhutan. In terms of foreign aid contribution, bilateral assistance has been prominent throughout and with regard to aid effectiveness, Bhutan has been following the principles of the PD as other South Asian countries. The chapter concludes that dependence on foreign aid has declined over the years, but foreign aid plays an important role as Bhutan's domestic revenue has not been able to keep pace with the expenditure growth.

Chapter 11 is based on the role of aid in the LDC, Maldives. Starting from the very basic levels of development, the Maldives has managed to make considerable headway in the path of socio-economic development during the decades following its independence in 1965. With improved tourism industry, which is the country's economic backbone, Maldives has become a world renowned tourist destination. The rapid economic growth of the islands is driven by two sectors, viz., tourism and fishing industry.

Maldives has benefited from the donor countries across the world and had maintained high rates of aid utilization focusing on key social sectors. This has led Maldives to graduate from the UN's LDCs category to a developing country. Maldives is, in this sense, at a development paradox where, due to HDIs and the LDC graduation, donors are reluctant to extend assistance despite the current fiscal difficulties in the country. However, the rapid development has also resulted in several fallouts that are discussed in the chapter. These effects have been compounded with the 2004 tsunami disaster, which physically washed away bulk of the GDP.

In terms of aid, foreign grant receipts to the Maldives have been decreasing over the last decade. However, unprecedented levels of aid flowed to the country following the tsunami disaster. The fragility and vulnerability of the country is apparent with the profoundness of the impact of the tsunami disaster on the entire nation. In terms of the aid composition, multilateral loans account for the bulk followed by bilateral loans. Grant assistance also plays an indispensable role in the development of human resources. The chapter highlights the role of the traditional donors, such as Japan as well as the new donors such as China and India on Maldivian economic development.

Whilst referring to the most visible indicators of effectiveness of aid in the Maldivian context, the chapter ventures into the costs of foreign aid such as lack of community participation and increased cost of project inputs, etc. In terms of aid effectiveness, it is evident from the chapter that Maldives is in line with the principles set by the PD. While highlighting the role of governance, the chapter argues that a clearer division of responsibility and closer coordination needs to be worked out in order to ensure that aid is utilized effectively. A five-point outline of approaching donors is also presented, in the chapter. It concludes that being a Small Island state, Maldives will continue to be highly susceptible to exogenous shocks and, hence, the cooperation and assistance from the international community are vital.

Concluding Remarks

The overall message that comes out of these chapters is that individual South Asian countries have to get their act together for the best use of aid. There are aid absorptive problems in many South Asian countries that need attention. Moreover, in almost all South Asian countries, aid has not been mainstreamed to the overall development strategy other than some ad hoc mainstreaming in various national plans. The experience of South Asia also throws challenges for aid donors since the stages of development and initial conditions in the South Asian countries are different and, thus, a 'one size fit all' type of an aid donor strategy will not work in the region.

The PD outcomes in South Asian countries are still not clear—many of the changes triggered by the PD will take several years to show up in development outcomes. Lack of evidence also reflects slow progress in implementing the commitments. Assessing the impact of aid has been difficult in all circumstances in South Asia. Despite methodological improvements, it remains difficult to pinpoint the causal relationship between the aid provided and the output achieved. The measurement of results is also an aid effectiveness issue, and, as aid comes increasingly under scrutiny for impact and value for money—the next HLF in Busan in late 2011 should consider how to improve measurement of aid effectiveness. Decision makers at the next HLF will, therefore, need to raise a broader range of analysis, including thorough investigation of existing evaluations and development experiences to see how aid effectiveness principles have played a role in supporting development over the past decades.

The PD with the AAA is the only international framework on the quality of aid—the essential counterpart to the commitments in the MDGs and UN/G8 commitments on development finance. The next HLF in Busan will assess how the effectiveness principle has affected development. It will take stock of how aid delivery has changed since 2005 and whether this has led to better developmental outcomes. On this basis, the HLF will make recommendations on future quality of aid framework, at least for the period up to the MDG date of 2015. If international aid architecture is to be designed using this framework with the PD providing the basic foundation, the South Asian experience should be carefully studied as it provides a number of lessons to donors and other stakeholders.

NOTE

1. See, for instance, Sobhan (1990).

REFERENCES

Addison, T. and M. Baliamoune-Lutz (2006), 'Economic Reform When Institutional Quality Is Weak: The Case of the Maghreb', *Journal of Policy Modeling*, 28(9): 1029–43.

Alesina, A. and B. Weder (2002), 'Do Corrupt Governments Receive Less Foreign Aid?' *American Economic Review*, September, 92(4): 126–37.

Burnside, C. and D. Dollar (2000), 'Aid, Policies and Growth', *American Economic Review*, American Economic Association, 90(4): 847–68, September.

Collier, Paul and David Dollar (2002), 'Aid Allocation and Poverty Reduction', *European Economic Review*, 46(8): 1475–1500.

Devarajan, S., D. Dollar and T. Holmgren (2001), *Aid and Reform in Africa*, World Bank, Washington, D.C.

Easterly, W., R. Levine and D. Roodman (2004), 'Aid, Policies, and Growth: Comment', *American Economic Review*, 94(3): 774–80.

Kharas, H., K. Makino and W. Jung (2011), *Catalyzing Development: A New Vision for Aid*, Brooking Press, USA.

McGillivary, M., M.S. Feeny, N. Hermes and R. Lensink (2006), 'Controversies Over the Impact of Development Aid: It Works; It Doesn't: It Can, but It Depens', *Journal of International Development*, 18(7): 1031–50.

Moyo, D. (2009), *Dead Aid: Why Aid Is Not Working and How There Is a Better Way for Africa*, Farrar, Straus, and Giroux, New York.

ROA (2008), *The Reality of Aid: An Independent Review of Poverty Reduction and Development Assistance*, IBON International, Philippines, www.realityofaid.com (accessed on January 2011).

———— (2010), 'South-South Cooperation: A Challenge for the Aid System', The Reality of Aid (ROA): Special Report on South-South Cooperation, IBON International, Philippines, www.realityofaid.com (accessed on January 2011).

Rajan, R. and A. Subramanian (2005), 'Aid and Growth: What Does the Cross-country Evidence Really Show?' IMF Working Paper 127, International Monetary Fund, Washington, DC.

Sobhan, R. (ed.) (1990), *From Aid Dependence to Self Reliance: Development Options for Bangladesh*, Dhaka University Press, Dhaka.

Tandon, Y. (2009), 'Ending Aid Dependence', in Y. Tandon (ed.) *Development and Globalization: Daring to Think Differently*, Pambazuka Press, UK.

United Nations (2003), 'Monterrey Consensus on Financing for Development', the final text of agreement and commitments adopted at the International Conference on Financing for Development, Monterrey, Mexico, 18–22 March 2002, http://www.un.org/esa/ffd/monterrey/MonterreyConsensus.pdf (accessed on January 2011).

AID DEBATE AND EMERGING DONORS

2

Overview of Global Reforms in Foreign Aid

INDRAJIT COOMARASWAMY

INTRODUCTION

The international aid architecture may be defined as the world's agencies, institutions and systems for managing the transfer of resources (finance and expertise) to low-income countries. In recent years, the aid industry has been experiencing significant changes. Aid volumes have increased since the Millennium Summit and subsequent commitments made by G-8 leaders at their Gleneagles meeting. However, the recession in the US and Europe is constraining future prospects for aid volumes. At the same time, the aid architecture is characterized by a proliferation of agencies and special purpose vehicles. The United Nations Development Programme (UNDP) has estimated that there are over 1000 financing mechanisms.

Since 2002 there have been several multilateral initiatives that have focused on the quantity and quality of aid. These include the Monterrey Consensus (2002) on the modalities of increasing development finance; the Rome High Level Forum (HLF) (2003) on harmonization of aid; the Paris HLF (2005) resulting in the Declaration on Aid Effectiveness which focused on ownership, alignment, harmonization, managing for results and mutual accountability; and the Accra HLF (2008) which highlighted enhancing predictability of aid, ownership (partner countries engaging more with parliament and civil society), use of country systems in aid delivery, untying aid, country-led division of labour among donors to avoid aid fragmentation and increased transparency in reviewing aid.

KEY FEATURES OF THE AID SYSTEM

Despite these initiatives, there is still a substantive unfinished agenda for reform of the aid system. The key features of the current aid system include

- an unplanned proliferation of agencies and special purpose vehicles (over 40 bilaterals, 20 global regional financial institutions, 15 UN agencies and a growing number of vertical funds);
- a high proportion of bilateral aid, much of it, particularly technical assistance (TA), still tied;
- substantial capital increases for the multilaterals in the aftermath of the global economic crisis (though their soft loan windows have had somewhat more modest replenishments);
- an expanding role for non-governmental organizations (NGOs); and
- the increasing importance of philanthropic capital (the Gates Foundation now provides more support for the health sector than the World Bank) (Commonwealth Secretariat, 2007).

EMERGENCE OF NEW DONORS

Historically, the Development Assistance Committee (DAC) countries have accounted for about 95 per cent of the Overseas Development Assistance (ODA). However, in recent years there has been the emergence of major non-traditional donors. China has committed to providing US$10 billion in concessional loans and preferential buyers' credits over a three-year period. India has been increasing its provision to Africa to roughly 10 times the level five years ago. It is also increasing its support for countries in South Asia. South Korea is aiming to reach US$1 billion ODA per year by 2011. Partner countries have indicated that new donors respond more quickly and have less 'intrusive' conditionality. The 'hassle factor' of dealing with them is, therefore, significantly less. However, traditional donors fare better on aid effectiveness. The challenge going forward is to develop an aid system that draws on the relative strengths of both traditional and non-traditional donors.

KEY COMPONENTS OF THE AID SYSTEM

Bilateral aid constitutes over two thirds of the ODA. Despite the Paris Declaration (PD) Process, it is not well coordinated, involves high transaction costs, has no binding rules or norms and delivers a large volume of tied and largely ineffective technical assistance.

The UN Development System has greater legitimacy. However, it is short of core funds. It has failed to win the trust of large donors who prefer to deal with organizations that are seen as being more 'effective'. However, these organizations have governance structures that lack legitimacy. The reforms intended to facilitate the UN Development System 'to deliver as one' are still a work in progress (UN, 2006). While there has been improvement, it has tended to be uneven across countries. The UN continues to face challenges in organizing effectively and prioritizing at the country level, with too many agencies still operating with insufficient coherence. There is an unfinished agenda in bringing together the UN's normative and analytical expertise, its operational and coordination capabilities and its advocacy role, more effectively at the country, regional and global levels.

The International Financial Institutions (IFIs), particularly the World Bank and the Regional Development Banks, have emerged from the global crisis with a higher funding base. Much of the intellectual input into the discourse on development and the formulation of policies comes from the IFIs, which often act as gatekeepers for the traditional bilaterals (ODI, 2009). It is encouraging that lending for agriculture and infrastructure is being given higher priority. Lending for these sectors has been revived as growth strategies have become more important after the triple crises (food, finance and energy) in 2008. There is now greater recognition that the Millennium Developments Goals (MDGs) are necessary but insufficient conditions for sustained growth and development. Their achievement has to be supplemented by a strategy to enhance growth, investment and employment.

The European Union (EU) is the largest provider of the ODA. The Partnership Frameworks, through which the EU provides its assistance, particularly to the African, Caribbean and Pacific (ACP) countries and North Africa, allows for greater 'voice' on the part of partner countries. However, both the EU members and recipients have raised concerns regarding effectiveness. These include bureaucratic and time-consuming procedures and a preoccupation with middle-income countries due to fears regarding immigration from North Africa.

SYSTEMIC ISSUES

There are a number of systemic issues that need to be addressed in reforming the aid system (Burall and Maxewell with Menocal, 2006).

1. Overall aid allocation has a number of shortcomings. There is the issue of 'donor darlings' and 'donor orphans', reflecting asymmetric treatment of partner countries. From a South Asian perspective, it is a matter of concern that there is no systematic framework that addresses the graduation from low-income to lower middle-income country status. This increases uncertainty regarding aid flows into the region in the future.
2. Aid flows to individual countries continue to be volatile, particularly multilateral assistance.
3. Historically, aid flows have tended to be pro-cyclical, thereby exacerbating the effects of shocks. However, the response to the recent crises has been different, with the multilaterals being used to provide counter-cyclical liquidity. It is to be hoped that this is not a one-off approach and that this change is institutionalized within the aid system.
4. The aid system has tended to lack flexibility and is generally slow in picking up new ideas. Strategies for dealing with single purpose funds and private philanthropy are unclear.
5. Low-income countries continue to lack voice within the system. The emergence of the G-20 is encouraging. Reform of the Bretton Woods institutions has increased the role of the major emerging economies in their governance. However, poor and vulnerable countries still continue to lack voice. The developing countries now participate in the DAC committee meetings but have no effective voice. The UN Development Cooperation Forum has been ineffectual so far.
6. Humanitarian assistance accounts for a growing share of the ODA. However, it has even fewer rules and norms than other

forms of the ODA. Furthermore, there is not even a unifying set of objectives, like the MDGs in this segment of the aid industry.

PRINCIPLES FOR AN EFFECTIVE AID SYSTEM

The main principles for an effective aid system may be stated as follows (DFID, 2006):

1. Improved accountability through effective voice and relevance for poor countries.
2. Balancing donor coordination and competition to avoid 'ganging-up' on the part of donors.
3. Medium-term predictability of aid flows at the country level. There is merit in working towards 5 or 10 year development partnerships or compacts based on shared commitments related to the MDGs, international covenants and obligations, and strengthening financial management and accountability.
4. Flexibility, including strengthening the capacity for counter-cyclical assistance to smooth over the effects of shocks.
5. Balancing need and performance. There should be a greater weight for poverty indicators in aid-allocation models. These models should also take greater account of country priorities rather than a 'one-size-fits-all' view of what constitutes a good policy environment.
6. Addressing market failures.
7. Promoting harmonization and alignment.

Overall, there is a need to continue the move away from supply driven instruments and approaches. There is also a need to mainstream political analysis and engagement. The aid system tends to be weak in analysing and understanding potential opportunities and threats associated with political processes in partner countries.

MOVING BEYOND AID DEPENDENCE

While continuing reform of the aid system is a major priority, the conclusion of a development-friendly Doha Round of Multilateral Trade Negotiations would do more than anything else to improve the prospects of low-income countries. However, the protectionist pressures that have been generated by the Great Recession mean that it is unlikely there will be a successful conclusion to the Round in the immediate future. Instead, the focus is now on preventing a sliding back on existing commitments.

As incomes rise and the financial services sector develops, domestic resource mobilization can and should play an increasingly important role, particularly in South Asia.

Those countries that can prudently do so can take advantage of the historically very low interest rates that are likely to prevail in the medium term to undertake commercial borrowing. It is important that such borrowing is used productively to earn the rates of return required to service commercial borrowing.

CONCLUSION

The PD has the potential to empower partner countries (OECD, 2006). However, it is important that these countries gear themselves up to take advantage of its provisions. Change has been relatively slow due to, at least in part, recipient countries not developing the necessary capacity and institutional arrangements. Low-income countries need to take stock of the role of the ODA in their development processes and clearly identify its niche in long-term planning. In this context, they need a clear policy on the ODA in terms of prioritizing the sectors where foreign aid is essential and weighing the benefits of the ODA in relation to other sources of finance.

However, even if the PD is implemented effectively, it will not address the issue of how the overall structure of the aid system should be rationalized. That is a task for which one needs an 'architect' rather than a 'tinker'. This introductory section has sought to explore how this could be done. The remainder of this publication sets out the priorities of the South Asia region for the next HLF in Korea.

REFERENCES

Burall, S. and Maxwell, S. with A. Rocha Menocal (2006), 'Reforming the International Aid Architecture: Options and Ways Forward', London, Overseas Development Institute.

Commonwealth Secretariat (2007), 'Reform of the International Aid Architecture', Paper for Commonwealth Finance Ministerial Meeting prepared by B. Mukherjee.

DFID (2006), 'Strengthening the Aid System', Discussion Paper, Department for International Development (DFID), UK.

ODI (2009), 'Bretton Woods Reform: Shifting through the Options in the Search for Legitimacy', Overseas Development Institute (ODI), Briefing Paper, Paris.

OECD (2006), 'Paris Declaration on Aid Effectiveness', High Level Forum, Organization for Economic Cooperation and Development (OECD), Paris.

UN (2006), 'Delivering as One', Report of the Secretary General's High Level Panel on System-wide Coherence in the Areas of Humanitarian Assistance and the Environment, United Nations (UN), New York.

3

South–South Cooperation

Aid Effectiveness and India

RAJIV KUMAR, MICHAEL DICKERSON AND SURABHI TANDON

INTRODUCTION

It is unfortunately clear from even a cursory look at the relevant evidence that the worthy objective of the Millennium Challenge Process of eliminating poverty by 2015 will not be achieved. South Asia, which is perhaps home to more than half the world's poor, is nowhere near meeting its Millennium Development Goals (MDGs). This inadequate progress in eliminating the demeaning scourge of degrading and dehumanizing poverty is despite the increase in aid flows and serious attempts at making these flows more effective. This is demonstrated by the resolve made at the Paris Conference, its follow-up with the Accra Agenda for Action (AAA) and the setting up of detailed time bound targets for each of the five principles[1] enunciated at Paris. But the goal still eludes us. This should encourage the development community to once again re-visit the issue of the role of aid in poverty elimination and achieving sustainable development in all its aspects and in an honest, transparent and inclusive manner.

In this context, the main argument of this chapter is that while there is sufficient recognition of the weaknesses in the present dominant paradigm of 'North–South' aid,[2] the next logical steps of better integrating the role of South–South Cooperation (SSC),[3] and even making it the dominant modality[4] for achieving greater aid effectiveness have not yet been taken. This chapter tries to provide the raison d'être for moving in this direction of a greater role of the SSC, both on an apriori basis and on the basis of empirical evidence. This evidence unambiguously demonstrates that the SSC has the potential to contribute significantly to making aid more effective. We also give some recommendations in the concluding section on how to make the SSC and trilateral cooperation a core component of global aid flows and integrate better emerging donors in the framework of global aid flows.

SSC and Aid Effectiveness

The SSC's role in aid effectiveness has been already recognized in the literature that has emerged since the PD.[5] As the AAA (2008, p. 4) acknowledged:

> The contributions made by all development actors, and in particular the role of middle-income countries as both providers and recipients of aid. We recognise the importance and particularities of South-South cooperation and acknowledge that we can learn from the experience of developing countries. We encourage further development of triangular co-operation.

The role of the SSC was further emphasized at the High Level Event on Aid Effectiveness in Bogotá, which will feed into the Fourth High Level Forum (HLF) on Aid Effectiveness in Seoul in 2011. As articulated in the Bogotá Statement, a non-binding recommendatory document, 'South-South cooperation is an important instrument of effective and inclusive partnerships … [and we] acknowledge its role in building capacity and advancing development … and [aim to] promote a greater role for, and increased effectiveness in, SSC' (OECD, 2010).

There were some initial apprehensions that aid from the so-called 'new or emerging donors' will reverse some of the gains by offering recipients soft terms, incentivizing them to increase their indebtedness and not adopt appropriate development policies. This was the reason for the AAA to emphasize that the SSC would have to also follow the five principles laid out in the PD and not deviate from well-established norms.[6] This apprehension has, however, been shown to be somewhat of an exaggeration and as Woods concludes, 'emerging donors are not overtly attempting either to overturn the rules of multilateral development assistance or to replace them' (Woods, 2008, 1221). Therefore, there is little reason to believe that emerging donors will not abide by the established practices for aid which include non-interference in internal affairs, respecting sovereignty, giving the leadership to recipients to ensure ownership and neither insisting on discredited conditionalities nor permitting a free run that encourages misutilization of aid resulting in rising indebtedness. As the AAA (2008) acknowledged, 'The contributions of all development actors are more effective when developing countries are in a position to manage and coordinate them. We welcome the role of new contributors and will improve the way all development actors work together.'[7]

With the role of emerging economies in pulling the global economy out of the post-Lehman recession now becoming increasingly evident, the HLF is taking place at a time when there has been a perceptible shift in the gravity of economic activity to emerging economies. Therefore, it may indeed be the opportune time to push the SSC centre stage for achieving greater aid effectiveness, through better capacity building and sustainable development. In this chapter, therefore, we focus on the issues that are critical to promoting the role of the SSC in addressing these issues.

In our view, the five pillars for aid effectiveness as enshrined in the 2005 PD have perhaps been overtaken by recent events in as much as they do not give the SSC a central and integral role in improving both the quantum and quality of aid flows. This could be due to these principles having been enunciated primarily from the advanced country perspective which saw aid effectiveness as being achieved through a process in which advanced country donors still retained the status of the principal actors with recipients as passive players who would, for example, be allowed greater country ownership and helped through better coordination and harmonization amongst donors. The principle of recipients *leading* the effort in designing and implementing the aid programme with donors playing a supportive role was of course highlighted but as the Organisation for Economic Co-operation and Development (OECD) was itself to admit five years later, this commitment was more easily said than achieved.[8] The role of emerging donors, which hardly merited a passing reference in the PD, was substantially strengthened in the AAA. However, this too, continued to focus principally on the five pillars for aid effectiveness as laid down in the PD.

The statement that 'the most effective aid is one that makes aid itself redundant' is both a truism and perhaps even a cliché. However, in our understanding, the statement reflects the immutable objective of all aid practices and remains the most important guiding principle for determining the nature and direction of global aid. Its centrality is because it underscores the importance of both capacity development and sustainable development of recipient developing economies, the two issues which have been particularly highlighted in recent literature.[9] But the OECD document (http://www.oecd.org/dataoecd/4/36/36326495.pdf, accessed on June 2010) also rightly emphasizes that 'rising to the challenge of capacity development is not going to be easy'. This is principally because both capacity building and sustainability are complex and sometimes elusive concepts in themselves. To achieve them depends on a host of factors, many of which—like an enabling environment or political will for making appropriate policies—are generally not within the control of donors and often not even of the recipient government. They may depend upon the state of supporting institutions, the dynamism of the civil society, the level of trust and mutual understanding between the donors and recipient agencies. But it is clear from a large number of actual case studies that sustainability and capacity building (and the latter can be seen as one of the instruments to achieve the former) are the two most important challenges in making aid more effective.

SSC, SUSTAINABILITY AND CAPACITY BUILDING

The OECD defines sustainable development as 'a development path along which the maximization of human well-being for today's generations does not lead to declines in future well-being'.[10] In both scholarly and popular discourse, sustainable development often refers to minimizing the impact on the environment during the process of economic growth. While environmental sustainability is an increasingly important aspect of development, the importance of achieving self-sustaining development should not be overlooked. Therefore, an accurate definition of sustainable development should include both environmental sustainability as well as the notion of being self-sustaining. One of the keys to achieving sustainable development (particularly with regard to self-sustaining development) is to build capacity locally (i.e., helping people to help themselves).[11]

The SSC has a special role in achieving both sustainability and capacity building. One of the fundamental features of sustainable development is that it is based as far as possible on locally available resources or on the economy's ability to efficiently absorb imported inputs into its production and distribution systems. Moreover, aid results in greater sustainability if it is integrated with the investment and trade regimes that are either already in place or are emerging as a part of the overall development practice.[12] As can be expected on a priori grounds and as indeed has been demonstrated plentifully by case studies from Africa, Latin America and Asia, emerging donors, having gone through the experience relatively recently themselves, are more likely to have an ab initio better understanding of ground realities and development challenges in recipient countries in comparison to donors from advanced partners. In addition, emerging donors would also be expected to make greater efforts at trying to understand the ground realities in recipient countries and use their own experience in adapting the technical cooperation package to suit these conditions. The better understanding and appreciation of ground realities and the rather easier transfer of their own recent development experience implies that the SSC can contribute more readily to sustainable development. By enhancing the role of inputs from local areas, the SSC also ensures larger spillover effects or positive externalities for recipient economies.

The SSC also helps sustainable development in another indirect manner by minimizing the chances for 'brain or resource drain' from recipient to donor economies. This is because of the relatively lower income differentials between the donor and recipient countries and the pressure on emerging donors to give a preference for employing their own resources in the domestic economy. Project implementation units, when established by emerging donors, offer somewhat higher but comparable salaries and working conditions as they obtain in the local economy. Thus, the distortion that often results from the Parallel Implementation Units (PIUs) being established by advanced economy donors and multilateral organizations is minimized in the case of the SSCs.

There can be an argument that emerging donors are not sufficiently aware of emerging concerns like global warming, gender empowerment, recognition of individual human rights, observance of labour standards, etc., and may not give sufficient heed to them in their aid practices. As the recent discourse leading up to the Copenhagen Summit and the stalemated Doha Round have shown, emerging economies are not only fully aware of these issues but also active participants in the debate on them. In some cases, they have taken significant steps within their own jurisdictions to address these issues to the extent possible. They would, therefore, not be expected to ignore these issues in aid-recipient countries. Admittedly, however, in some cases, emerging donors can be seen to turn a blind eye on violations of established norms and this has to be identified and prevented. This will be facilitated by bringing the new donors firmly into the fold of the donor community aid.

Capacity building in developing economies and capacity creation in failed states or in fragile and post-conflict economies is the other critical aspect and indeed the Siamese twin of sustainable development. One can hardly be disassociated from the other.[13] The OECD study on Capacity Development cited above (OECD, 2006) has highlighted the crucial role of capacity development and comprehensively discussed the challenges in achieving it. Its emphasis that 'a good understanding of context is fundamental' and that this can be achieved by using one of the three analytical tools of 'institutional analysis', 'power analysis' or 'drivers of change analysis' is well taken. So also are its other major conclusions including 'building shared understanding about what works and what doesn't' and 'consolidat[ing] the new consensus on capacity development as an endogenous process, make it reach all parts of the aid system and become a central topic of policy dialogue at country level'. While agreeing with all its major conclusions, we want to point out four additional aspects in the context of highlighting the role of emerging economies and the SSC in capacity building through aid to developing economies.

First, it is important to recognize, as this has not been sufficiently done so far, that there can be cases where donors have to build capacity virtually from scratch in critical sectors of the economy. In such cases of post-conflict and fragile states, it is crucial to quickly identify these critical sectors and not hesitate from direct action. This can be best done in consultation with local leaders and opinion makers but on occasions, on the basis of the donors' own judgement. From practical experience in many developing aid-receiving countries, it can be said with some confidence that this task will be more effectively and efficiently undertaken by emerging donors and their agents.[14]

Second, in actual experience, the identification of critical sectors in fragile states or that of critical weaknesses in existing institutions and practices in other developing economies can best be done by a sustained interaction and engagement between development agents and local residents. This can be achieved if donors insist on keeping their staff and consultants on the ground for long periods rather than bring them in for short durations.[15] Given all its complexities and non-tangible aspects, capacity building is best achieved by a process of sustained 'osmosis' between the recipients and experts which enables the former to observe and learn on the job.[16] In this case as well, emerging donors would have an added advantage as their resource persons would be more likely to agree for long-term stay in recipient countries and would be more affordable. Because of likely cultural and social overlap, they will also have a higher possibility to communicate their experience and lessons to the recipients. This is perhaps most important in improving the enabling environment for sustainable development and capacity building. Clearly, the SSC scores over the North–South paradigm in achieving aid effectiveness.

Third, emerging economy experts often demonstrate a greater tolerance for and the flexibility to adopt the 'second best' solution, which is often the best that can be achieved in the given circumstances of a developing or fragile economy. This often implies a dilution of the results that are *ex ante* expected to be achieved through a given programme of technical cooperation. This often becomes the critical difference between success and failure of the capacity-building exercise. The second best solution often conforms more closely to the absorptive capacity of the recipient agencies and produces tangible though diluted results. On the other hand, insisting on the first best solution could result in a breakdown of communications and demoralization of local staff. These three are important basis for giving the SSC a greater role in capacity building efforts in aid receiving countries.

Finally, if it is accepted that building capacity locally (i.e., training) is a cost-effective method of facilitating long-term, self-sustaining (i.e., sustainable) development, another question arises—what comparative advantages do certain countries have over others in delivering the training/technical assistance? The Government of India's comparative advantage with regard to providing technical assistance (through programmes like ITEC) is *value*.[17] There are two main factors contributing to the cost effectiveness of such programmes: *(a)* there is little overhead, and *(b)* the cost of services (i.e., education) is less than that of the

North.[18] India also has a wide range of technical expertise that can be of value to other developing countries.

SSC AND CONDITIONALITIES

Apart from the two central reasons of sustainable development and capacity building, the SSC's better role in improving aid effectiveness emerges from two other factors. First, there is a lower likelihood of imposing 'discredited or fashionable' conditionalities in the case of the SSC. Instead, emerging donors stand a better chance of getting the recipients' buy in for critical conditionalities that ensure successful outcomes. Second, the SSC permits a greater possibility of enforcing mutual accountability of both donors and recipients.

There has, in recent years, been strong resistance to and departure from imposing conditionalities on borrowers or aid recipients. The trend gathered strength in the wake of the Asian and Latin American crises during the latter half of the 1990s. In that phase, unnecessary suffering and economic malaise were brought about by an insistence by the donors on a set of conditionalities that were later seen to be unsuited to the prevailing conditions. This was also true of African, East European and Central Asian economies where the imposition of conditionalities drawn from the Washington Consensus had resulted in mounting debt, stagnant or even regressing MDGs and emergence of systemic corruption for which the onus was on the donors. To our mind, this experience of the latter half of the 1990s resulted in the demise of the Washington Consensus.[19] This trend has been further reinforced by the recent post-Lehman crisis which erupted at the very epicentre of global capitalism but affected nearly every country in varying degrees. The ostensible inability of any International Financial Institutions (IFIs) or multilateral agency to either foresee the crises or to prevent the spread of the contagion or respond effectively to minimize damage has taken a severe toll of both the credibility and the legitimacy of these institutions. This has left them quite incapable of imposing conditionalities on aid recipients.

However, emerging economies led by Brazil, China and India have weathered the crisis far better and come out of it with enhanced credibility. Their economic policies and approach to development is attracting significant attention in developing countries. These leading emerging economies have consequently far more credibility and legitimacy at this stage than their advanced economy counterparts. This enhanced stature can now be used by emerging donors to persuade recipients even to accept certain critical conditionalities that are essential for inclusive and rapid development. Emerging donors are more likely to ensure that such critical conditionalities are rooted in the ground realities and are arrived at after sustained interaction and analysis that results in them being mutually acceptable programmes.

One of the best examples of aid effectiveness has been the post-Second World War experience of the US aid to Europe under the Marshall Plan. This not only had strict conditionalities (including a complete tying to specified procurement sources) but also included US aid workers and resource persons taking over the running of particularly critical departments and agencies for a stipulated time period. It is important to cite this historical example to impress the need for similar actions by donors in specific circumstances. These could arise in countries where because of systemic corruption, institutional collapse, decimation of capacity and resources due to prolonged ethnic, and ideological or external strife, existing capacities may simply not suffice for delivering expected outcomes. Emerging donors will perhaps be less reluctant to take on a direct role in such cases where imposing a set of critically needed conditionalities is essential for achieving the desired outcomes.[20] It will also be more feasible for them to negotiate such an arrangement with the local ruling coalitions as they may be perceived as being more empathetic and understanding of the prevailing conditions.

SSC and Mutual Accountability

Building mutual accountability is clearly critical to putting in place a system of management that is focused on results. Developing country recipients will find emerging donor agencies to be relatively more accessible in negotiating such mutually acceptable benchmarks. Emerging donors may also be more amenable to being measured against those jointly agreed norms. As mentioned earlier, the SSC will perhaps generate more suitable or appropriate norms for enforcing accountability as they are more likely to accept the second-best as the acceptable outcome. The advantage of the SSC in enforcing mutual accountability and indeed for achieving better aid outcomes, as argued above, derives principally because of a 'shorter distance' between the recipients and donors across a range of parameters relative to the North–South paradigm. The distance or the gap between the emerging donor and the recipient is, for example, shorter in the case of development or transition experience which in advanced economies happened several centuries ago when, say, carbon imprint was not an issue and the world was not a global village!

Accountability generally refers to development actors (i.e., donors, recipients, etc.) being accountable to each other; however, recipients' accountability to their citizens can be a useful tool for development as well. Generating awareness among civil society in developing countries can play an important role in putting pressure on governments to implement policy reforms by leading to greater incentives for the provision of public goods. Bottom-up pressure in combination with outside pressure (i.e., international) can be a catalyst for effective reform.

THE STRONG CASE FOR TRILATERAL COOPERATION

While the SSC does have the above advantages which should propel it to centre stage in the aid architecture in the coming period, there are some possible downside risks as well. First, some emerging donors could possibly connive or collude with recipients to agree to highly diluted norms for mutual accountability. They may also agree on adoption of weak and non-transparent governance practices. These could (and are reportedly already in some cases) generate resentment among actual beneficiaries who may not receive the full benefit of the aid programme. Second, emerging donors may, in some cases, be tempted to not observe some of the accepted pillars of aid practices and not accept even the minimally required level of coordination, again to the detriment of recipients. For these and similar reasons, it will be useful to co-opt the SSC in the general architecture of global aid flows. This can be most effectively done by giving a greater role to trilateral cooperation[21] that brings together donors from advanced and emerging economies to work jointly on projects in developing countries. There are by now several examples of successful trilateral cooperation in nearly all of which the financial help from 'northern partners' has helped to replicate or scale up a successful development experience in an emerging or another developing country.[22]

Trilateral cooperation has the potential to exploit the comparative advantages of development partners (i.e., funding from the North, experience, expertise and value from the South), having important implications with regard to aid effectiveness. Using the limited resources of traditional donors to facilitate development as effectively as possible is a core goal of the international development community. One of the most effective ways to achieve this goal is to shift the role of traditional donors and to create more effective partnerships between traditional donors, emerging donors and recipients. Emerging donors have a wealth of expertise and experience in development; rather than 'reinventing the wheel' in other countries, it is possible to replicate and adapt successful interventions using the trilateral cooperation model.

The trilateral cooperation model can hopefully be made the norm rather than the exception as it is today. The necessary condition to achieve this transition for making trilateral collaboration the core modality of aid architecture is perhaps to accept 'poverty alleviation' as a global public good. This could result in all possible players accepting aid as an instrument for achieving this public good and a 'cooperative game' rather than see it as a tool for pursuing geostrategic national interests, which will quite often be perceived as a non-cooperative exercise.[23] This can be seen as the fourth rationale for aid which is in contrast to the threefold typology of aid serving geostrategic interests, undertaken as pure philanthropy or extended to achieve better governance. When seen as an instrument to achieve a global objective which generates extensive externalities for all concerned, aid can become a cooperative rather than a competitive game in which the SSC can be more easily co-opted as a component in the dominant paradigm of trilateral cooperation for managing global aid flows.

INDIA AS AN EMERGING DONOR

India is, and will continue, to shift from a recipient of aid to a donor. However, despite rapid growth, poverty remains a serious problem within India and it is not the case that India 'cannot use' aid (and, in fact, still receives considerable funding). However, donors from the

Global North will find it increasingly difficult to continue sending aid to India, particularly post-2008; while growth stagnates and unemployment rises, constituents within the UK, for example, are finding development assistance in India, which has quickly rebounded from the financial crisis and continues its torrid growth, to be less of a priority. Accordingly, there are reports that the Department For International Development (DFID) may substantially reduce or possibly stop providing aid to India. Meanwhile, India's outward assistance flows will continue to rise in an attempt (among other things) to counter China's influence within the developing world, although it will hardly be possible for India to keep pace with China's aggressive assistance strategy anytime soon.

According to the recently published Multidimensional Poverty Index, there are more poor people (according to their index, 421 million people) in 8 of the poorest states in India than in the 26 poorest countries in Africa combined. Accordingly, despite impressive growth, the Global North should continue to provide development assistance to India, particularly in the poorest states. Furthermore, aid agencies might consider channelling assistance directly to the poorest states, rather than the central government.

Despite the need for continued assistance, India can help improve the delivery and effectiveness of aid to the Least Developed Countries (LDCs) and can function as a conduit between the Global North and the LDCs. As noted, India has a comparative advantage in providing assistance in certain capacities (e.g., training/education) that should be taken advantage of through trilateral arrangements. Furthermore, certain developing countries, including India, are well suited to address development challenges (e.g., climate change adaptation). Since certain challenges faced by developing countries are unique to developing countries, developing countries might, in some instances, be more able to effectively address the issue. For example, water issues in developing countries are different from those in developed countries; as water stress continues to rise rapidly, transferring effective strategies and know-how will be of increasing importance.

CONCLUSION

With the ongoing shift in global balance of economic activity, larger emerging economies are destined to play a greater role both in driving forward the global economy and consequently in the management and implementation of global aid programmes. The emergence of new or emerging donors opens up several interesting possibilities in improving aid effectiveness. This leads us to conclude that it is the opportune time for moving the SSC from the sidelines to the centre stage of the discourse and delivery of aid globally. This is both timely and necessary. The most effective modality for bringing about this transition may be 'trilateral cooperation' which brings together both emerging and advanced economy donors in a common endeavour to facilitate the development process in recipient countries. Trilateral cooperation combines the comparative advantages of different categories of donors and also minimizes downside risks.

If the SSC is to emerge as a core component of future aid flows, some institutional changes in the governance architecture for managing global aid flows may be desirable. At present, the Development Assistance Committee (DAC) of the OECD is principally responsible for tracking and monitoring aid flows and for ensuring coordination among donors and harmonization of policies and delivery mechanisms. For the last decade, the DAC has also been engaging with the larger emerging economies in an attempt to bring them within the OECD framework that governs aid flows. These efforts have had mixed results so far, with emerging economies being largely on the margins of the governing global architecture. The prevailing modality is still that of the DAC extending its invitation for emerging economies to join the global effort instead of recognizing the central role it can be playing in making aid more effective.

Such an approach that is based on an 'Us and Them' distinction between advanced and emerging economy donors is somewhat archaic in present times. This is especially true in context of the changes already made and in the pipeline with respect to the global economic and financial architecture. Emerging economies have already been integrated, for example, in the enlarged Financial Stability Forum at the Bank of International Settlements and in the so called 'New Quad' that leads negotiations in the World Trade Organization. It is now well established that the G-20 is destined to be the apex global body for dealing with economic and financial issues. Therefore, in keeping with emerging trends, it would be appropriate for the DAC to give way to a larger G-20 committee for managing global aid flows. This is perhaps the only way forward to ensure that emerging donors are brought into the mainstream of global aid practices and contribute substantially to the design and delivery of aid and in tracking its flows and monitoring outcomes. This will also give a strong fillip to trilateral cooperation as a common forum will encourage greater interaction and a better appreciation of the role of aid flows in poverty alleviation, which will have a better chance of being recognized as a global public good in a forum that is more globally representative and relevant.

NOTES

1. These well-known five principles as per the Paris Declaration (PD) (2005) are ownership, alignment, harmonization, monitoring and mutual Accountability.
2. 'Donor-driven projects fit in with the myth of Western superiority—and indeed even reinforce it. We lecture, you listen; we give, you receive; we know, you learn; we take care of things—because you can't. Undermining Africans' own responsibilities, we take over. The attitude that "we" (i.e., donors, with our money and experts) will save Africa, and that "we" will end poverty undermines incentives for poor people to demand action from their own government'—Eveline Herfkens, Executive Coordinator, UN Millennium Campaign.
3. 'An analysis of the evolution of SSC indicates three trends. The first, refers to the explosion of networking made possible with the advent and "democratization of access"… the second, to mobilization of southern countries and institutions around strategic issues like global governance, financing for development … and the last, concerns seeking a "middle-ground" between traditional form of technical cooperation and the "soft" SSC in an effort to capture the best of both'—Ekoko and Benn, 2002.
4. Earlier rationales for the SSC in the 1960s believed that the North had been exploiting the resources of the South for its own benefits, and as such the SSC would provide to the South the strength of collectivism for bargaining its positions in the multilateral fora of negotiations (http://www.unescap.org/pdd/publications/apdj_12_1/7_escap.pdf, accessed on 8 March 2010).
5. See Woods (2008). Also, 'Implementing the Monterrey Consensus in the Asian and the Pacific Region: An Agenda for South-South regional Development Cooperation', http://www.unescap.org/61/English/E1332e.pdf (accessed on 8 March 2010).
6. 'South-South co-operation on development aims to observe the principle of non-interference in internal affairs, equality among developing partners and respect for their independence, national sovereignty, cultural diversity and identity and local content. It plays an important role in international development co-operation and is a valuable complement to North-South co-operation'—AAA, 2008.
7. Also, the Paris Declaration on Aid Effectiveness (2005).

8. 'The commitment in the Paris Declaration that countries should lead and donors support is more easily said than done. It is clear, however, that the interactions between donors and domestic actors can generate either vicious or virtuous circles of change in regard to the ownership of capacity development efforts. The key thing is to interrupt any vicious circles, in which ownership and capacity are progressively eroded, and build on any tentative steps that might result in the establishment of a more positive trend'—OECD, 2006, 8.

9. See for example, OECD (2006).

10. OECD Sustainable Development Glossary, http://www.oecd.org/glossary/0,3414, en_2649_37425_1970394_1_1_1_1,00.html#1970340 (accessed on September 2010).

11. The benefits of building capacity locally are well documented in the OECD-DAC Working Party on Aid Effectiveness Task Team on South-South Cooperation's analytical work for the Bogotá HLE (e.g., Barefoot College, ASER, BRAC and ITEC case stories).

12. Apparently the Chinese aid effort in Africa, which was earlier seen to lead the recipients away from the path of sustainable development, is now seen to be more effective as it has been entwined with the emerging trade and investment flows in the recipient countries. These are also often targeted to China but not exclusively to it, and in any case, results in income generation and employment whose benefits are more widely spread.

13. It can be argued that the two are indeed co-terminus in as much as if capacity development is achieved, sustainable development will invariably follow. This can, however, be seen as an over-reach because it can be visualized, for example, that policymaking capacity can be put to designing and implementing 'bad policies' in cases when there is a governance or regulatory capture by sectional interests. Many examples from South Asia can be given in support of this malutilization of capacity, created originally through aid including military capability.

14. This observation is based on the principal author's experience of working as a staff of the Asian Development Bank (ADB) in Mongolia, Myanmar and the Central Asian Republics over a period of seven years. The ADB staff was considered more accessible and also more appreciative of local conditions by officials of recipient countries. In some cases, the ADB staff would find themselves being approached to advise senior policymakers in developing and transition economies on how best to negotiate with representatives of advanced economy donors or organizations based in advanced countries. This would often result in a virtual trade-off between achieving greater harmonization of donor positions against safeguarding recipient interests. This perhaps explains the rather lukewarm support that emerging donors and regional multilateral organizations may have for some of the five pillars of the PD. The case of Asian donors' aid to Myanmar and Turkmenistan are perhaps exemplary in this regard and deserve to be studied in further detail to get a better understanding of these implicit trade-offs and their impact on aid effectiveness.

15. The short-term engagement is best captured by the fact that as pointed out by the OECD Report, there were 15,229 missions in 2007 by donor agencies to recipient developing economies.

16. This can be surely observed from studying the impact of different types of technical cooperation and isolating those where the resource persons stayed for extended periods.

17. ITEC Case Story, http://www.impactalliance.org/ev_en.php?ID=48720_201&ID2=DO_TOPIC (last accessed on September 2010).
18. Ibid.
19. See the work of Easterly (2006) for more details (for example, *The White Man's Burden: Why the West's Effort to Aid the Rest Have Done So Much Ill and So Little Good*).
20. This implies that one of the five pillars of the PD viz., 'non-interference in the internal affairs of the recipient country' will have to be suitably interpreted to allow for such a direct role which is mutually seen to be necessary. The next step should also be envisaged when in the case of a 'rogue regime' which prevents humanitarian aid from reaching the affected people, the global community will have to decide on the basis of some norms, reached hopefully through a consensus amongst donors, to act unilaterally to prevent avoidable major disasters.
21. 'Triangular Cooperation is supposed to rest on four principles:

    - The development priorities between two or more developing countries are identified and set by them.
    - The options for solving the particular development challenges are decided by the countries involved.
    - The development activity is managed by the developing countries.
    - Developed countries provide financial resources or other inputs'—Ekoko and Benn, 2002).

22. For example, the case of drip irrigation technologies being transferred from India to Pakistan with funds from Acumen Fund, US. Also, the work done by BRAC and Barefoot in different developing economies (based on a common working methodology) but funded by donors in the north.
23. This view is in contrast to that of Thérien (2002) who writes about the Right holding the fight against poverty ultimately a duty incumbent upon each state, not of the international community. Seen from this viewpoint, aid is often considered inefficient.

References

AAA (2008), 'Accra Agenda for Action (AAA)—Statement', http://siteresources. worldbank.org/ACCRAEXT/Resources/4700790-1217425866038/AAA-4-SEPTEMBER-FINAL-16h00.pdf (accessed in December 2011).

Dickerson, Michael (2010), 'ITEC Case Story', Task Team on South-South Cooperation, http://www.impactalliance.org/ev_en.php?ID=49445_201&ID2=DO_TOPIC (accessed on September 2010).

Easterly, William (2006), *The White Man's Burden: Why the West's Effort to Aid the Rest Have Done So Much Ill and So Little Good*, Penguin Press, New York.

Ekoko, Francois and Dennis Benn (2002), 'South South Cooperation and Capacity Development', *Development Policy Journal*, 2, UNDP.

Moyo, Dambisa (2009), *Dead Aid: Why Aid Is Not Working and How There Is a Better Way for Africa*, Farrar, Straus, and Giroux, New York.

OECD (2006), The Challenge of Capacity Development: Working towards Good Practice, Network on Governance, 35 DAC, Paris.

OECD (2010), 'Bogota Statement Towards Effective and Inclusive Development Partnerships', The High Level Event on South-South Cooperation and Capacity Development, 25 March, http://www.oecd.org/dataoecd/1/23/45497536.pdf (accessed in December 2011).

Woods, Ngaire (2008), 'Whose Aid? Whose Influence? China, Emerging Donors and the Silent Revolution in Development Assistance', *International Affairs,* 84 (6).

Thérien, Jean-Phillippe (2002), 'Debating Foreign Aid: Right Versus Left', *Third World Quarterly,* 23(3):449–6.

4

Aid and Growth in India

Some Evidence from Disaggregated Aid Data[1]

GEORGE MAVROTAS

INTRODUCTION

In this chapter we focus on the impact of aid on growth through the use of a new approach in the aid-effectiveness literature related to the composition of foreign aid. We present a model of the impact of aid on growth in an aid-recipient economy to derive a reduced-form growth equation, which is subsequently estimated by using time-series data for India over the period 1970–92. This chapter improves upon earlier work in the area of aid effectiveness by focusing on a neglected, though important issue, namely aid disaggregation and the way it affects the empirics of aid effectiveness. Fully disaggregated aid data has been constructed by the OECD for the first time to test the relevance of the aid-disaggregation hypothesis to aid effectiveness for India. Furthermore, the chapter employs modern time-series econometric analysis based on general-to-specific modelling and cointegration to shed more light on a highly debatable topic. The empirical results obtained seem to suggest that the composition of aid matters for deriving robust conclusions on aid effectiveness in the case of India and, at the same time, call for further work in this promising area within the context of more individual country studies.

A central problem with the existing empirical studies in the vast literature of aid effectiveness is their neglect of the heterogeneous character of foreign aid. The employment of a single figure for aid has been a key feature of the above literature. However, it has been rightly argued that the conclusions on aid effectiveness through the use of a single figure may be misleading, since we can distinguish at least four different categories of aid:

- Project aid with a relatively lengthy gestation period
- Programme aid which disburses rapidly as free foreign exchange
- Technical assistance (TA)
- Food aid and other commodity aid which adds directly to consumption (Cassen, 1994)

To the above four types of foreign aid, emergency or relief aid could be added as a separate category, given its increasing importance in recent years.

There are three key points here (Mavrotas, 1998):

1. First, different types of aid operate in a different way (and with different lag-structure) in the recipient country, thus, resulting in different macro effects.
2. Second, because of different conditions relating to each in different countries, there is also an extra reason to expect different effects of aid in each country—the *ceteris paribus* assumptions of the econometrics of aid may be disturbed by such considerations.
3. Third, and perhaps most importantly, aid composition might not matter so much if the proportions of different types of aid were constant; in such a case, there could be sense in a coefficient relating aid (measured by one number) to some aspect of effectiveness; but if the proportions are changing, as they are, and changing in different degrees for different countries, this will definitely disturb the econometric results.

Although an in-depth analysis of the impact of each type seems to be important, as the existing literature appears to suggest, a rigorous empirical analysis of the effectiveness of the above types of aid, being considered together, has been neglected by the existing literature. This has important implications for aid effectiveness studies (Mavrotas, 1998).[2]

The rest of the chapter proceeds as follows. In the next section, we present a model of the impact of aid on growth in an aid-recipient economy, with a particular focus on the composition of aid; thereafter, the chapter briefly discusses key features of the effectiveness of aid in the case of India; following this discussion, the chapter deals with data issues as well as with issues related to the econometric methodology. Thereafter, we report empirical findings from the estimation of a growth equation for India over the period 1970–92. The final section concludes the chapter and suggests some directions for further research in this area.

THE MODEL

The model I developed in this section is rooted in one aspect of the aid-effectiveness literature, which focuses on the response of the fiscal sector in the aid-recipient country in the presence of aid—namely the 'fiscal response' literature.[3]

We assume that the aid-recipient government has the following objective function:

$$U = f\,(I_g, T, B, G_c, G_s, A_1, A_2, A_3)$$

where,

U	:	welfare of public-sector policymakers
I_g	:	public investment expenditure for development purposes
T	:	tax revenue
B	:	public borrowing from domestic sources
G_c	:	government civil expenditure (non-developmental expenditure)
G_s	:	government socio-economic expenditure (developmental expenditure)
A_1	:	total programme aid to the public sector from all sources
A_2	:	total project aid to the public sector from all sources
A_3	:	total technical assistance to the public sector from all sources

The policymakers, therefore, have a set of alternative uses of public resources (i.e., public investment expenditure for development purposes, public socio-economic expenditure and public civil expenditure), alternative types of domestic financing (i.e., public borrowing and tax revenue) and alternative types of external assistance (i.e., programme aid, project aid and technical assistance.

We further assume that the public-sector policymaker is maximizing the following quadratic utility function:

$$U = a_0 - (a_1/2)(I_g - I_g^*)^2 - (a_2/2)(T - T^*)^2 - (a_3/2)(G_c - G_c^*)^2 -$$
$$(a_4/2)(G_s - G_s^*)^2 - (a_5/2)(B - B^*)^2 \qquad [2.1]$$

where,

$a_i > 0, i = 1, 2, ..., 5$ and the "*" variables stand for target levels of the variables defined above.

Deviating from the above planned variables is undesirable for the government policymaker.[4]

To go further, we draw on earlier work in this area by Mosley, Hudson and Horrell (1987) and Mosley and Hudson (1995, 1996) by incorporating a production function into the previous model and deriving the reduced-form equation for Gross Domestic Product (GDP) growth from a similar utility-maximization problem to the one used in the fiscal-response model above. However, we improve substantially on earlier work in this area by including a different private investment equation in the model and considering the role of uncertainty in both the growth and investment processes (see below).

Along these lines, the target values associated with the variables I_g, T, G_c, G_s and B in equation [2.1] above are defined as follows:[5]

$$I_g^* = a_6 Y + a_7 I_p \qquad [2.2]$$

where,

I_p is domestic private investment.

$$T^* = 0 \qquad [2.3]$$

That is, the aid-recipient government aims at minimising the tax burden.

$$B^* = 0 \qquad [2.4]$$

The underlying assumption in this case is that the aid-recipient government tries to minimize borrowing.

$$G_s^* = a_8 Y + a_9 G_{s, t-1} \qquad [2.5]$$

That is, it is assumed that government socio-economic expenditures (developmental expenditures) are determined by income level as well as their level a year ago.

$$G_c^* = a_{10} G_{c, t-1} \qquad [2.6]$$

Similarly, government civil expenditure (non-developmental expenditure) is determined by taking into account its level in the previous year.

The aid-recipient government now faces the following constraints:

$$I_g = B + (1 - a_{11})T + (1 - a_{12})A \qquad [2.7]$$

That is, the budget constraint. It is worth noting that the above budget constraint is the final outcome of the combination of the two sets of constraints below:

$$I_g + G_s + G_c = T + B + A \qquad [2.7.1]$$

and

$$G_s + G_c = a_{11}T + a_{12}A \qquad [2.7.2]$$

where,

$$0 \le p_i \le 1 \quad \text{and} \quad i = 1, 2$$

Furthermore, $1 - a_{11}$ stands for the portion of tax revenue going to government investment in the presence of aid, and $1 - a_{12}$ is the portion of total aid directed to government investment. .

We further assume that:

$$T = a_{13}Y \qquad [2.8]$$

Another feature of budget constraint [2.7] above is the use of the total aid variable A which is the sum of variables A_1 (programme aid),

A_2 (project assistance) and A_3 (technical assistance), i.e., $A = A_1 + A_2 + A_3$. For estimation purposes (see section on empirical findings from the estimation of a growth equation) we use disaggregated aid data figures given the focus of the chapter on the aid disaggregation issue. However, the use of a single figure for aid in the model above can facilitate the building of the model without raising problems in the estimation stage which will follow. Furthermore, we assume that total aid (A) and its components, A_1, A_2 and A_3, are exogenously determined.[6]

The Growth Constraint

The government's production function is of the following type:

$$Y = f\{K_g, K_p, L, H, \kappa(H, A), \sigma, UN\} \qquad [2.9]$$

where,

Y is national income; K_g is public sector physical capital stock; K_p is private sector physical capital stock; L stands for labour; H stands for total stock of human capital in the country; κ is technical progress and depends in turn on the available human capital stock in the country as well as foreign aid coming into the country; σ is an efficiency parameter which determines the position of output in relation to the production possibility frontier; finally, UN is an index of uncertainty in the recipient country (to capture mainly macroeconomic and sociopolitical instability). The above production function, similar to the one used by Mosley and Hudson (1995, 1996), reflects in a way recent developments in new growth theory, in which the level of human capital stock in the country is linked with output.

L can be omitted from equation [2.9] above given that in most developing countries labour is not a binding constraint on output. Therefore, we may end up with the following production function:

$$Y = f\{K_g, K_p, H, \kappa(H, A), \sigma, UN\} \qquad [2.10]$$

We further assume, following Mosley and Hudson (1995, 1996), that credit expansion (CR) in the aid-recipient country depends on the level of domestic savings (S), other financial flows (OFF) and the change in exports (ΔX):

$$CR = a_{14}\Delta X + a_{15}OFF + a_{16}S \qquad [2.11]$$

Contrary to what is assumed in most studies on aid effectiveness, domestic savings is assumed to be an endogenous variable in the model, being determined by GDP, aid and other financial flows:

$$S = a_{17}Y + a_{18}A + a_{19}OFF \qquad [2.12]$$

The Private Investment Constraint

In view of the theoretical and empirical literature of the determinants of private investment in developing countries the following specification is adopted:

$$I_p = a_{20}\Delta Y + a_{21}A + a_{22}OFF + a_{23}CR + a_{24}I_g + a_{25}UN \quad [2.13]$$

where,

ΔY is the change in the GDP (accelerator-type effect), CR stands for credit to the private sector, I_g is public investment (crowding-in or crowding-out effect), A and OFF stand for foreign aid and other foreign capital flows (Direct Foreign Investment or DFI, etc.) respectively (the external constraint) and UN stands for uncertainty related to macroeconomic instability or political instability.[7]

Before we go any further it is rather important at this stage to comment on the relationship between investment and growth in equation [2.13] above. The presence of ΔY variable in the right-hand side of the above equation clearly raises an important issue, debated for years in the relevant empirical literature, namely the direction of causation between investment and the GDP growth. For many years it has been argued that investment is an important determinant of the entire growth process. However, recently the above view has been challenged by a number of studies which have argued that the co-movement of investment ratios and growth rates may be mainly the result of a third crucial factor namely technological innovation which drives both output expansion and capital accumulation.[8] Along the above lines, capital accumulation is a consequence rather than a cause of the growth process. The above seem to suggest that the flexible accelerator model of investment used in this chapter, in which the GDP growth determines investment, is in line with recent findings in the relevant empirical literature.

The efficiency parameter σ, in the production equation [2.10], is also assumed to be dependent on foreign capital, namely foreign aid and other financial flows. In other words:

$$\sigma = a_{26} + a_{27} A + a_{28} OFF \qquad [2.14]$$

Following Mosley and Hudson (1995, 1996), we assume that the efficiency parameter σ will have upper and lower bounds of 1 and 0, where 1 stands for full efficiency; in addition the constant, a_{26} in equation [2.14] stands for the 'normal' level of efficiency which may depend on the socio-economic system.

Furthermore, technical progress κ is assumed to be determined by two variables only, namely foreign aid and stock of human capital available in the country, which together generate increasing returns to the stock of human capital along the lines of the new growth literature:[9]

$$\kappa = a_{29} + a_{30} A + a_{31} H \qquad [2.15]$$

The last equation completes the model.

We can now derive the reduced-form growth equation for the above aid-recipient economy by maximizing utility function [2.1] subject to constraints.

Maximizing [2.1] subject to constraints [2.7.1] and [2.7.2] and forming the Lagrangean, we take:

$$L = a_0 - (a_1/2)(I_g - I_g^*)^2 - (a_2/2)(T - T^*)^2 - (a_3/2)(G_c - G_c^*)^2 - (a_4/2)(G_s - G_s^*)^2 - (a_5/2)(B - B^*)^2 + \lambda_1\{I_g + G_s + G_c - T - B - A\} + \lambda_2\{G_s + G_c - a_{11}T - a_{12}A\}$$

And, the first-order conditions can now be derived as follows:

$$\partial L/\partial I_g = -a_1(I_g - I_g^*) + \lambda_1 = 0 \qquad [2.16]$$

$$\partial L/\partial G_c = -a_3(G_c - G_c^*) + \lambda_1 + \lambda_2 = 0 \qquad [2.17]$$

$$\partial L/\partial G_s = -a_4(G_s - G_s^*) + \lambda_1 + \lambda_2 = 0 \qquad [2.18]$$

$$\partial L/\partial T = -a_2(T - T^*) - \lambda_1 - \lambda_2 a_{11} = 0 \qquad [2.19]$$

$$\partial L/\partial B = -a_5(B - B^*) - \lambda_1 = 0 \qquad [2.20]$$

The final model solution can be obtained by taking into account the growth constraint and the private investment constraint (aforementioned). Finally, we end up with the following reduced-form estimable growth equation:[10]

$$\Delta Y/Y = b_0 + b_1\Delta X/Y + b_2 A/Y + b_3 OFF/Y + b_4 UN + b_5 dH \quad [2.21]$$

And, by decomposing total aid flows A in three main components, namely A_1 (programme aid), A_2 (project assistance) and A_3 (technical assistance), we end up with the following growth equation:

$$\Delta Y/Y = b_0 + b_1\Delta X/Y + b_2 A_1/Y + b_3 A_2/Y + b_4 A_3/Y + b_5 OFF/Y + b_6 UN + b_7 dH \quad [2.22]$$

In the light of equation [2.22] above, the GDP growth is determined by a set of factors which include the share of aid variables in the GDP, foreign capital directed to the private sector (as percentage of GDP), the share of exports in GDP, the change in human capital stock in the aid-recipient country and an uncertainty variable to capture macroeconomic instability or uncertainty stemming from socio-political instability.[11] By using the above equation we try to capture some of the most important developments in the growth literature recently with a particular focus on the impact of foreign aid on growth.

The Impact of Human Capital

Going back to our growth equation (equation [2.22]), the inclusion of a human capital variable in the equation reflects the centrality of the human capital factor in the theoretical and empirical growth literature. The development of human capital through education and vocational training increases productivity which in turn increases output. Furthermore, given that investment in human capital has benefits which are external to the individual, it will result in increasing returns to scale which in turn raise the long run rate of growth along the lines of some new growth models (Barro, 1991; Lucas, 1988; Obstfeld, 1989; Romer, 1986 among others).

The Role of International Capital Flows

Foreign capital going to the private sector (other financial flows variable in equation [2.22]) is expected to affect growth positively, particularly through policies which encourage DFI and international capital in general, as shown in Findlay (1978) and Wang (1990).

Trade and Growth

The presence of the export variable in our growth equation is associated with trade aspects of the growth literature. Studies by Balassa and Associates (1982), Bhagwati (1978), Edwards (1989), Krueger (1995) and Moschos (1989) among others, suggest a strong positive link between trade openness (as measured by export performance) and the GDP growth. Export performance as a proxy for trade openness has also been used in studies by Dollar (1992), Greenaway and Sapsford (1994) as well as Heitger (1987).

The Impact of Uncertainty on Growth (and Investment)

The appearance of the uncertainty variable in our growth equation [2.22] above reflects the increasing attention which has been paid by empirical studies recently to the potential negative effects of uncertainty on the GDP growth. The available studies in the growth literature (not necessarily related to the effectiveness of aid) define uncertainty either by considering democracy aspects in the growth process (see studies by Alesina and Rodrik (1994); Helliwell (1992) and, more recently, Mauro (1995) on the relationship between corruption and growth) or uncertainty in terms of socio-political instability (see Barro (1991); Cukierman, Edwards and Tabellini (1992); and Ozler and Tabellini (1992) among others). In this chapter, uncertainty is defined in terms of macroeconomic instability following an increasing literature recently and in the light of the severe problems involved in the measurement of other types of uncertainty. Measurement and definition issues are discussed in section where data and methodology issues are discussed.[12]

Do Policies Matter for Growth?

A particularly rich strand of the new growth literature has considered the important role of policies in the entire growth process. Although policy issues have widely been acknowledged as central ones for improving the effectiveness of foreign aid in aid-recipient economies, little has been done in the relevant empirical literature to test the impact of foreign aid on growth in the presence of macroeconomic policies. Even most importantly, nothing has been done so far, to test the growth impact of disaggregated aid series in the presence of policies.[13]

The recent World Bank (1998) study with a clear focus on the role of macroeconomic policies in aid effectiveness (though not using an aid disaggregation approach) is an important contribution in this interesting area. The main conclusion of the report is that 'aid works in a good policy environment'. However, the robustness of the empirical analysis of Burnside and Dollar (1997), on which the World Bank study is based, has been under attack recently by a number of studies, which cast serious doubts on the validity of empirical analysis in the above study, with significant implications for policy in the area of aid effectiveness. More precisely, the Burnside-Dollar 'solution' of the micro–macro paradox is statistically delicate, to say the least, has been contradicted by other recent studies (e.g., Hansen and Tarp, 2000; Killick, 1998; and Guillamont and Chauvet, 1999) and cannot be seen as robust (Tarp and Hjertholm, 2000; Lensink and White, 2000).

In this chapter we try to address this important issue as well, in the context of the aid disaggregation approach. We do this by adding a number of policy variables in the growth equation [2.22] above. These include government consumption as a percentage of the GDP, budget surplus as a percentage of the GDP and money supply as a percentage of the GDP (in order to capture possible distortions in the financial system as suggested by King and Levine (1994)—an institutional/political variable as well).[14] Finally, trade policy (in terms of trade openness) has already been captured in our growth equation by the use of the export variable (as a percentage of the GDP). The importance of trade policy for growth has been stressed very recently in studies by Sachs and Warner (1995) and Krueger (1995).

AID IN INDIA[15]

India has recently been shrinking as a focus of aid donors' attention, although it has been one of the main aid recipients in the 1960s and the 1970s. Total Overseas Development Assistance (ODA) assistance (gross ODA, disbursements) to India was on average about 1.5 per cent of the GDP over the period 1970–92. It reached its peak in 1975 (2.38 per cent of the GDP), following the 1974 crisis year. Since then, it has steadily declined, around 1 per cent on average throughout the 1980s, to recover slightly in the early 1990s, mainly due to the crisis of 1991 and the related Structural Adjustment Programmes (SAP) aid flows which followed.[16]

As an important study on aid effectiveness in India has shown, aid donors have never been willing to provide the massive absolute sums of money required to render India's aid, per person or as a proportion of Gross National Product (GNP), comparable to that of other low income countries (Lipton and Toye, 1990). This 'large country effect', according to the authors, partly results from the geo-political motivation behind aid giving in the sense that most aid donors wish to appear generous in as many different countries as possible and within this context, they can win allies in 20 medium-sized poor countries by economizing on aid to one large country like India.[17]

Aid flows, however, have been of macroeconomic importance for that they have released a savings or a foreign exchange constraint and, thus, have been valuable for the economy despite their modest size; aid financed a significant, though declining, share of gross domestic capital formation, imports of plant and machinery and central government capital expenditures. Foreign aid's contribution to the Green Revolution in India was also something more than significant. Furthermore, India's experience of aid offers useful lessons for aid to other countries today, particularly in the areas of aid management, sectoral policies, rural credit, agricultural research and poverty-oriented schemes (see Cassen, 1978, Cassen, 1994; Sukhatme, 1989).[18]

During the period 1980–92 (of relevance to this chapter), the main donors of aid to India were the World Bank/International Development Organization (IDA) (35 per cent), Germany (9 per cent), Japan (8 per cent), United Kingdom (8 per cent), the US (7 per cent), the Netherlands (5 per cent), the European Commision or EC (4 per cent) and Sweden (3 per cent). Furthermore, most of the overall aid went to infrastructural projects (including power, coal, transport and communications). Major aid donors, such as the World Bank, Germany and Japan, offered mixed credits for such projects which involved imports from the donor countries. Finally, about 50 per cent of the World Bank/IDA aid primarily involved irrigation and 'general agriculture' (OECD, various issues; Netherlands Development Cooperation, 1994).

During the period 1980–90, multilateral and bilateral donors provided almost equal shares on average. At the beginning of the 1980s, bilateral donors started to direct an increasing part of their aid budgets to social sectors in India. It is notable that almost 70 per cent of these social-sector projects were concentrated in seven states only. That was not the case with multilateral donors, which rather concentrate on nation-wide programmes (Netherlands Development Cooperation, 1994).[19, 20]

Turning to the composition of aid in India, and in particular the proportions of each aid category employed in the chapter in total aid, they changed dramatically during the period 1970–92. Project assistance remained the main type of aid throughout the period, with an average share in total aid at the level of 65 per cent, although it fluctuated dramatically during the above period, moving between 40 per cent in 1976 to almost 77 per cent in 1982 and 1990. Programme aid also fluctuated sharply during the above period following a downward trend since 1976 and averaging around 20 per cent of total aid for the remaining years. It grew rapidly in 1991, reaching almost 30 per cent of total aid, due to the macroeconomic crisis in that year.[21] Finally, the technical assistance's share in total aid was on average 5 per cent throughout the 1970s to increase at about 10 per cent on average during the remaining years, reaching 13.5 per cent in 1992.

Regarding the share of the above aid categories in the GDP over the period under examination, project assistance is well above the two other types of aid as percentage of the DP throughout most of the period, followed by programme aid and technical cooperation grants. The share of project aid is on average less than 1 per cent for the entire period, whereas the programme aid's share was below 0.25 per cent on average over the same period, to increase to 0.41 per cent in 1991. The TA was relatively modest as a percentage of the GDP, as compared to the other two types of aid flows to the country during the period 1970–92. This may be partly due to India's own large stock of skilled and trained people in many sectors of the economy, although technical cooperation grants were particularly significant for the development of agricultural research institutes (Cassen, 1994; Lipton and Toye, 1990).

Previous aid effectiveness studies in India concluded that overall, aid had a positive impact on the Indian economy.[22] Aid was found to have a strong positive impact on investment in India in the study by Chaudhuri (1978), by regressing investment on net national product and aid.

The overall effect of food aid from the US on India's agricultural sector in the 1950s and the 1960s was also considered to be positive. The period of food aid in India opened with the US Agriculture

Trade and Adjustment Act of 1954, better known as PL 480. During the period 1955–76, India received the most food aid of any country under PL 480: over 50 million tonnes of agricultural commodities—only slightly less than the combined shipments to Pakistan, South Korea, South Vietnam and Egypt (Sukhatme, 1989).[23]

Finally, turning to the impact of particular types of aid on the Indian economy, by reviewing more than 60 evaluations of project aid to India, a major aid effectiveness study found that overall World Bank projects show good returns (Lipton and Toye, 1990); it also found that more recent World Bank projects showed better results than earlier ones. However, several evaluation inadequacies were identified and the need for more rigorous project evaluations was stressed.[24]

DATA ISSUES AND ECONOMETRIC METHODOLOGY

Data series on disaggregated aid flows (programme aid, project aid and TA) were constructed by the OECD in Paris (Reporting Systems Division) by drawing on two separate databases: the Development Assistance Committee (DAC) and the Creditor Reporting System (CRS). As programme aid and commodity aid are not identifiable by recipient country in the DAC data, the CRS data were used for individual commitments. Then, the series were transformed into disbursements by aggregating the commitments and applying their percentage share in total CRS grants/loans (minus food aid and technical cooperation) to total DAC disbursements of grants/loans (minus food aid and technical cooperation).[25, 26] It is notable that data availability on aid figures (of crucial significance in this chapter) was the main factor for determining the sample size (1970–92)of the present study.

Total Programme Aid (A1)

Figures are in gross disbursements and in millions of US dollars (current prices). The series cover the period 1973–92; data on programme aid is not available before 1973. The series include the following programme aid sub-categories: balance-of-payment support, current import finance, general imports, programme assistance, budget support, agricultural buffer stock financing, other buffer stock financing and commodity aid.

Total Project Aid (A2)

As in the case of Programme Aid above, the series are in gross disbursements and in millions of US dollars (current prices); they also cover the period 1970–92. The series include project aid in terms of both grants and loans.

Total Technical Assistance (A3)

Data is in gross disbursements and in millions of US dollars. The series cover the period 1970–92. Note also that before 1973, TA is included in Project Aid; from 1973 onwards TA (or technical cooperation grants) is a separate aid category.

GDP

Data series are drawn from the World Tables (various issues) of the World Bank over the period 1970–92.

Other Financial Flows (OFF)

The series cover financial flows directed to the private sector, mainly in the form of Foreign Direct Investment (FDI) and portfolio flows. The source is the Geographical Distribution of Financial Flows to Aid Recipient Countries of the OECD (various issues).

Exports (X)

Data on exports are derived from the World Tables (various issues) of the World Bank for the period 1970–92; for India, see line 'exports of goods and services'.

Human Capital Variable

The choice of an appropriate human capital variable to be included in the estimation of our growth equation was a difficult one. Quite recently, the International Economic Department of the World Bank, has prepared a new database on annual education stocks for 85 industrial and developing countries (including India) over the period 1965–87.[27] The method used to build the new database on human capital draws on earlier approaches by Lau, Jamison and Louat (1991) among others, in which years of schooling are used as a proxy measure for human capital (school enrolment data). Although the database is quite long, the series terminate in 1987 and, therefore, could not be used in our econometric analysis since they would reduce an already small sample size dramatically.

The variable we decided to use in the present study in order to capture human capital effects in the growth equation for India is the secondary school enrolment ratio, which is available from the World Bank (World Tables, various issues). Although problems do also exist with this particular measure of human capital, the choice seems to be appropriate in the light of the incomplete series related to the existing human capital stock databases and the extensive use of school enrolment ratios in the empirical literature.[28]

Policy Variables

We recall from the discussion in the previous section that a number of policy variables will be considered at the final stage of the estimation of the growth equation. The policy variables we consider in our econometric analysis include government consumption as a percentage of the GDP, budget surplus as a percentage of the GDP and money supply as a percentage of the GDP. Data on government consumption (general government consumption) were derived from the World Tables (various issues) of the World Bank for the period 1970–92. The same source was also used to derive data on money supply. Finally, concerning the third policy variable tried, namely budget surplus/deficit as a percentage of the GDP, it was constructed by the author from the existing series on total tax revenue (T) and total current expenditure (G) (IMF, various issues).

Uncertainty Variables

As is well known, it is notoriously difficult to use uncertainty variables in empirical research, in the light of the severe measurement problems which are involved in the construction of this sort of series. The existing databases on uncertainty variables mainly in the form of socio-political instability do not cover long time periods and are much more appropriate for cross-section or panel data analysis.[29]

Given the lack of sufficiently long data series on uncertainty (in terms of socio-political instability) in the case of India, we tried to construct a set of uncertainty variables associated with macroeconomic variables to capture macroeconomic instability effects. More precisely, we decided to construct three uncertainty variables in order to experiment with their possible negative impact on the growth equation: uncertainty variable UN1 was constructed as a three-year moving average of the standard deviation of the change in real GDP; uncertainty variable UN2 was obtained as a three-year moving average of the standard deviation of the change in terms of trade; and, finally, uncertainty variable UN3 was constructed as a three-year moving average of the standard deviation of the change in the real exchange rate. Data on Terms of Trade (used in the construction of UN2 uncertainty variable) covering the period 1970–92 was derived from the World Tables (various issues) of the World Bank (index, 1987 = 100). Finally, we used the following definition of real exchange rate in order to obtain the uncertainty variable UN3 above:

$$RER = \{ER(Px + Pm)/2\}/GDPdeflator$$

where ER stands for nominal exchange rate, Px represents the export unit price index derived from the World Tables (various issues) of the World Bank over the period 1970–92, Pm stands for the import unit price index drawn from the World Tables (various issues) over the same period and GDP deflator represents the GDP deflator (1987= 100) (see the section on data and methodology). The use of the above formula for the derivation of real exchange rate reflects a trade-oriented definition of RER.

Finally, the local GDP deflator (1987 = 100) has been used to deflate the series (source: World Tables, World Bank).

On the estimation front, in this chapter we build on two important developments in applied econometrics in recent years namely general-to-specific methodology and cointegration (Hendry, 1995). Along these lines, we employ unit root tests to test the stationarity of the series followed by cointegration tests (see Johansen, 1988; Johansen and Juselius, 1990).[30]

Johansen's approach is the best available to estimate the growth equation of our extended model since it is asymptotically more efficient. However, given our relatively small sample size and the number of variables involved in the growth equation, the employment of Johansen's full-information procedure would give rise to a practical problem in the estimation stage. More precisely, the growth equation to be estimated consists of the dependent variable and a set of 7 regressors, not to mention the policy variables. The estimation of the complete Variance (VAR)system in this case would involve an eight-equation system. However, parameter estimation in the context of this system would be dramatically affected by the relatively limited degrees of freedom we have for estimation purposes (Heargraves, 1994). Moreover, it has been argued quite rightly by Urbain (1995) that economic interpretation of empirical relations in such a large system is problematic due to the common inability of economic theory to offer sufficient guidance for a complete structural specification. Furthermore, given that the VAR model is a statistical model of a reduced form, it cannot offer insight into the short-run dynamics, in case someone is interested not only in the long-run parameters but also in the short-run ones—the reduced form parameters may be of a limited structural as well as economic interest in this case.

Along the above lines, although we use Johansen's approach to search for cointegrating vectors in the equation under consideration, we do not go further to estimate the complete VAR. Instead, we focus on the estimation of the General Unrestricted Model procedure (GUM) in case only one cointegrating vector is present (see Hendry, 1995; Boswijk, 1995; Serven, 1996 among others). At a final stage, we can rearrange and simplify the GUM in order to arrive at an error-correction specification with all the advantages it implies for the empirical estimates derived.

The above methodology is the most appropriate in our case, since it combines the strengths of both the Johansen approach and the error-correction specification and thus can result in robust econometric analysis and economically meaningful estimates as well. However, when the reduced rank regression procedure of Johansen suggests the presence of more than one cointegrating vector, the use of the GUM cannot be justified. In this case, we can focus on the cointegrating vector which is theory consistent and at the same time statistically meaningful and then employ the instrumental variables technique to estimate the error correction model. This can help us to tackle interpretation problems, which would arise if we used the full Maximum Likelihood approach of Johansen to estimate the complete VAR system, and at the same time to capture a possible simultaneity bias in the empirical models concerned. The above reasonable compromise in the estimation methodology of the growth equation can help us to derive empirical results which would be interpretable and meaningful in an economic sense as well as econometrically robust.

ESTIMATION RESULTS

We can now turn to the estimation of the central equation of our model, i.e., growth equation [2.22]. The list of determinants include foreign capital flows directed to the private sector (per cent of GDP), exports (per cent of GDP), the change in human capital stock, an uncertainty variable to capture macroeconomic instability and the three types of foreign aid (all as per cent of GDP) which we are using in our econometric analysis. Unit-roots associated with DF and ADF test-statistics are reported in Table 4.1. The tests seem to suggest that the series A1/Y, A2/Y, A3/Y, ΔX/Y and OFF/Y are all integrated of order one, but the series ΔGDP/Y and ΔH are rather stationary ones.

We can now proceed with the next stage, i.e., tests for the presence of a long-run relationship among our series in the growth equation. A working assumption that has been made, in view of the significance of the series ΔGDP/Y (our dependent variable) and ΔH for our growth equation, was to treat these series as I(1) ones and include them in the VAR. We also decided to use uncertainty variable UN2 in the VAR in light of preliminary regressions carried out.[31] Results obtained within the context of the maximum likelihood procedure of Johansen are reported in Table 4.2. Cointegration seems to be present among the series in the growth equation and two cointegrating vectors were identified.[32]

In view of the discussion in data and methodology, we focus on one cointegrating vector, which is theory consistent and econometrically robust, in order to estimate a restricted error correction model for the GDP growth by employing the instrumental variables estimation procedure.[33] Empirical results from the estimation of the

Table 4.1
Unit Root Tests for the Variables ΔY/Y, A1/Y, A2/Y, A3/Y, OFF/Y, ΔX/Y, ΔH, India, 1970–92

GDP growth (ΔY/Y)		
Statistic	Without trend	With trend
DF	–3.757 (–3.003)	–4.657 (–3.633)
ADF(1)	–0.766 (–3.011)	–1.645 (–3.645)
ADF(2)	–0.189 (–3.019)	–1.028 (–3.659)
ADF(3)	–1.140 (–3.029)	–2.358 (–3.674)

95% critical values in brackets

Programme Aid as % of GDP (A1/Y)		
Statistic	Without trend	With trend
DF	–1.915 (–3.003)	–2.396 (–3.633)
ADF(1)	–1.884 (–3.011)	–2.774 (–3.645)
ADF(2)	–2.418 (–3.019)	–4.549 (–3.659)
ADF(3)	–2.389 (–3.029)	–4.357 (–3.674)

95% critical values in brackets

Project Aid as % of GDP (A2/Y)		
Statistic	Without trend	With trend
DF	–2.708 (–3.003)	–2.735 (–3.633)
ADF(1)	–4.851 (–3.011)	–4.812 (–3.645)
ADF(2)	–2.705 (–3.019)	–2.666 (–3.659)
ADF(3)	–2.020 (–3.029)	–1.167 (–3.674)

95% critical values in brackets

Technical Assistance as % of GDP (A3/Y)		
Statistic	Without trend	With trend
DF	–0.756 (–3.003)	–2.601 (–3.633)
ADF(1)	–0.183 (–3.011)	–2.749 (–3.645)
ADF(2)	0.721 (–3.019)	–1.516 (–3.659)
ADF(3)	1.230 (–3.029)	–0.521 (–3.674)

95% critical values in brackets

Other Financial Flows as % of GDP (OFF/Y)		
Statistic	Without trend	With trend
DF	–2.079 (–3.003)	–2.206 (–3.633)
ADF(1)	–1.987 (–3.011)	–2.866 (–3.645)

(continued table 4.1)

(continued table 4.1)

Statistic	Without trend	With trend
ADF(2)	−1.317 (−3.019)	−1.563 (−3.659)
ADF(3)	−1.102 (−3.029)	−1.289 (−3.674)

95% critical values in brackets

Change in Exports as % of GDP (ΔX/Y)

Statistic	Without trend	With trend
DF	−2.682 (−3.003)	−3.180 (−3.633)
ADF(1)	−2.433 (−3.011)	−2.984 (−3.645)
ADF(2)	−1.498 (−3.019)	−2.169 (−3.659)
ADF(3)	−1.788 (−3.029)	−2.493 (−3.674)

95% critical values in brackets

Change in Human Capital (ΔH)

Statistic	Without trend	With trend
DF	−3.703 (−3.003)	−3.844 (−3.633)
ADF(1)	−2.761 (−3.011)	−2.797 (−3.645)
ADF(2)	−2.609 (−3.019)	−2.623 (−3.659)
ADF(3)	−1.821 (−3.029)	−1.386 (−3.674)

95% critical values in brackets

Table 4.2
Testing for Cointegration: Growth Equation
(without Policy Variables), India, 1970–92

Johansen Maximum Likelihood Procedure—Cointegration LR Test based on Maximal Eigenvalue of the Stochastic Matrix; maximum lag in VAR = 1

Null	Alternative	Statistic	95% critical value
$r = 0$	$r \geq 1$	186.53	157.10
$r \leq 1$	$r \geq 2$	125.27	124.25
$r \leq 2$	$r \geq 3$	81.22	95.17
$r \leq 3$	$r \geq 4$	52.15	70.59
$r \leq 4$	$r \geq 5$	29.36	48.28
$r \leq 5$	$r \geq 6$	11.97	31.52
$r \leq 6$	$r \geq 7$	5.05	17.95
$r \leq 7$	$r = 8$	0.14	8.17

Table 4.3
Instrumental Variable Estimates of the *Error Correction Model* (ECM)—Growth Equation, India, 1973–92

Dependent Variable: $\Delta(\Delta Y/Y)$		
Regressors	Coefficient	t-ratio
constant	−10.67	−2.38
$\Delta(\Delta Y/Y)$ (−1)	−0.61	−3.48
$\Delta(\Delta X/Y)$	−10.18	3.87
$\Delta(A2/Y)$	−12.80	−1.64
ECM (−1)	−0.32	−2.03
adjusted $R^2 = 0.70$	DW-statistic = 2.20	Sargan's $\chi^2(9)$: 5.11 [0.82]

Diagnostic Tests*		
Test Statistics	LM version	F version
Serial Correlation (a)	$\chi^2(1)$: 3.35 [0.54]	not applicable
Functional Form (b)	$\chi^2(1)$: 0.41 [0.52]	not applicable
Normality (c)	$\chi^2(2)$: 0.42 [0.81]	not applicable
Heteroscedasticity (d)	$\chi^2(1)$: 0.15 [0.69]	not applicable

* Figures in square brackets are rejection probabilities.

Notes: (a) Lagrange multiplier test of residual serial correlation; (b) Ramsey's RESET test using the square of the fitted values; (c) based on the test of skewness and kurtosis of residuals; (d) based on the regression of squared residuals on squared fitted values.

restricted error correction model appear in Table 4.3. We end up with a final parsimonious error correction model for GDP growth in India, in which the main determinants of growth (in terms of short-run effects) are only exports, project assistance (A2/Y) and the lagged dependent variable. The remaining variables did not appear in the final restricted error correction model on the basis of a general-to-specific approach that was followed. Indeed, LM, LR and F-tests, which were carried out, clearly indicated that the series A1/Y, A3/Y, UN2, ΔH and OFF/Y (and their lag values up to two years) were not significant in all the less restricted error correction models which we estimated.

However, they all appear in the final model, in an indirect way, through the error correction term, ECM (−1), reported in Table 4.3. It is notable that the coefficient of the error correction term is 0.32, which suggests that the adjustment to the long-run equilibrium is relatively slow; the coefficient for the ECM (–1) is also significant at 5 per cent as it happened with all the less restricted models tried.

Turning to the discussion of the findings related to the variables appearing in the Table (short-run effects), the lagged dependent variable (one-year lag) has a negative short-run effect on the GDP growth; it is notable, however, that the lagged dependent variable had a positive sign when longer lags were tried (though non-significant) in more general error correction models. The export variable takes the expected positive sign (short-run effect on growth) and it is significant at 5 per cent significance level; this finding is in line with empirical findings reported in the vast empirical literature related to the impact of exports on growth. The only aid variable with short-run effects on growth is project assistance; it has a strong and negative short-run effect on the GDP growth in India over the period 1970–92, and it is significant at 10 per cent level only. This finding is consistent with the one obtained in Mosley and Hudson (1995), in which a negative, though non-significant, coefficient for total aid was reported (total aid as an average of five years since current year) from the estimation of a similar growth equation for India covering the period 1965–90.

Finally, our parsimonious, restricted error-correction model of the GDP growth for India passes all misspecification tests related to functional form, autocorrelation, heteroscedasticity and normality as well as Sargan's test associated with the rejection of the overidentifying restriction. The model's explanatory power is relatively good with an adjusted R^2 around 0.70 as is also the case with the model's predictive power.

Aid and Growth in India: The Role of Policies

Following the discussion of the impact of aid on growth in an aid-recipient economy, we will try to go further in our examination of the impact of different types of aid on growth in India by considering the role of policies in our growth equation. The question which we will try to address here is whether policies adopted in the aid recipient country have an impact on the overall effect of aid on the GDP growth.

We use as policy variables the share of government consumption in GDP (C/Y), budget-surplus/budget-deficit as per cent of GDP (TG/Y) and the money supply's share in GDP (MS/Y). Two main scenarios will be considered: *(a)* use of policy variables (one at a time) in the growth equation, but without the uncertainty variable UN2 being included in the equation; and *(b)* use of policy variables (one at a time) in the growth equation with the uncertainty variable UN2 being included in the model.

Scenario I: Policies in the Presence of Aid without Uncertainty

In Table 4.4 we report standard unit root tests for the policy variables MS/Y, TG/Y and C/Y. In the light of the reported DF and ADF test-statistics, all policy variables seem to be I(1) series.

Table 4.4
Unit Root Tests for the Policy Variables C/Y, TG/Y, MS/Y, India, 1970–92

Government Consumption as % of GDP (C/Y)		
Statistic	*Without trend*	*With trend*
DF	−1.104 (−3.003)	−1.828 (−3.633)
ADF (1)	−0.944 (−3.011)	−3.434 (−3.645)
ADF (2)	−0.729 (−3.019)	−1.651 (−3.659)
ADF (3)	−1.599 (−3.029)	−1.498 (−3.674)

95% critical values in brackets

Budget Surplus as % of GDP (TG/Y)		
Statistic	*Without trend*	*With trend*
DF	−0.836 (−3.003)	−2.775 (−3.633)
ADF (1)	−0.566 (−3.011)	−2.406 (−3.645)
ADF (2)	−0.655 (−3.019)	−2.278 (−3.659)
ADF (3)	−0.781 (−3.029)	−2.285 (−3.674)

95% critical values in brackets

Money Supply as % of GDP (MS/Y)		
Statistic	*Without trend*	*With trend*
DF	−1.051 (−3.003)	−1.385 (−3.633)
ADF (1)	−0.795 (−3.011)	−2.491 (−3.645)
ADF (2)	−0.779 (−3.019)	−2.212 (−3.659)
ADF (3)	−1.257 (−3.029)	−2.061 (−3.674)

95% critical values in brackets

We proceed next by reporting cointegration tests associated with the Johansen approach of reduced rank regression. Table 4.5 presents cointegration tests in case the three policy variables are included in the list of variables in the growth equation but with the uncertainty variable UN2 being excluded. The right lag for the VAR in all cases is one year, given the long list of explanatory variables in our growth equation. Johansen's maximum likelihood approach seems to suggest the presence of a long run relationship among the series in question, i.e., the series are cointegrated and one cointegrating vector was identified in each case.

Given the presence of one cointegrating vector in each case, the right next step should be the estimation of a GUM, followed by the estimation of the final restricted error correction model. However, in all the above three different cases associated with our policy variables, the derivation of a robust model on econometric grounds was not possible. More precisely, in the case of MS/Y policy variable, although the estimation of the GUM provided us with the necessary long-run solution for the estimation of the error-correction model, the error-correction term obtained from the estimation of the restricted model was well above unity, thus suggesting inappropriate specification. In the

Table 4.5
Testing for Cointegration: Growth Equation
(with Policy Variables C/Y, TG/Y, MS/Y), India, 1970–92

Johansen Maximum Likelihood Procedure—Cointegration LR Test based on Maximal Eigenvalue of the Stochastic Matrix; maximum lag in VAR = 1

	C/Y Policy Variable		
Null	*Alternative*	*Statistic*	*95% critical value*
$r = 0$	$r = 1$	72.89	51.07
$r \le 1$	$r = 2$	32.22	44.91
$r \le 2$	$r = 3$	28.16	39.42
$r \le 3$	$r = 4$	23.58	33.31
$r \le 4$	$r = 5$	18.93	27.13
$r \le 5$	$r = 6$	7.35	21.07
$r \le 6$	$r = 7$	2.52	14.90
$r \le 7$	$r = 8$	1.40	8.17

(continued table 4.5)

(continued table 4.5)

Johansen Maximum Likelihood Procedure—Cointegration LR Test based on Maximal Eigenvalue of the Stochastic Matrix; maximum lag in VAR = 1

TG/Y Policy Variable

Null	Alternative	Statistic	95% critical value
r = 0	r = 1	71.95	51.07
r ≤ 1	r = 2	38.95	44.91
r ≤ 2	r = 3	30.34	39.42
r ≤ 3	r = 4	23.92	33.31
r ≤ 4	r = 5	17.93	27.13
r ≤ 5	r = 6	6.36	21.07
r ≤ 6	r = 7	4.76	14.90
r ≤ 7	r = 8	0.28	8.17

Johansen Maximum Likelihood Procedure—Cointegration LR Test based on Maximal Eigenvalue of the Stochastic Matrix; maximum lag in VAR = 1

MS/Y Policy Variable

Null	Alternative	Statistic	95% critical value
r = 0	r = 1	60.51	51.07
r ≤ 1	r = 2	31.44	44.91
r ≤ 2	r = 3	28.71	39.42
r ≤ 3	r = 4	22.92	33.31
r ≤ 4	r = 5	18.19	27.13
r ≤ 5	r = 6	7.31	21.07
r ≤ 6	r = 7	4.45	14.90
r ≤ 7	r = 8	0.36	8.17

case of the budget surplus variable, TG/Y, the problem was different, in the sense that the GUM model failed to pass both Ramsey's test for functional form and the misspecification test for serial correlation; the estimation of an error-correction model by using the instrumental variables procedure also failed to give robust econometric evidence, mainly due to the presence of a non-significant coefficient for the error correction term, ECM(-1).[34] Finally, a similar problem to the one appeared with variable TG/Y above, was present when dealing with the policy variable C/Y.[35]

The only case in which we managed to get meaningful results was related to the policy variable MS/Y, when an empirical growth model in first differences was estimated. Empirical results obtained from the final parsimonious model which we tried, within the context of a general-to-specific methodology are reported in Table 4.6. The findings are quite interesting indeed. The export variable retains its positive and strong short-run effect on GDP growth and the policy variable MS/Y (lagged one year) has the expected positive sign and it is significant at 5 per cent.[36] However, there is a major change concerning the impact of different aid types on growth in the presence of the financial variable MS/Y. The coefficient for project aid (lagged one year) is still negative as before, but not significant even at 10 per cent level; but under this policy scenario, the other two aid variables, A2 and A3 appear to have strong and significant effects on growth, although with a different sign in each case. More precisely, programme aid (lagged two years) has a positive and significant impact of the GDP growth in India in the presence of the financial variable MS/Y (significant at 5 per cent) unlike what happened when the same variable was not lagged; in the latter case, the impact was negative and significant. However, the overall impact of the programme aid variable turns to be positive, if we take into account the much larger magnitude of the coefficient in the lagged case. Finally technical assistance appears to have a very strong negative coefficient, significant at 5 per cent, in the presence of the policy variable MS/Y. The above findings clearly suggest that aid disaggregation matters, in terms of a differential impact of the different aid variables on growth, in the presence of particular financial policies in India over the period 1970–92. However, any generalization of the above conclusion would be rather inappropriate in this case, given the severe estimation problems with policy scenarios in India over the above period which we faced. It is notable that our empirical model here passes all misspecification tests and it is overall satisfactory in terms of goodness of fit, predictive power and stability of parameter coefficients.

Scenario II: Policies in the Presence of Aid with Uncertainty

Under this scenario, we tried to consider the impact of the three policy variables on growth in the presence of aid and uncertainty at the same time. We used uncertainty variable UN2 (based on a three-year moving average of the standard deviation of terms of trade in India) for this purpose. On the basis of the previous discussion, all variables appear to be I (1) series, and therefore, the next stage was testing for a

George Mavrotas

Table 4.6
Estimation of the Growth Equation with Policy Variable MS/Y, India, 1973–92

Dependent Variable: $\Delta(\Delta Y/Y)$		
Regressors	*Coefficient*	*t-ratio*
constant	−2.24	−1.71
$\Delta(\Delta Y/Y)$ (−1)	−0.69	−6.62
$\Delta(\Delta X/Y)$	8.92	4.55
$\Delta(A1/Y)$	−9.87	−2.43
$\Delta(A1/Y)$ (−2)	17.28	4.26
$\Delta(A2/Y)$ (−1)	−6.93	−1.55
$\Delta(A3/Y)$	−146.97	−2.05
$\Delta(MS/Y)$ (−1)	143.97	2.03
adjusted $R^2 = 0.91$	DW-statistic = 1.86	Durbin's h – st.:0.36 [0.72]

Diagnostic Tests*		
Test Statistics	*LM version*	*F version*
Serial Correlation (a)	$\chi^2(1)$: 0.02 [0.87]	$F(1,11)$: 0.01 [0.91]
Functional Form (b)	$\chi^2(1)$: 0.93 [0.33]	$F(1,11)$: 0.54 [0.47]
Normality (c)	$\chi^2(2)$: 2.28 [0.32]	not applicable
Heteroscedasticity (d)	$\chi^2(1)$: 0.008 [0.93]	$F(1,18)$: 0.007 [0.74]

* Figures in square brackets are rejection probabilities.

Notes: (a) Lagrange multiplier test of residual serial correlation; *(b)* Ramsey's RESET test using the square of the fitted values; *(c)* based on the test of skewness and kurtosis of residuals; *(d)* based on the regression of squared residuals on squared fitted values.

possible long-run relationship among the series involved in the growth equation. Complete results related to Johansen's maximum likelihood procedure appear in Table 4.7. Again, cointegration was present and one cointegrating vector was identified among the variables in the growth equation in each case. However, the severe estimation problems which we faced with the previous policy scenario were present with this policy scenario, too.

The estimated GUM model which was appropriate in each case, in view of the results of Table 4.7 above, was rejected in the light of a number of misspecification tests which were carried out in all three cases (in most of the cases the model failed to pass tests for functional form); also, the numerous error-correction models which were tried in each case were rejected due to the presence of quite inappropriate error-correction terms.

Table 4.7

Testing for Cointegration: Growth Equation (with Policy Variables C/Y, TG/Y, MS/Y and Uncertainty Variable), India, 1970–92

Johansen Maximum Likelihood Procedure—Cointegration LR Test based on Maximal Eigenvalue of the Stochastic Matrix; maximum lag in VAR = 1

	C/Y Policy Variable		
Null	*Alternative*	*Statistic*	*95% critical value*
$r = 0$	$r = 1$	98.20	56.99
$r \leq 1$	$r = 2$	45.63	51.07
$r \leq 2$	$r = 3$	32.57	44.91
$r \leq 3$	$r = 4$	26.16	39.42
$r \leq 4$	$r = 5$	22.55	33.31
$r \leq 5$	$r = 6$	18.98	27.13
$r \leq 6$	$r = 7$	8.26	21.07
$r \leq 7$	$r = 8$	2.66	14.90
$r \leq 8$	$r = 9$	0.37	8.17

Johansen Maximum Likelihood Procedure—Cointegration LR Test based on Maximal Eigenvalue of the Stochastic Matrix; maximum lag in VAR = 1

	TG/Y Policy Variable		
Null	*Alternative*	*Statistic*	*95% critical value*
$r = 0$	$r = 1$	84.62	56.99
$r \leq 1$	$r = 2$	48.58	51.07
$r \leq 2$	$r = 3$	37.85	44.91
$r \leq 3$	$r = 4$	26.87	39.42
$r \leq 4$	$r = 5$	22.71	33.31
$r \leq 5$	$r = 6$	17.26	27.13
$r \leq 6$	$r = 7$	6.45	21.07
$r \leq 7$	$r = 8$	4.82	14.90
$r \leq 8$	$r = 9$	0.53	8.17

(continued table 4.7)

(continued table 4.7)

Johansen Maximum Likelihood Procedure—Cointegration LR Test based
on Maximal Eigenvalue of the Stochastic Matrix; maximum lag in VAR = 1

	MS/Y Policy Variable		
Null	*Alternative*	*Statistic*	*95% critical value*
r = 0	r = 1	69.76	56.99
r ≤ 1	r = 2	48.29	51.07
r ≤ 2	r = 3	30.99	44.91
r ≤ 3	r = 4	28.62	39.42
r ≤ 4	r = 5	23.63	33.31
r ≤ 5	r = 6	16.41	27.13
r ≤ 6	r = 7	6.85	21.07
r ≤ 7	r = 8	4.47	14.90
r ≤ 8	r = 9	0.17	8.17

CONCLUSIONS AND ISSUES FOR FURTHER RESEARCH

This chapter has attempted to improve upon earlier work in the area of
aid effectiveness by focusing on a neglected, though important issue,
namely the aid disaggregation and the way it affects the econometrics
of aid effectiveness. For this purpose, we used disaggregated aid data
(project, programme and technical assistance) on India over the period
1970–92, constructed by the OECD Office in Paris. We further adopted
modern applied time-series econometrics to estimate a reduced-form
growth equation derived from the model we presented in this chapter.

Does aid composition matter for the effectiveness of aid in India?
The answer appears to be that, it partly does. More precisely, in view of
the results obtained, both programme aid and project assistance series
seem to exert a rather negative influence on growth in India during the
period under examination. Further scenarios, which we tried in our
econometric analysis of aid effectiveness in India, that is the inclusion
of a set of policy variables in the model with or without uncertainty
variables, did not shed much light on the important issue of aid's growth
impact in the presence of policies, due to severe estimation problems.
However, an important exception concerned the scenario of a financial
policy defined as the share of money supply in the GDP—a measure of

financial deepening and financial sector development in the country. In this case, the composition of aid seems to matter, given the different impact on growth of the three aid categories we used in our econometric analysis.

The results obtained in this chapter raise a number of important issues for future research work in this promising area.

The presence of policies seem to have an important impact on aid effectiveness and the way aid disaggregation operates; this is rather in line with recent work in this area (see the World Bank study (1998), *Assessing Aid*), although in the present study the focus is on time-series econometric analysis and an aid-disaggregation approach. This clearly calls for further work in this area which will properly explore the role of policies (and institutions) for aid effectiveness and a better understanding of the overall aid-policies-institutions nexus.

Furthermore, individual country studies and time-series base analysis may offer a better picture concerning the macroeconomic impact of aid in aid-recipient economies, given that the plethora of cross-section studies in the aid-effectiveness literature cannot capture properly the numerous heterogeneous characteristics of the countries included in the sample. Along these lines, since the macroeconomic impact of foreign aid is likely to vary substantially from country to country, the need for more individual country studies (using an aid-disaggregation approach) is more important than ever.

Last but not least, disaggregation of the three categories of aid which were used in this chapter into grants vis-à-vis loans for each category as well as the use of separate data on food aid (where appropriate) could be beneficial for a better understanding of the macroeconomic impact of each aid type in aid-recipient countries. At the same time, longer time-series data on different aid categories would be also extremely helpful in empirical analysis. Data availability has been the key inhibiting factor so far in both the above cases. Aid agencies could help (in collaboration with aid-recipients) towards this direction by collecting, preparing and publishing disaggregated aid data for research and policy purposes.

NOTES

1. I am most grateful to Dr Saman Kelegama and the editors of the journal *South Asia Economic Journal*, 3(1) for helpful comments and suggestions on an earlier draft.

I would like also to thank Bernard Wood, Bevan Stein and Peter Ellehoj of the Reporting Systems Division of the OECD/DAC Secretariat for their invaluable assistance with aid data. Needless to say, all the remaining errors are my own responsibility.

2. Mavrotas (1988) develops a new model of foreign aid and fiscal response with a primary focus on the aid-composition issue. The author reports evidence according to which different types of aid operate in different ways and with different effects on the fiscal sector of the economy in two aid recipient countries, Kenya and India, for which disaggregated time-series data has been constructed by the Organisation for Economic Co-operation and Development (OECD) Office in Paris for this purpose.

3. The term is attributed to White (1992).

4. The above utility function, also used in Mavrotas (1998) with a focus on aid disaggregation, is a clear departure from the utility function used in a number of studies in the fiscal response literature such as Heller (1975), Gang and Khan (1991), Khan and Hoshino (1992) and, more recently, Otim (1996). The utility function used in the above studies has been rightly criticized in Binh and McGillivray (1993) and White (1994). It is also notable that Mosley, Hudson and Horrell (1987) use a utility function similar to [2.1] above; however, they do not consider the important issue of aid disaggregation. Finally, a utility function like [2.1] above has been used quite recently by Franco-Rodriguez, Morrissey and McGillivray (1998); the authors shed light on the nexus between aid and the public sector in Pakistan by endogenizing aid within the context of a fiscal response model. However, the study does not use an aid-disaggregation approach.

5. For a detailed discussion concerning the derivation of similar target values in the aid effectiveness literature see Mosley, Hudson and Horrell (1987).

6. Endogenizing foreign aid might add an interesting dimension to the above approach. However, given the centrality of aid disaggregation in the present study endogenizing the different types of aid I am using in the chapter, although in some sense desirable, is technically almost unthinkable. Note that Franco-Rodriguez, Morrissey and McGillivray (1998) as well as the World Bank study, *Assessing Aid* (1998), endogenize foreign aid, though not in the context of an aid-disaggregation approach.

7. See Mavrotas (1997) for a discussion.

8. See studies by King and Levine (1994), Benhabib and Jovanovic (1991) and, more recently, Blomstrom, Lipsey and Zejan (1996).

9. A linear specification is adopted for modelling purposes.

10. The detailed algebraic derivation of the model solution is not reported here for reasons related to economy of space. However, it is available by the author upon request.

11. Clearly, there are important causality issues in the growth literature which has been the subject of a voluminous, though problematic, empirical literature. See Mavrotas and Kelly (2001a) on an innovative econometric test used to explore causality issues between growth and savings in India and Sri Lanka.

12. Apart from the growth equation, uncertainty is also used in the private investment equation [2.13] in the above model, following a rather interesting recent literature associated with irreversibility aspects of investment decisions. For details, see Dixit and Pindyck (1994), Hubbard (1994) and Mavrotas (1997).

13. The vast literature related to the impact of Structural Adjustment Loans (SALs) on the GDP growth in developing countries with Structural Adjustment experience, does address, of course, policy issues; however, the studies involved focus on the impact of programme aid only and not on the impact of different types of aid in the presence of macroeconomic policies.

14. This is a proxy for the level of financial sector development/level of financial deepening used extensively in the vast financial sector development literature—see Mavrotas and Kelly (2001b) for a discussion.

15. There exists a voluminous literature related to the Indian economy. Obviously, it is beyond the scope of this chapter to cover issues concerning the Indian economy but, instead, to provide the reader with a brief discussion of the major trends in foreign assistance. Interested readers should refer to Singh (1974), Bhagwati and Srinivasan (1975), Cassen (1978), Chaudhuri (1978), Frankel (1978), Goldsmith (1983), Chakravarthy (1987), Bhagwati (1992) and Joshi and Little (1994) among others.

16. For an excellent detailed discussion of the aid history in India see Lipton and Toye (1990). Sukhatme (1989) provides also an interesting, although brief, discussion.

17. According to a relatively recent study (Cassen, Joshi and Lipton (1993)), India has been receiving progressively less concessional assistance from the multilateral system. For instance, in some past years, IDA disbursements were above 40 per cent; this declined to about 17 per cent by 1990. Furthermore, average net disbursements of IDA assistance were US$3,575 million in 1980–81, US$4,545 million in 1985–86 and US$3,783 million in 1989–90.

18. It is notable, that the aid process in India is much more orderly than in other countries, in the sense that control of aid receipts is centralized in one department of government, investment planning takes account of anticipated aid receipts, and considerable experience has been built up in the field of international price comparisons (Cassen, 1994; Toye and Lipton, 1990).

19. Examples include UNICEF's aid which was involved in sponsoring India's national immunisation programme, the EC's assistance with a focus on the agricultural sector and the World Bank/IDA aid being mainly involved in irrigation and general agriculture projects (Netherlands Development Cooperation, 1994).

20. It is notable, that, since India was excluded from the Asian Development Fund (the Asian Development Bank's [ADB] soft loan window), IDA is the main source of multilateral concessional funding by providing over 40 per cent of India's total concessional aid in 1990. Furthermore, in recent years, the overall terms on which India borrowed from official sources have hardened dramatically, given the increased share of World Bank (International Bank for Reconstruction and Development or IBRD) loans in India's borrowing from the World Bank group, the shortened maturities of IDA loans and the increased share of non-concessional finance in bilateral lending (Cassen, Joshi and Lipton, 1993).

21. It is notable that the downward trend of programme aid since 1976 can be partly explained from the fact that the figures include food aid, which fell sharply after 1976 in India.

22. Aid effectiveness studies on India include Lipton and Toye (1990), Lele and Agarwal (1991), Sukhatme (1989) and Cassen, Joshi and Lipton (1993) among others.

23. It has been argued that the US assistance to India from independence to mid-1960s played two key roles: first, it helped to maintain food consumption until domestic agricultural production could expand, and, second, it contributed significantly to the Green Revolution by providing the necessary funds and technical assistance. However, the US efforts, related to the policy dialogue for the use of aid in the mid-1960s, were less successful (Lele and Agarwal, 1991).
24. See Cassen (1994) for a summary of findings and Lipton and Toye (1990, Chapter 5) for a detailed discussion.
25. The figures associated with the above aid categories encompass assistance from the DAC member countries, multilateral organizations and Arab countries and agencies.
26. It is notable that further disaggregation of the above aid categories into grants and loans over the entire time period was not possible due to several gaps in the series.
27. See Nehru, Swanson and Dubey (1993).
28. See Behrman (1997) for an excellent discussion of the problems involved in human capital data on school enrolments.
29. See for instance Cukierman, Edwards and Tabellini (1992) and more recently Mauro (1995).
30. The Johansen approach has two important elements, namely, the *vector error-correction model* (VECM) and the *method of reduced rank regression* to test for cointegration.
31. Uncertainty variables UN1 and UN3 were non-significant and had the wrong sign in most of the preliminary regressions which were carried out.
32. A VAR with lag-length = 1 was used given the number of regressors in our growth equation—estimation of a VAR with more than one lags was not possible.
33. The estimation of the GUM is not possible here, given the presence of two cointegrating vectors.
34. It is notable that the error-correction term was not significant in all the more general versions of the error-correction model which were tried.
35. We want to make clear at this stage that the above conclusion is the final outcome of numerous experiments, regressions and specifications which we have tried in order to find a meaningful way out of the above problems which we faced with the policy-scenario case; the complete set of empirical results obtained are available by the author upon request.
36. It is notable that a lagged MS/Y may well capture a possible endogeneity of this policy variable here.

REFERENCES

Alesina, A. and D. Rodrik (1994), 'Distributed Politics and economic growth', *Quarterly Journal of Economics*, 109: 465–90.
Balassa, B. and Associates (1982), *Development Strategies in Semi-Industrial Countries*, Johns Hopkins University Press, Baltimore.
Barro, R. (1991), 'Economic Growth in a Cross-section of Countries', *Quarterly Journal of Economics*, 106: 407–44.

Behrman, J. (1997), 'Simple Analytical Considerations for Skill Development for International Competitiveness', in M. Godfrey (ed.) *Skill Development for International Competitiveness*, Edward Elgar.

Benhabib, J. and B. Jovanovic (1991), 'Externalities and Growth Accounting', *American Economic Review*, 81: 82–113.

Binh, T. N. and M. McGillivray (1993), 'Foreign Aid, Taxes and Public Investment: A Comment', *Journal of Development Economics*, 41: 173–76.

Bhagwati, J. (1978), *Anatomy and Consequences of Exchange Control Regimes*, NBER, Cambridge, M.A.

—— (1985), *Dependence and Interdependence: Essays in Development Economics*, Basil Blackwell Oxford.

—— (1992), 'India's Economy: The Shackled Giant', The Radhakrishnan Lectures, Oxford, Mimeo.

Bhagwati, J. and T. Srinivasan (1975), *India*, Columbia University Press, New York.

Blomstrom, M., R. E. Lipsey and M. Zejan (1996), 'Is Fixed Investment the Key to Economic Growth?', *Quarterly Journal of Economics*, 111: 269–76.

Boswijk, H. (1995), 'Efficient Inference on Cointegration Parameters in Structural Error Correction Models', *Journal of Econometrics*, 69: 133–58.

Burnside, G. and D. Dollar (1997), 'Aid, Policies and Growth', Policy Research Working Paper No.1777, World Bank, Washington DC.

Cassen, R. (1978), *India: Population, Economy and Society*, Oxford University Press. Oxford.

—— (1994), *Does Aid Work?* Oxford University Press (2nd edn), Oxford.

Cassen, R., V. Joshi and M. Lipton (1993), *Stabilisation, Structural Reform and IDA Assistance to India*, Thomson Press.

Chakravarthy, S. (1987), *Development Planning: The Indian Experience*, Oxford University Press, Oxford.

Chaudhuri, P. (1978), *The Indian Economy: Poverty and Development*, Crosby Lockwood, London.

Cukierman, A., S. Edwards and G. Tabellini (1992), 'Seignorage and Political Instability', *American Economic Review*, 82: 537–55.

Dixit, A. and R. Pindyck (1994), *Investment under Uncertainty*, Princeton University Press, Princeton.

Dollar, D. (1992), 'Outward-oriented Developing Economies Really Do Grow More Rapidly: Evidence from 95 LDCs, 1976-85', *Economic Development and Cultural Change*, 40(3): 523–44.

Edwards, S. (1989), 'Openness, Outward Orientation, Trade Liberalisation and Economic Performance in Developing Countries', Policy Research Department Working Paper No.191, World Bank, Washington DC.

Findlay, R. (1978), 'Relative Backwardness, Direct Foreign Investment and Transfer of Technology', *Quarterly Journal of Economics*, 92: 1–16.

Franco-Rodriguez, S., O. Morrissey and M. McGillivray (1998). 'Aid and the Public Sector in Pakistan: Evidence with Endogenous Aid', *World Development*, 26(7): 1241–50.

Frankel, F. (1978), *India's Political Economy 1947-77: The Gradual Revolution*, Princeton University Press.

Gang, I. N. and H. A. Khan (1991), 'Foreign Aid, Taxes and Public Investment', *Journal of Development Economics*, 24: 355–69.

Goldsmith, R. (1983), *The Financial Development of India, 1860–1977*, Yale University Press, New Haven.

Greenaway, D. and D. Sapsford (1994), 'What Does Liberalisation Do for Export and Growth', *Weltwirtschaftliches Archiv*, 130(1): 157–74.

Guillamont, P. and L. Chauvet (1999), 'Aid and Performance: A Reassessment', CERDI, CNRS and University of Auvergne, mimeo.

Hansen, H. and F. Tarp (2000), 'Aid Effectiveness Disputed', *Journal of Internation Development*.

Heargraves, C. (1994), 'A Review of Methods of Estimating Cointegrating Relationships' in C. Heargraves (ed.) *Non-Stationary Time-Series Analysis and Cointegration*, Oxford University Press, Oxford.

Heitger, B. (1987), 'Import Protection and Export Performance: The Impact on Economic Growth', *Weltwirtschaftliches Archiv*, 123(2): 249–61.

Heller, P. S. (1975) 'A Model of Public Fiscal Behaviour in Developing Countries: Aid, Investment and Taxation', *American Economic Review*, 65: 429–45.

Helliwell, J. (1992), 'Empirical Linkages between Democracy and Economic Growth', NBER Working Paper 4066.

Hendry, D. (1995), *Dynamic Econometrics*, Oxford University Press, Oxford.

Hubbard, R. (1994), 'Investment under Uncertainty: Keeping One's Options Open', *Journal of Economic Literature*, 92: 1816–31.

IMF (various issues), *Government Financial Statistics Yearbook*, International Monetary Fund (IMF) publication, Washington D.C.

Johansen, S. (1988), 'Statistical Analysis of Cointegrating Vectors', *Journal of Economic Dynamics and Control*, 12: 231–54.

Johansen, S. and K. Juselius (1990), 'Maximum Likelihood Estimation and Inference on Cointegration', *Oxford Bulletin of Economics and Statistics*, 52: 169–210.

Joshi, V. and I. M. D. Little (1994), *India: Macroeconomics and Political Economy (1964–1991)*, The World Bank, Washington, D.C.

Killick, T. (1998), *Aid and the Political Economy of Policy Change*, Routledge, London and New York.

King, R. and R. Levine (1994), *Capital Fundamentalism, Economic Development and Economic Growth*, mimeo, the World Bank, Washington D.C.

Khan, H. and E. Hoshino (1992), 'Impact of Foreign Aid on the Fiscal Behaviour of LDC Governments', *World Development*, 20: 1481–88.

Krueger, A. (1995), *Trade Policies and Developing Nations*, Brookings Institution, Washington D.C.

Lau, L., D. Jamison and F. Louat (1991), 'Education and Productivity in Developing Countries: An Aggregate Production Function Approach', Policy Research Department, Working Paper No. 612, World Bank, Washington D.C.

Lele, U. and M. Agarwal (1991), 'Four Decades of Economic Development in India and the Role of External Assistance', in U. Lele and I. Nabi (eds), *Transitions in Development*, ICS Press, San Francisco.

Lensink, R. and H. White (2000), 'Assessing Aid: A Manifesto for Aid in the 21st Century?' *Oxford Development Studies*, 28(1): 5–17.

Levine, R. and S. Zervos (1992), 'Looking at the Facts: What We Know about Policy and Growth from the Cross-country Analysis', mimeo, World Bank, Washington D.C.

Lipton, M. and J. Toye (1990), *Does Aid Work in India?*, Routledge, London.

Lucas, R. (1988), 'On the Mechanics of Economic Development', *Journal of Monetary Economics*, 22: 3–42.

Mauro, P. (1995), 'Corruption and Growth', *Quarterly Journal of Economics*, 110: 681–712.

Mavrotas, G. and R. Kelly (2001a), 'Old Wine in New Bottles: Testing Causality between Savings and Growth', *The Manchester School*, 69: 97–105.

———— (2001b), 'Savings Mobilisation and Financial Sector Development: The Nexus', *Savings and Development*, XXV(1): 33–65.

Mavrotas, G. (1998), 'Foreign Aid and Fiscal Response: A New Model', School of Economic Studies, University of Manchester, Working Paper No. 9802.

Mavrotas, G. (1997), 'Uncertainty and Private Investment in Developing Countries: An Assessment', School of Economic Studies, University of Manchester, Working Paper No. 9707.

Moschos, D. (1989), 'Export Expansion, Growth and the Level of Economic Development: An Empirical Analysis', *Journal of Development Economics*, 30: 93–102.

Mosley P. and J. Hudson (1995), 'Aid Effectiveness: A Study of the Effectiveness of Overseas Aid in the Main Countries Receiving ODA Assistance', Report to the ODA, November.

———— (1996), 'Effectiveness of Overseas Aid Flows: A Study of 29 *ACP* Countries', Report to the European Commission, July.

Mosley, P., J. Hudson and S. Horrell (1987), 'Aid, the Public Sector and the Market in LDCs', *Economic Journal*, 97: 616–41.

Nehru, V., E. Swanson and A. Dubey (1993), 'A New Database on Human Capital Stock: Sources, Methodology and Results', Policy Research Department, Working Paper No.1124, World Bank, Washington D.C.

Netherlands Development Cooperation (1994), 'Evaluation of the Netherlands Development Programme with India: 1980–92', Evaluation Report, Operations Review Unit.

Obstfeld, M. (1989), 'Saving, Investment and Long-run Growth', University of Berkeley, processed.

OECD (various issues), OECD Reports, OECD, Paris.

Otim, S. (1996), 'Foreign Aid and Government Fiscal Behaviour in Low-income South Asian Countries', *Applied Economics*, 28: 927–33.

Ozler, S. and G. Tabellini (1992), 'External Debt and Political Instability', UCLA, Department of Economics, processed.

Romer, P. (1986), 'Increasing Returns and Long-run Growth', *Journal of Political Economy*, 94: 1002–37.

Sachs, J. and A. Warner (1995), 'Economic Reform and the Process of Global Integration', Brookings Papers of Economic Activity, No.1, pp.1–18.

Serven, L. (1996), 'Does Public Capital Crowd out Private Capital? Evidence from India', Policy Research Working Paper No.1613, World Bank, Washington D.C.

Singh, T. (1974), *India's Development Experience*, Macmillan, London.

Sukhatme, V. (1989), 'Assistance to India' in Krueger et al. (eds.) Aid and Development, Johns Hopkins University Press, Baltimore.

Tarp, F., with P. Hjertholm (ed.) (2000), Foreign Aid and Development: Lessons Learnt and Directions for the Future, Routledge Studies in Development Economics 17: London.

Urbain, J. (1995), 'Partial versus Full-system Modelling of Cointegrated Systems: An Empirical Illustration', *Journal of Econometrics*, 69: 177–210.

Wang, J. (1990), 'Growth, Technology Transfer, and the Long-run Theory of International Capital Movements', *Journal of International Economics*, 29: 255–71.

White, H. (1992), 'The Macroeconomic Impact of Development Aid: A Critical Survey', *Journal of Development Studies*, 28: 163–240.

———— (1994), 'Foreign Aid, Taxes and Public Investment: A Further Comment', *Journal of Development Economics*, 45: 155–63.

World Bank (1998), *Assessing Aid, A World Bank Policy Research Report*, World Bank and Oxford University Press.

NEXUS BETWEEN AID AND SECURITY

5

Pakistan

VAQAR AHMED AND MUHAMMAD ABDUL WAHAB[1]

INTRODUCTION

Foreign aid in developing economies has become an indispensable source of financing economic growth and development. The narrow fiscal space and low levels of foreign exchange earnings imply less financing for infrastructure and social sector development. Successful aid experiences suggest countries achieving higher human capital growth, faster capital accumulation and improved welfare levels (Chowdhury and Garonna, 2007).

Critics of the existing aid regime have highlighted negative implications of foreign aid which in many countries gets diverted to non-development expenditures and servicing of debt overhang. Furthermore, political instability, frequent changes in policies, misaligned public sector priorities and inefficiency of institutions neutralizes the effect of aid on growth, thereby having less than expected impact on poverty reduction. The study on sources of ineffectiveness of aid has occupied substantial attention in the recent literature and explains the slow progress towards Millennium Development Goals (MDGs).

Pack and Rothenberg (1993) argued that aid ineffectiveness in developing countries is because of diversion of aid from development to deficit financing (which is largely owed to rising current expenditures) and debt servicing. Burnside and Dollar (2000) find the positive impact of aid in developing countries in the presence of prudent policies. However, Easterly, Levine and Roodman (Forthcoming), find no support that aid works well under good policy environment. Chong, Gradstein and Calderon (2009) show the significant effect of aid on inequality and poverty reduction. Furthermore, they suggest that good institutions may be necessary for aid to reach the poor. When studied for specific indicators, Masud and Yontcheva (2005) show that non-governmental organizations' (NGOs') aid reduces infant mortality more effectively than official bilateral aid.

In the case of Pakistan, a two-gap framework might justify the need of foreign assistance (Saeed, 1995). Like most developing countries, Pakistan's domestic resource mobilization is not sufficient to overcome the rising government expenditures which have recently also ballooned due to the financing of the war on terror and destruction due to devastating flash floods. In order to keep the growth momentum going during times of conflict, one requires multisectoral foreign assistance. Upon independence in 1947, the country inherited obsolete or minimal infrastructure in most productive sectors leading to Pakistan approaching the donors relatively early in history. Pakistan's association with, for example, the World Bank, goes back to 1950. The World Bank has been the largest provider of development assistance to Pakistan. Between 1952 and 2006, the World Bank has approved 266 financing arrangements for Pakistan, totalling more than US$15.7 billion, of which about US$9 billion remains outstanding.

In 1960, the World Bank organized the Aid-to-Pakistan Consortium to facilitate coordination among the major providers of international assistance. The consortium's members included the US, Canada, Japan, Britain, Germany, France and organizations such as the Asian Development Bank (ADB). Most non-consortium funding came from Saudi Arabia and other oil-producing Middle Eastern countries. The US has been a major provider of aid since independence and was the largest donor until the 1980s.

It can be observed in Pakistan's history that periods of intense conflict were not followed by sustainable growth. Due to this the macroeconomic situation remained fragile. Since 1988, almost eleven loan arrangements (including the recent US$7.6 billion in 2008) have taken place under various International Monetary Fund (IMF) programmes. Almost six loan arrangements were made during the regimes of the Pakistan People's Party including Standby Arrangements, Structural Adjustment Programmes (SAP), Poverty Reduction and Growth Facility (PRGF) and Extended Structural Adjustment Programme. Two IMF loan arrangements were made during the Pakistan Muslim League regime and two Standby Agreements and PRGF were contracted under military regimes (post-1999) to stabilize the economy. There is a significant difference between the loans promised and disbursed under the aforementioned arrangements, because national governments were unable to fulfil the stringent conditionalities. Later, between 2001 and 2005, Pakistan successfully implemented two IMF-supported programmes.

In 2010, the World Bank approved a lending facility of US\$6.2 billion for four years focusing on specific areas such as energy management and development, revenue generation and aid to terror-stricken areas. In energy, the World Bank plans to assist the government in making the power sector more efficient by optimally harnessing the potential of the hydropower sector. The natural gas system will also receive much awaited attention, which presently suffers from higher costs of leakages owing to dilapidated operations management. This arrangement comes at an apt time when the productive sectors are suffering from power shortages and the input costs of industry, particularly small and medium enterprises (SME), have led to substantial business closures.

The earthquake of 2005 and destruction in Khyber-Pakhtunkhwa province due to war on terror has led to mass suffering in the region. The World Bank along with other donors are aiming for intervention in health and education. The overall strategy focuses on putting Pakistan back on a broad-based pro-poor growth path which ultimately creates employment and reduces poverty. One of the cornerstones of the macroeconomic framework will be increasing the tax to the Gross Domestic Product (GDP) ratio which currently ranks as one of the lowest in the world. It is essential that Value Added Tax (VAT) reforms are undertaken at the earliest which can form a basis for longer term requirements of human capital and related social sectors. These reforms which also intend to focus on broad basing of the tax regime will also reduce reliance on foreign aid.

In this chapter, we study the link between aid, development and security. We start with briefly describing the role of aid in Pakistan's economy, including a review on how aid is motivated by geopolitics and security concerns. Next we have results from a linked computable general equilibrium (CGE), microsimulation model where we simulate an increase in foreign savings and see its macro–micro impact. We also discuss the current aid regime in Pakistan and how effective it is in the provision of services and infrastructure. We then focus on some key aid experiences of Pakistan with respect to specific programmes initiated during different phases of the country's history. Lastly we provides a checklist of priorities for aid policy reform in Pakistan.

AID, SECURITY AND DEVELOPMENT

Role of Aid in the Pakistan Economy

The Pakistan economy has grown at an average growth rate of 5 per cent between 2001 and 2010. This period saw the doubling of merchandise exports and remittances from abroad while imports more than doubled. For most part of the decade, the improved fiscal discipline helped to maintain a high level of poverty related government expenditure. However, in the wake of food, fuel and financial crisis, the economy saw a decline in aid and Foreign Direct Investment (FDI) inflows (see Ahmed and O' Donoghue, 2010). The size of external debt and liabilities ballooned and due to the hike in inflation and deteriorating exchange rate, high inflation after 2007 eroded the gains made towards poverty reduction (Table 5.1). With dwindling foreign exchange reserves, Pakistan resorted to IMF standby arrangements and gradually moved towards a recovery phase during 2008–09. However

Table 5.1
Pakistan—Macroeconomic Situation, 2001–10

Indicators	2001	2005	2006	2007	2009	2010*
GDP growth (%)	2.0	9.0	5.8	6.8	1.2	4.1
Merchandise exports (US$ billion)	9.2	14.4	16.4	17.1	18.9	19.6
Merchandise imports (US$ billion)	10.7	20.6	28.6	26.6	31.4	30.5
FDI (US$ billion)		1.5	3.5	5.1	3.7	2.2
Remittances (US$ billion)		4.2	4.6	5.5	7.8	8.9
External debt and liabilities (US$ billion)		34.0	35.9	39.0	50.7	52.7
Poverty headcount ratio	34.5	23.9	22.3		3.5	
Poverty related expenditure (US$ billion)		5.3	6.3	7.0	3.8	
Exchange rate	58.4	59.4	59.9	60.6	78.5	83.6

Source: Government of Pakistan (n.d.a); State Bank of Pakistan (n.d.).
Note: *Provisional estimates.

in 2010, the economy was also hit by a domestic energy crisis, where inter-corporate debt crippled the energy sector and led to electricity and gas shortages for commercial purposes as well as households. With some recovery in large scale manufacturing, the growth in 2009–10 crossed 4 per cent and exports remained robust despite the looming global recession. The devastating flash floods of September 2010 destroyed US$9 billion worth of infrastructure, in turn putting downward pressure on economic growth and increasing Pakistan's expectation from donors for higher levels of aid.

The history of foreign borrowing in Pakistan goes back to the 1950s. The major chunk of aid has come under project assistance which in most cases was tied to source and utilization. The initialization process of project assistance also required participation by the government. The second most important type of aid to Pakistan was in the form of commodity assistance. Various governments preferred this type of inflows as these were not tied to utilization. However, Saeed (1995) indicates that commodity assistance to Pakistan as a ratio of total aid had decreased from 34 per cent in 1965 to 23 per cent by 1980. Within this category, Pakistan also received food aid which initially included wheat and edible oils from the US government. Finally, technical cooperation remained high on Pakistan's agenda as this allowed technical help from sectoral experts as well as training of officials abroad. Brecher and Abbas (1972) provide an analysis of the early period when Pakistan received US$3.5 billion in assistance from the US over 15 years (1952–67). Out of this amount, loans accounted for 38 per cent, food aid was 37 per cent and other grants constituted 25 per cent. The majority of aid was concentrated in industrial commodities, power, irrigation and transport sectors.

Rahim and Khan (1993) found an inconclusive relationship between aid, savings and economic growth. There is a negative coefficient between aid and domestic resource mobilisation. However, aid plays a definite role in determining overall savings behaviour in Pakistan. Khan (1997) taking account of falling concessional aid as a percentage of the total higher overtime average interest rates, falling maturity periods and lower grant element, argues that aid has a negative causal impact on the GDP and aid has a negative impact on economic growth after controlling the supply side shocks. The harsher terms of aid made it all the more difficult to retire debt in the medium to long run. The factors identified for ineffectiveness of aid include project selection biases towards poorly identified and large projects, foreign exchange intensive development programmes, longer gestation infrastructure rather than productive projects, lack of government-donor and intra-donor coordination.

Iqbal (1997) discovered that foreign capital flows channelled through the public sector have a strong positive impact on social and non-development expenditures. However, foreign aid has little effect on development expenditure. The non-development expenditure has strong interdependence with social sector expenditures. Furthermore, foreign assistance increases the potential of tax revenue generation. As the flow of foreign capital increases, the GDP increases at a decreasing rate. However, rising aid flows substituted for domestic savings ultimately increasing the debt burden. Ishfaq (2004) explains that foreign aid, though in a limited manner, has assisted poverty reduction in Pakistan. Vos (1998) suggests that aid flows tend to generate strong Dutch disease effects in the case of Pakistan.

Figure 5.1 shows the outstanding debt stock of Pakistan from 1980 to 2009. The government's domestic borrowing increased much faster than external borrowing and crossed US$50 billion in 2008. Whether or not the rising debt stock is good for the country largely

Figure 5.1
Debt Stock Outstanding

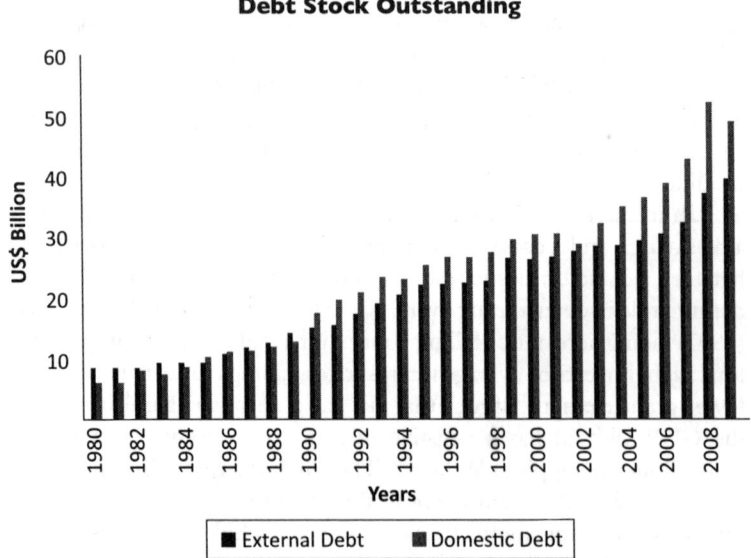

Source: Government of Pakistan (n.d.a); Government of Pakistan (n.d.b).

depends upon how these borrowings are spent. If the government fails to channelize debt flows in efficient public investment (which in turn provides enabling infrastructure and facilitation to the private sector), there is a possibility that the country ends up embracing a debt trap situation which also brings with it a Dutch disease phenomenon. After 2005, Pakistan's dependence on aid increased substantially, primarily due to two reasons: *(a)* food, fuel and financial crisis, and *(b)* war on terror. At the same time, Pakistan's involvement in the war against terror has worsened the business environment in the country which in turn led to reduced or stagnant domestic revenue generation (see Table 5.2).

Husain (1992) highlighted the Pakistan economy's repeated reliance on foreign savings for bridging the gap between domestic savings and investment. However, the rising debt burden of Pakistan[2] required a gradual shift away from this persistent reliance on foreign resources. In order to avoid the debt crisis, the author suggested a strategy where emphasis should be on increasing domestic saving rates, export receipts, foreign investment and a reflow of foreign assets held by Pakistanis abroad. Husain (1999) explains that a major change in Pakistan's debt profile was when the composition of external financing changed from bilateral grants and concessional lending towards multilateral and non-concessional flows. The percentage of grant in total assistance declined from 77 per cent in 1960 to 9.6 per cent during the late 1990s (see Table 5.3). Baqai (1973) while discussing the dominant role of foreign

Table 5.2
Pakistan Tax to GDP Ratio

Year	Tax to GDP ratio
2003	11.4
2004	10.8
2005	10.1
2006	10.5
2007	10.3
2008	10.3
2009	9.5

Source: Government of Pakistan (n.d.a.).

Table 5.3
Pakistan—Decade-wise Loans and Grants Disbursed (US$ Million)

Year	Loans	Grants	Total	% of grants in total
I. Up to 30-06-1960	192	650	842	77.2
II. 2nd Plan (1961–65)	1,232	1,162	2,394	48.5
III. 3rd Plan (1966–70)	2,324	719	3,043	23.6
IV. Non-Plan (1971–78)	5,083	634	5,717	11.1
V. 5th Plan (1979–83)	4,418	1,375	5,793	23.7
VI. 6th Plan(1984–88)	5,158	2,025	7,183	28.2
VII. 7th Plan (1989–93)	9,540	2,541	12,081	21.0
VIII. 8th Plan (1994–98)	11,522	1,226	12,748	9.6
IX. 1999–2007	12,824	5,380	18,204	29.6
Grand Total	52,293	15,712	68,005	23.1

Source: Economic Affairs Division, www.ead.gov.pk (accessed on 30 October 2010).

aid in Pakistan's earlier plans, explains that choice is not yet open to developing countries to adopt a development strategy based on aid flows (which Pakistan actually did in the Second Five Year Development Plan). The developed countries are unwilling to provide assistance on such a scale.

The rate of interest remained relatively low during 1960s to 1970s (Table 5.4). During 1970s and most part of 1980s, grants constituted around 35 to 50 per cent of external financing requirements. However by 1995, this ratio was down to 5 per cent. The main factors responsible for this were frequent change in political orientations and 'donor fatigue' leading to increase in debt servicing costs during 1990s. By 1995, most of the debt as part of official financing was being channelled through international financial institutions and bilateral debt only accounted for less than 35 per cent. Out of the total debt stock, around 80 per cent was for financing of longer term projects and commodity aid and the remainder was credits by banks and the IMF.

Ahmed and Amjad (1984) discuss that most aid to Pakistan was tied to source and utilization, ultimately resulting in Pakistan purchasing desired goods and services on credit and at uncompetitive prices. The

Table 5.4
Term Structure of Loans

Period	Interest (%)	Payment (years)	Grace period (years)
1950s	4.6	21	2
1960s	3.3	30	7
1970s	3.6	25	6
1980s	4.8	28	7
1990s	4.4	21	6
2005–09	1.3	25.1	–

Source: Government of Pakistan (n.d.a.).

interest rates in most cases were equal to the commercial rates (see also Hamid, 1970; Alavi and Khusro, 1970).

Pakistan managed to keep a sound current account balance during the early phase of this decade. However, one can observe a recent jump in external debt to the GDP ratio from 27 per cent in 2007 to 30.4 per cent in 2010. The key contributors to this increase are the IMF Standby Arrangement and multilateral loans (Table 5.5). While the contribution of the Paris Club only increased by US$1 billion during 2005 to 2010, the contribution of multilaterals went up from US$15.4 billion in 2005 to US$23.2 billion in 2010. In the Paris Club group, Pakistan has contracted loans and signed grant agreements with Canada, Japan, the UK and the USA in 2009. In the non-Paris Club group, Saudi Arabia, Kuwait and China are the main donors. In multilaterals, the main sources were the ADB, the European Union (EU) and International Development Organization (IDA). In mid-1990s, when public debt to the GDP ratio was hovering around 87 per cent with a higher share of external debt, Pasha and Ghaus (1996) explained that the key fiscal management goal in Pakistan should be to keep primary budget deficit at a level which prevents the public debt to income ratio from rising.

For functional use, we could bifurcate aid into project aid and non-project aid. Food, non-food, relief and balance of payments aid constitute non-project aid. The project aid almost equalled the non-project aid in the earlier phases of the economic history of Pakistan

Table 5.5
External Debt and Liabilities, 2005–10 (US$ Billion)

	2005	2006	2007	2008	2009	2010*
1. Public and Publically Generated Debt	31.1	32.8	35.3	40.2	42.2	42.4
A. Medium- and Long-term (>1 year)	30.8	32.6	35.3	39.5	41.6	41.8
Paris Club	13.0	12.8	12.7	13.9	14.0	14.0
Multilateral	15.4	16.8	18.7	21.6	23.1	23.2
Other Bilateral	0.8	0.8	1.0	1.2	2.0	2.5
Euro/Other Bonds	1.3	1.9	2.7	2.7	2.2	1.6
Military Debt	0.2	0.1	0.1	0.0	0.2	0.2
Commercial Loans/ Credits	0.2	0.2	0.1	0.1	0.2	0.3
B. Short-term (<1 year)	0.3	0.2	0.0	0.7	0.7	0.6
IDB	0.3	0.2	0.0	0.7	0.7	0.6
2. Private Non-guaranteed Debt (>1 year)	1.3	1.6	2.3	2.9	3.3	3.2
3. IMF	1.6	1.5	1.4	1.3	5.1	7.2
(of which) Central Government						1.1
Monetary Authorities	1.6	1.5	1.4	1.3	5.1	6.1
Total External Debt (1 through 3)	34.0	35.9	39.0	44.5	50.7	52.7
(of which) Public Debt	31.1	32.8	35.3	40.2	42.2	43.5
4. Foreign Exchange Liabilities	1.4	1.3	1.3	1.7	1.3	1.2
Total External Debt and Liabilities (1 through 4)	35.4	37.2	40.3	46.2	52.0	53.9
(of which) Public Debt	32.1	33.8	36.5	40.7	42.2	43.5
Official Liquid Reserves	9.8	10.8	13.3	8.7	9.5	11.2

(continued table 5.5)

(continued table 5.5)

	2005	2006	2007	2008	2009	2010*
	(In % of GDP)					
Total External debt (1 through 3)	31.1	28.2	27.3	27.0	31.3	30.4
1. Public and Publically Guaranteed Debt	28.4	25.8	24.7	24.5	26.0	24.4
A. Medium- and Long-term (>1 year)	28.1	25.6	24.7	24.0	25.6	24.1
B. Short-term (<1 year)	0.2	0.1	0.0	0.4	0.4	0.3
3. IMF	1.5	1.2	1.0	0.8	3.2	4.1
4. Foreign Exchange Liabilities	1.3	1.1	0.9	1.0	0.8	0.7
Total External Debt and Liabilities (1 through 4)	32.3	29.2	28.2	28.1	32.0	31.1

Source: Government of Pakistan (n.d.a).
Note: *Data up to March 2009–10.

(see Table 5.6). However, project aid increased much faster from the Fifth to Eighth Plan period. After which, increased Balance of Payments (BoP) support led to an increase in the non-project aid component.

Table 5.7 shows the disbursement of project aid in different sectors of the economy between 2000 and 2009. The sectors that have received the highest foreign assistance include power, water, transport and communication and rural development. However, it seems that Pakistan has received low levels of aid for development of science and technology, human resource development and information technology. These neglected areas are critical for sustaining short-term growth spurts in developing countries.

Extracting rankings from disbursements shown in Table 5.7, we see that the sectoral preference of donors kept changing between 2000 and 2009. The power sector that ranked first in 2000 had slid to second in 2009 when the priority sector now was transport and communication. The increased focus on rural development and education was seen only recently in 2009. Both sectors were not amongst the top five in 2000 (see Table 5.8).

Table 5.6
Project and Non-project Aid Disbursed (US$ Million)

	Project aid	Non-food aid	Food aid	BoP support/ Cash receipts	Others aid	Total non-project aid	Total disbursement
	1	2	3	4	5	6=(2+3+4+5)	7=(1+6)
Up to 30 June 1960	406	244	192	–	0	436	842
Second Plan (1961–65)	1,209	420	765	–	0	1,185	2,394
Third Plan (1966–70)	1,811	763	469	–	0	1,232	3,043
Non-plan (1971–78)	2,543	1,299	785	1,090	0	3,174	5,717
Fifth Plan (1979–83)	3,363	950	306	531	643	2,430	5,793
Sixth Plan (1984–88)	4,882	791	776	–	734	2,301	7,183
Seventh Plan (1989–93)	7,643	1,922	1,558	413	545	4,438	12,081
Eighth Plan (1994–98)	9,564	61	1,923	1,139	61	3,184	12,748
1999–2009	13,269	255	538	1,6129	51	16,973	30,242
Total	44,691	6,707	7,315	1,9306	2,039	35,353	80,043

Source: Economic Affairs Division, Government of Pakistan.

Table 5.7

Sector-wise Disbursement of Project Aid (US$ Million)

Sectors	2000	2001	2002	2003	2004	2005	2006	2007	2008	2009	Total
Agriculture	68.5	37.7	44.3	10.9	17.7	9.0	19.2	26.0	27.3	32.2	292.8
Education and Training	102.7	74.6	60.4	43.1	57.2	46.2	93.0	111.3	54.3	84.2	727.0
Environment	13.1	8.8	14.7	3.1	11.7	7.2	6.2	15.5	9.9	7.2	97.3
Fuel	164.1	14.9	1.5	0.0	1.5	51.0	0.8	0.2	0.0	0.0	234.0
Governance, Research and Statistics	17.5	41.3	29.4	29.6	35.3	82.7	85.1	84.4	54.9	77.5	537.7
Health and Nutrition	31.2	22.2	14.9	59.8	52.4	78.7	54.3	47.2	51.1	31.0	442.9
Industry and Production	6.6	5.3	–	2.2	0.5	6.7	3.0	7.9	1.0	6.6	38.3
Information Technology	0.1	0.0	0.0	0.0	0.0	0.0	0.0	0.0	0.0	0.0	0.1
Manpower, Employment and HRD	0.0	0.0	0.0	0.0	0.0	0.0	2.2	0.4	0.1	0.0	2.8
Physical Planning and Housing	65.2	31.3	29.0	27.9	37.3	32.5	46.0	51.8	34.5	29.5	385.1
Population Welfare	63.4	5.4	5.8	9.1	5.9	17.6	27.2	27.1	15.6	56.4	233.6
Power	211.7	303.9	176.6	250.6	112.4	59.2	143.6	119.0	116.4	208.3	1702.0
Rural Development and Poverty Reduction	23.0	35.2	45.8	63.3	50.2	228.8	272.8	97.9	83.3	111.0	1011.0
Science and Technology	0.3	0.1	0.0	0.3	0.6	0.0	0.0	0.0	0.0	0.0	1.4
Social Welfare	200.8	188.8	92.3	79.6	7.5	15.1	9.2	20.0	20.3	14.3	647.8
Transport and Communication	172.8	152.0	110.9	184.1	129.0	136.7	159.8	197.7	234.9	311.5	1789.0
Water	121.7	106.8	114.0	68.6	94.6	143.7	121.9	113.4	44.1	91.1	1020.0
Women Development	0.2	1.3	3.0	13.5	8.4	2.6	0.7	2.6	1.8	1.9	35.9
Total	1263.0	1030.0	741.2	845.8	622.4	917.7	1045.0	922.4	749.2	1063	9199.0

Source: Economic Affairs Division, Government of Pakistan.

Table 5.8
Top Five Sectoral Disbursements, 2000–09

Rank	2000	2009
1	Power	Transport and Communication
2	Social Welfare	Power
3	Transport and Communication	Rural Development and Poverty Reduction
4	Fuel	Water
5	Water	Education and Training

Source: Planning & Development Division, Government of Pakistan.

Foreign Assistance and Regional Security

The link between aid and security and how both impact service delivery, poverty and welfare indicators has received substantial attention in the literature. The work done by the Development and Assistance Committee (DAC) Fragile States Group Secretariat requires special mention here. The DAC (2008a) provides an understanding of the mutual influence of security and service delivery and provides recommendations on how to strengthen service provision and governance. The report also identifies the challenges faced by international development partners in countries with security issues (see also DAC, 2008b).

Carment, Samy and Prest (2008) while examining the effects of state fragility on aid allocation, explain that aid is usually directed towards states on the basis of their capacity and authority and not on the basis of their legitimacy. Ehrenfeld, Kogut and Hove (2003) explain that the potential of aid conditionality to positively influence peace processes depends on successful coordination among donors, understanding of the political situation, willingness to act on threats, and suitable rewards and pledges to enhance credibility (see also Boyce, 2002; Goodhand and Sedra, 2007). Suhrke and Buckmaster (2005) discuss the patterns and purposes of post-war aid. Hansen and Borchgrevink (2006) highlight the intentions and effectiveness of aid sanctions and provide analysis on cutting aid to promote peace and democracy. Svensson (2000) explains that expectation of aid in the future may increase *rent dissipation* and reduce the public goods provision. There seems to be no existence of donors systematically allocating aid to countries with less corruption. Alesina and Weder (1999) show that according to some measure of corruption, more corrupt governments are receiving more aid and there is no evidence that an increase in aid reduces corruption.

Aid flows in Pakistan have suffered from unpredictability, in turn affecting the country's development plans as well as ongoing projects. The per capita aid flows on average have increased between 1960 and 2006. However, as shown in Figure 5.2, these flows followed sharp spikes which made foreign financing an unreliable option for growth over the longer term. There is some evidence that Pakistan's dependence on aid has decreased over time. Figure 5.3 exhibits the declining aid receipts as a percentage of Gross National Income (GNI).

Figure 5.2
Net ODA Received Per Capita (Current US$)

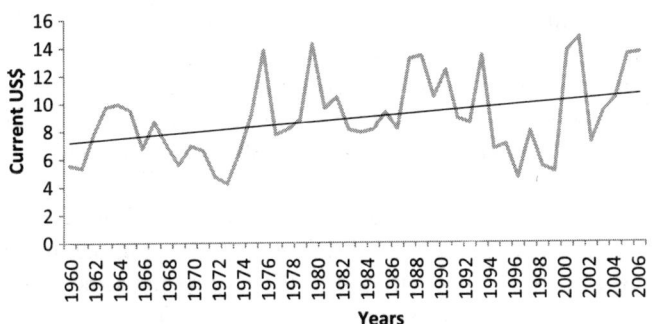

Source: Government of Pakistan (n.d.a.).

Figure 5.3
Aid Received as Percentage of GNI, 1960–2006

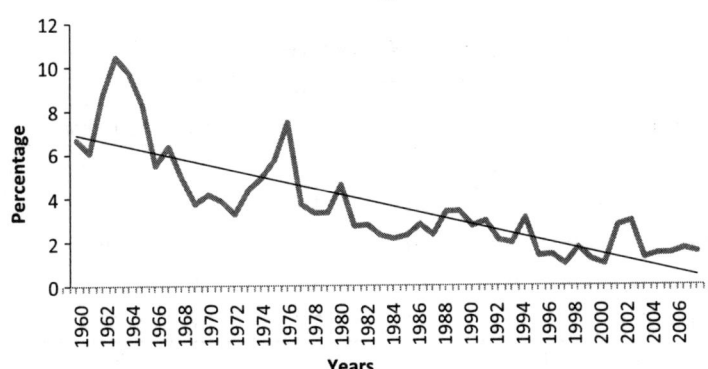

Source: Government of Pakistan (n.d.a.).

Table 5.9
Net ODA Received Per Capita

Years	Pakistan	India	Bangladesh	Sri Lanka	Indonesia	Afghanistan	Nepal
1960s	7.6	2.0	–	2.2	1.4	3.3	1.9
1970s	7.7	1.8	7.7	10.5	4.6	4.9	3.8
1980s	10.3	2.4	13.7	30.5	6.3	3.0	9.6
1990s	8.6	2.0	12.0	31.3	8.2	11.9	9.8
2000–07	11.0	1.2	8.4	30.0	6.4	65.1	6.2

Source: OECD (2010).

The argument of Pakistan receiving less aid in comparison with other economies currently facing security threat is strengthened, if per capita aid receipts are taken into account (Table 5.9). Recent statistics indicate that regionally, Afghanistan remains the highest recipient in terms of per capita receipts of aid followed by Sri Lanka. Similarly, in terms of aid as a percentage of GNI, Afghanistan, Nepal and Sri Lanka were the leading recipients (Table 5.10).

According to the South Asia Terrorism Portal (SATP) database, the total number of civilians killed during terrorist violence in Pakistan during 2003 to 2010 was around 8,597. During the same period, the number of security forces personnel killed was 3,141. Being a major partner in the war against terror, Pakistan's military forces killed 18,100 terrorists. The total number of suicide attacks during 2007 and 2009 was around 197 which took the lives of 735 civilians and 196 security forces personnel. This loss of life, destruction of infrastructure and uncertain

Table 5.10
Aid as Percentage of GNI

Years	Pakistan	India	Bangladesh	Sri Lanka	Indonesia	Afghanistan	Nepal
1960s	7.0	2.2	–	1.4	4.0	3.0	1.2
1970s	4.4	1.2	6.1	4.9	2.9	2.6	3.8
1980s	2.9	0.8	6.4	8.5	1.2	0.8	15.8
1990s	1.9	0.6	4.1	5.2	1.2	–	–
2000–07	1.7	0.2	2.2	2.7	0.6	32.6	16.9

Source: OECD (2010).

Table 5.11
Damage to Pakistan Economy (Rs Billion)

	2005	2006	2007	2008	2009	2010	Total 2005–10
Direct Costs	67	78	83	109	114	262	712
Indirect Costs	192	223	278	376	564	707	2340
Total	259	301	361	484	678	969	3052
Cost in US$ billion	4.4	5.0	6.0	7.7	8.6	11.5	43.2

Source: Government of Pakistan (n.d.a).

business environmental has collectively resulted in an economic loss of US$43 billion between 2005 and 2010 (Table 5.11). The leakage of domestic output still remains unaccounted for. Due to the porous borders and unrest in the neighbouring region with Afghanistan, substantial amount of agricultural items are illegally transported into Afghanistan which in turn makes Pakistan food insecure. This has in the short term led to sharp spikes in food prices. After 2005, industrial items such as cement and steel were being transported to Commonwealth of Independent States (CIS) countries via Afghanistan, ultimately escalating construction costs in Pakistan. Same was true for fertilizer upon which Pakistan had allowed a subsidy; however, it was priced much higher in CIS market. The price differential prompted smuggling of fertilizer to across the border. The food insecurity has led Pakistan to repeatedly resort to food aid. Table 5.12 indicates the unprecedented increase in food aid during the 1980s and 1990s.

Pakistan's involvement in anti-terror efforts also led to unemployment in regions which were already suffering economic slump. This

Table 5.12
Decade-wise Food and Non-food Aid

Period	Non-food aid	Food aid
1960s	127	134
1970s	167	92
1980s	207	157
1990s	145	321
2000–09	26	27

Source: Economic Affairs Division, www.ead.gov.pk (accessed on 30 October 2010).

not only increased rural poverty but also forced internal migration. In the Swat district alone, around 2 million people have been displaced, education of youth disrupted, economic infrastructure hampered, and the supply of items such as marble, furniture, gems and jewellery, fruits and vegetables has been affected. While conflict has substantially damaged infrastructure and added to business costs, reduced economic growth has also led to sharp challenges of debt servicing. Figure 5.4 shows how debt servicing as percentage of exports increased after 2008 when the military operations in northern areas were coupled with budget and BoP crises.

The nature of war-related damage in Pakistan and Afghanistan remains similar. However in Pakistan, it has cost the loss of established socio-economic infrastructure (see Jones, 2007). While there has been increased hype about pushing donors to do more in Afghanistan, Pakistan still awaits the fulfilment of promised pledges. Between 2003 and 2007, the US had spent US$22 billion in Afghanistan and US$42 billion in Iraq on aid and reconstruction (Tellis, 2008). Since 2002, the US provided Pakistan US$12.3 billion out of which less than 27 per cent has gone towards development and economic assistance. Annexure I also show the bilateral aid disbursed to a sample of countries along with the share of US in the global bilateral aid.

Whether or not aid has contributed towards rent seeking behaviour in Pakistan needs to be further evaluated. It has been argued by the civil society that aid was one of the factors that help military regimes become stronger. Table 5.13 shows that in terms of per capita aid, recent military

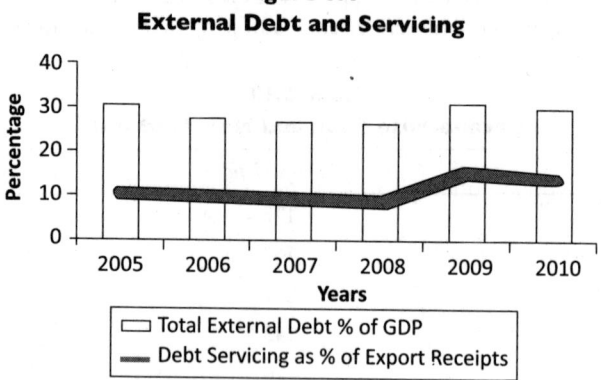

Figure 5.4
External Debt and Servicing

Source: Government of Pakistan (n.d.a).

Table 5.13
Aid Inflows during Various Political Regimes

Regime	From	To	Per capita aid (current US$)	Aid received percentage of GNI	Total aid (US$ million)
Ayub Khan (Military)	1958	1969	7.6	7.0	5,715
Yahya Khan (Military)	1969	1971	6.4	3.9	1,770
Zulfiquar Ali Bhutto (Civil)	1971	1977	7.5	4.7	4,861
Zia-ul-Haq (Military)	1977	1988	9.5	3.0	14,792
From 1988 to 1998 (Civil)	1988	1990	9.4	2.2	24,829
Pervez Musharraf (Military)	1999	2007	10.3	1.7	21,895

Source: Author's own calculations.

regimes in Pakistan received much higher inflows in comparison to the civilian rule.

MACRO–MICRO IMPACT OF FOREIGN RESOURCES

The role of foreign savings have been instrumental in leveraging short-term growth in Pakistan during the post 9/11 period. Using a linked Computable General Equilibrium (CGE) microsimulation model[3] based on 2002 Social Accounting Matrix (SAM), we show that a 50 per cent increase in foreign savings leads to an increase in real private consumption by 2.8 per cent. Given the greater amount of foreign exchange available, imports increase by 3.7 per cent; however, exports decline by 6.5 per cent. The declining exports indicate deterioration in trade balance. We can observe that trade deficit as per cent of nominal GDP increases by 1.8 per cent. In nominal terms, the foreign savings to the GDP ratio increased by 2 per cent while the investment and private savings to GDP decline by 0.3 and 2.4 per cent, respectively.[4]

These results, if seen in the light of economic theory, suggest that foreign savings can significantly alter the real exchange rate, that in turn causes the trade balance to change. This also implies that production of domestically consumed goods will alter. This happens in our results because absorption, which is defined as the total domestic spending on a good calculated at the prices paid by the domestic demanders, increases by 2.2 per cent in real terms. This increase to some extent is made possible through the domestic (non-tradable) price index which is decreasing.

The value-added prices in our simulation decline mostly for tradable goods. The sectors showing the highest decline are: leather (10 per cent), cotton lint/yarn (7.1 per cent) and manufacturing (6.9 per cent). The prices of several large sectors show an increase such as livestock, wheat milling, housing and private services. These are mostly non-tradable sectors. The direction of change is similar for the case of output prices; however, the magnitude of these changes is much smaller given the inclusion of other factors in output prices. Such a change seems pro-poor given that the prices of food and oil show a decline. However, the price of housing increases by 6.9 per cent in case of value added price and 5.5 per cent in case of output price. The decreased prices of cotton and textile also indicate towards increasing export competitiveness; however, we know from macroeconomic results above, that the overall exports did not increase because of an exchange rate appreciation.

The returns for labour with farm holding and returns for land decline. The return to capital does not change. Those who gain under this change are agricultural wage labour and non-agricultural unskilled wage labour, whose wages increase by 1.5 and 0.5, respectively. It is broadly recognized that agricultural wage workers are regarded as the poorest of the rural poor (ILO, 1996). The overall agriculture incomes are the second most important source, with almost 27 per cent of total per capita household income (see Adams, 1995). According to the Labour Force Survey, around 44 per cent of the employed persons (10 years age and above) are working in the agriculture, forestry and fishing sectors. Given these statistics, it seems that our simulation results indicate redistribution within the agriculture sector, where the returns for farm owners are declining, and the wages for employed labour in agriculture are increasing. The increase in the wages of non-agricultural unskilled labour also indicates a change in favour of urban poor.

The return to land declines for all land classifications in the model. The returns for non-irrigated land decline more than the irrigated land,

and within the latter, the decline is greater for large and medium farms in Punjab province.

For evaluating the changes in the welfare, we first see how household incomes change for our experiments. We can observe that the change mimics what we have seen for changes in factor returns. When foreign savings increase, large or medium farms are the main losers, while all other household groups gain, most notably rural agricultural workers who are landless and small farm owners. We had explained before that this also represents redistribution in favour of low income households. Household consumption, however, increases for all groups. The increase is greater for rural workers.

In line with the household welfare impact explained above, poverty decreases by 3.1 per cent when foreign savings increase by 50 per cent. Poverty gap and severity both show a decline. Poverty decreases in all provinces with Punjab having the highest decline by almost 3.3 per cent followed by Sindh (2.8 per cent). The inequality as measured by Gini coefficient declines by 0.3 per cent.

AID EFFECTIVENESS IN PAKISTAN

The fundamental notion behind the usage of aid facility should be ownership of development agenda and preferably home grown policies that are envisaged by the recipients of aid in alignment with national strategies. The delivery of aid requires transparency and effectiveness of national institutions, starting from the federal tier to the local or municipality level. Having a constant eye on results and outcomes requires continuous reiteration of development goals at all levels of public sector and civil society. The development parameters should be coordinated and synchronized in order to keep aid flows tractable. The predictability of aid should be accompanied with untied arrangements and finally, overarching development agenda of the country should be augmented through appropriate real sector and external account policies.

Most recent aid inflows for Pakistan are associated with geopolitical, law and order situation inside the country and the neighbouring region with Afghanistan. The security concern of donors however has hampered future aid flows to Pakistan particularly in long-term infrastructure projects. The volatility of assistance in turn, results in delayed disbursements, project closures, shifting of aid portfolio from budgetary support to project aid.

The development budget of 2007 indicated 17 per cent foreign funding. It is estimated that only one third external assistance appears in the budgetary record and forms a part of the Public Sector Development Programme (PSDP). The optimal absorption of these foreign resources largely depends upon the implementation capacity of federal, provincial and local governments. Donors have at times argued about the duplicity of development policy documents being issued by various government institutions. Apart from the main development dossiers such as medium-term plans by the Planning Commission, the federal ministries also have their own policy documents such as Annual Trade Policy developed by the Ministry of Commerce, Textile Policy designed by the Ministry of Textile, Investment Policy given by the Board of Investment and National Education, Health and Social Sector Policies designed by relevant ministries. This fragmented policy making makes the development implementation task all the more difficult for stakeholders and leaves foreign assistance misaligned.

The challenge of coordinating fragmented assistance in Pakistan is more difficult in sectors such as governance, education, health and nutrition, gender and environment which are receiving aid for small projects from a large number of donors. The donors should fast come to a conclusion about a manageable scale of programme and the manner in which delivery of aid is kept strongly grounded in the Paris Declaration (PD) Agenda. An understanding is also necessary regarding how much of assistance should be managed in a decentralized fashion. The Development Assistance Database (DAD) for 2006 indicates 20 donors who have been regular in assisting Pakistan in the recent past. Around five donors, which include the ADB, the World Bank, Japan, China and the US are providing 90 per cent of annual disbursement. These donors need to connect with each other on a more regular basis in order to ensure absorption of disbursed aid. The country representatives of most of the donors are still far from the principles of the PD being advocated in their top hierarchy.

The coordination between domestic institutions suffers due to lack of clarity regarding rules and responsibility of various authorities. The PD survey 2006 had revealed the small portion of coordinated technical cooperation. At the government level, careful attention should be given to formulation of aid policy, which should define the provision, allocation and coordination of aid. The aid policy once formulated should be able to ensure compliance with conditionalities. The Economic Affairs Division (EAD) working under the Ministry of Finance should also streamline internal procedures in order to ensure the aid effectiveness in line with international best practices. The policy should also streamline a plan for systematic dialogue between donors at various levels of government (currently three federal ministries deal with disbursement of foreign aid). At the national level, the Pakistan Development Forum (PDF) provided opportunity where donors may have detailed sectoral dialogue with recipient institutions. However, the inconclusive discussions at the PDF indicate the need to restructure this forum and make it more focused towards information sharing dialogue on crosscutting themes and impediments in aid implementation. The establishment of the new consortium led by the US, Friends of Democratic Pakistan (FoDP) resulted in discontinuation of the PDF. However, the reduced FoDP inflows have prompted the donors to demand a revival of PDF.

Malik (2009) splits the analysis of quality and coordination of the ODA into three main areas of concern namely: *(a)* composition of aid, *(b)* fragmentation of aid, and *(c)* aid volatility. Taking the lead from Easterly and Pfutze (2008) to highlight that some form of aid and technical assistance may be less effective than others, the author emphasizes the important role of aid-mix in determining flexibility of resources. There is limited need assessment, insufficient local efficiency and communication in design of technical cooperation and not much attention is given to the follow-up phase which should ideally ensure proper monitoring. Past experience suggests that China (whose aid accounted for 66 per cent of total aid commitments in Pakistan) during 2001–07 and the non-DAC donors do not participate in aid coordination forums.

The issue of aid fragmentation is most seen in the social sector such as governance and education. The higher transaction costs attributed to increased fragmentation take the form of time and money spent on compliance and coordination. Rabea (2007) shows for the education sector that aid since 1999 has come from numerous donors in small quantities. However, it becomes difficult to assess the donor influence due to lack of consistent data on performance indicators.

The volatility of aid poses problems that include poor planning, increased number of short-term projects, discontinuity of projects and cash flow issues with existing projects. The volatility of assistance has led to a large size of throw forward (public sector projects which stand approved but now lack liquidity). The current PSDP throw forward liability has exceeded Rs 3 trillion. The OECD DAC data shows that between 2000 and 2006, Pakistan faced 35 per cent more volatility as compared to an average recipient. The variation in aid composition accounted for 70 per cent of overall volatility during 1997–2006. Around 76 per cent of volatility in grants during 1998–2007 originated from the grants provided by the US. The unpredicted aid has translated into assistance falling short of the committed amount on occasions. Around 20 per cent of the ODA disbursed has never been released and 50 per cent of donors disbursed less than the committed amount (Malik, 2009).

The sources of aid volatility in Pakistan include limited implementation capacity, changing donor priorities and geopolitical conditions. The short-term orientation of aid flows has contributed toward unsustainability of development. Around 45 per cent of projects which carry 34 per cent of disbursement were of three years duration or less.

Pakistan participated in the PD monitoring survey 2006; however, it did not participate in the next round as the exercise coincided with the election cycle and shifts in development priorities. We may summarize here the results from the 2006 survey.[5]

1. Around 88 per cent of the total ODA disbursed by the government sector was recorded in the government system.
2. Out of the total ODA provided for technical cooperation in 2005, only 28 per cent was disbursed in support of coordinated capacity development programmes.
3. During 2005, 76 per cent of ODA was disbursed by using the public financial management system of the government. The government has set up a multi-donor working group to look at improving harmonization of donor financial management and procurement systems, and increasing the alignment and use of the government procedures.
4. Out of the total ODA disbursed in 2005, 68 per cent was disbursed by using the national procurement systems. In total, 7 out of 16 donors used the national procurement systems. However, only three of them (World Bank, ADB, United Sates Agency for International Development (USAID) account together for 97 per cent of the total ODA disbursed by using national procurement systems. The vast majority of donors disbursed none or very small amounts of the ODA by using the national procurement systems.
5. Out of the ODA disbursements planned for 2005, 83 per cent was recorded as actually disbursed by the government.

While overall predictability, according to the measure used in the survey, seems to be high, the government's experience suggests that in-year predictability of disbursements is rather low. At the time when the corresponding commitment is made, many donors do not indicate when (e.g., in which quarter) the disbursement is planned.

6. In 2005, 31 per cent of the total ODA was disbursed in support of initiatives adopting programme-based approaches. The majority of the funding disbursed through programme-based approaches was disbursed as budget support (84 per cent). There is very little use of programme-based approaches outside of direct budget support. Out of 16 donors, the World Bank accounts for 82 per cent of the total ODA disbursed in support of programme-based approaches.

7. The proportion of joint missions and joint analytical work is relatively low at 12 per cent and 41 per cent, respectively. Coordinated missions and analytical work are still only conducted on an ad hoc basis.

PAKISTAN-SPECIFIC CASE STUDIES IN AID EFFECTIVENESS

In this section, we discuss briefly the key aid experiences of Pakistan under specific programmes. In 1954, with the revamping of individual country programme under Foreign Aid Bill, the US stepped up aid for Pakistan which continued until the mid-1960s. The war of 1965 between India and Pakistan meant that the US administration wanted to impose statutory curbs on both countries—a move later vetoed in Congress. A similar action was initiated against Pakistan during the civil war of 1971 which called for banning the US economic and military aid to Pakistan (Kole, 1971).

By end 1970s, as the Soviet Union flexed its strength in Afghanistan, the US came forward with a series of aid packages for Pakistan which formally started in 1981 and lasted for most part of the military regime in 1980s. After the break-up of the Soviet Union, the US aid to Pakistan sharply diminished and 1990s saw Pakistan relying on non-concessional sources even to cover its past debt accumulated during the Afghan war period. This implied a movement away from bilateral sources of aid towards multi-donor programmes.

The Social Action Programme mainly designed and initiated by the World Bank in Pakistan in 1992 was aimed at improving human development status and improving socio-economic indicators in Pakistan. Initially, the programme's focus was through primary health services, education sector, population welfare, rural water supply and sanitation aimed to augment the quality and quantity of investment in social services (DFID, 2000). The government in partnership with donors agreed to raise spending, improve sectoral policies and make efforts towards removing initial constraints. Despite making progress in growth and investment, not much achievement was seen in the human development sphere during 1990s. Among the lapses indentified in optimal utilization of programme, predicaments included: inefficient resource allocation, poor design of social services and non-optimal utilization which was in part due to institutional weakness.

In various donor evaluations, these difficulties had been attributed to lack of ownership at both political and bureaucratic level. Furthermore, the federal administrative structure of the country implied that revenues and funds were being generated at the federal tier and the social sectors were being managed by provinces. This not only made the process of implementation more challenging but also required a high level of commitment at both tiers.

From the outset, this programme was being considered as a World Bank dominated programme, which not only implied the government following the World Bank style implementation but also meant that other donors did not come forward in a truly coordinated manner for financing the same or similar projects. Provincial governments had to go through mundane monitoring processes, where little attention was being paid to the overarching theme of social reforms. By 1997, after a review of the first phase, World Bank shifted the entire management of the Social Action Programme to Pakistan for initiation of the second phase. Only, this time the World Bank agreed on a more participatory approach among all stakeholders. In DFID (2000) it was again emphasized that the World Bank only held limited engagements.

In its country assistance evaluation (2006), World Bank highlighted the manner in which the bank's assistance strategy was changed over time. By 1998, when focus of the strategy was completely on service delivery through the vehicle of the Social Action Programme, targeted programmes were introduced for social protection and it was during this phase that the Pakistan Poverty Alleviation Fund (PPAF) was created in 1999 to facilitate in the provision of micro credit and small scale community infrastructure. However the 2001 country assistance strategy progress report informed that the programme outcome fell short of targets and despite significant investment from the government and donors, social sector indicators exhibited a dismal performance. In education, particularly primary education, poor governance was held responsible which in turn was an outcome of financial mismanagement and lack of accountability at teacher's level. In the health sector, the resistance to mobilize NGOs was termed as the main cause of weak result.

At this stage, the government adopted a new reform programme focused on expanding the devolution process. It was envisaged that accountability at the local level will improve service delivery. In order to address the gender issues raised by the civil society, while increasing the number of seats and capacity building programmes for women parliamentarians, the government with the support of donors also expanded at the micro level, lady health workers programme and conditional cash transfers to female students in primary schoolings.

Three years into the devolution programme World Bank, the ADB and Department For International Development (DFID) published a joint report in 2004 that focused on six districts and found evidence of change where citizens reported that their voices were now being heard at the administrative levels. Recommendations for further improvement emphasised incentives for efficiency, local accountability and efforts to gradually change existing practices and attitudes. For the overall decentralization process, Keefer, Narayan and Vishwanath (2005) suggested embedding of decentralization in the national constitution and improving voter information regarding actions of local officials. The process of political decentralization was supposed to follow fiscal decentralization. However, with the return of civilian rule in 2007–08, the new government in a bid to strengthen federal and provincial tiers abolished the local governments—a move which was resented by civil society and smaller political parties.

The aid experiences in Pakistan will be incomplete without the mention of rural support programmes. The Aga Khan Rural Support Programme (AKRSP) operational in northern Pakistan since 1982, provides an example of private development agencies working towards community-driven participatory rural development through indigenous self-help projects. The aim was to facilitate venture capital for rural enterprise; however, the prerequisites required a process of village organization. The villagers should choose leaders, set priorities and select fellow villagers to lead various teams focusing on economic and social ventures. In this process, the villagers learn to create a consensus amongst themselves and to keep the new infrastructure maintained (see De Spoelberch and Shaw, 1987; Padawangi, 2010).

Inspired by the AKRSP model, the government in 1992 launched a nationwide National Rural Support Program (NRSP). An important feature of scaling-up of Rural Support Programmes (RSPs) was that these were created as independent non-profit bodies. This implied that these RSPs would remain insulated from political and bureaucratic interference. At the initial stages of RSPs, the main commitment came from the Aga Khan Foundation, Canadian and the UK governments; however, at later stages federal government became the leading resource provider (Malik, 2009). Another important contribution of the Aga Khan Foundation along with the Orangi Pilot Project in Karachi was the initiation of the microfinance movement in Pakistan which ultimately became the main objective of establishing Pakistan Poverty Alleviation Fund (PPAF) (see Shah, 2009; Muhammad, 2010).

The PPAF largely focuses on enterprise development, water and community infrastructure, education and health. The government receives a soft loan from donors and forwards it to the PPAF under even softer terms. The PPAF then identifies NGOs or other civil society arrangements amongst which it disburses the funds. Currently, this fund has the largest support from the World Bank. While discussing possible implications for aid fragmentation, Malik (2009) argues that the PPAF model reduces duplication of programmes and internalizes the aid arrangement with multiple donors.

Another recent aid experience of Pakistan originates from the 2005 earthquake when almost 73,500 people were killed. The aftermath of the earthquake also saw 128,000 people with injuries and requiring immediate rehabilitation. Almost 3.3 million people had lost their homes and now required shelter and food. In terms of physical infrastructure the loss included 600,000 houses; 6,400 km of road network; 6,298 schools; 350 health facilities; 3,994 water supply lines and 949 public sector buildings. MacLeod (2006) indicates the success of the early recovery programme due to a cluster approach that allowed military and civilian efforts backed by the donor community to focus on: protecting the most vulnerable, restoring capacities, rebuild livelihoods, secure human development gains, reduce disaster risk, engage the private sector, promote self-sufficiency, ensure transparency and accountability, and remain coordinated at all levels of operations.

While documenting the history of aid in Pakistan, one has to also evaluate the impact of assistance for Afghan refugees. Hilali (2002) explains that the Afghan war had a detrimental impact on the internal and external security of Pakistan. After the Soviet invasion of Afghanistan in 1979, Pakistan saw a record influx of refugees entering its border. The refugee settlements created political, economic, social, environmental and ecological problems for Pakistan. In various areas of Pakistan, the refugees destroyed the ecological balance, causing desertification and soil erosion and promoted drug trafficking, Kalashnikov culture, sectarianism and law and order problems that still persist. The author also explains how the Afghan war corrupted Pakistani elites and provided political legitimacy to military rule and dictatorship in the country (see also Ibrahim, 2010). Figure 5.5 indicates how assistance to Pakistan towards Afghan relief declined prematurely. During the mid and late 1990s, when Pakistan was host to the highest number of refugees in the world, Afghan assistance was at its lowest.

Figure 5.5
Aid towards Afghan Relief

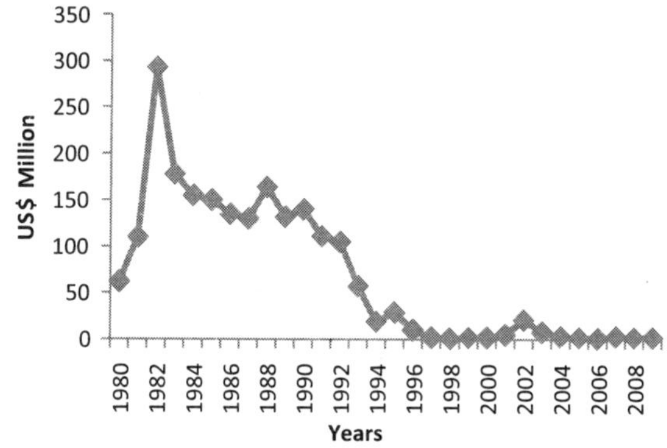

Source: Government of Pakistan (n.d.a).

PRIORITIES FOR AID POLICY REFORM IN PAKISTAN

PD and Aid Policy Framework

In September 2008, representatives from developing and developed countries met in Accra, Ghana, to reinforce the commitments towards aid effectiveness in the PD. It was realized that real progress has been made towards improving lives of those under extreme poverty, however rising commodity prices now posed a greater challenge if countries are to successfully accomplish MDGs. According to the 2008 PD survey, developing countries had started to improve management of public funds and donors were now working in a more coordinated manner. The world leaders in Accra established consensus towards three main factors that can play a vital role in improving aid effectiveness.

First, the strengthening of country ownership over development should take the form of deepening country-level policy dialogue on development, expanding the capacity of developing countries to lead and manage development processes and using the institutions and systems available in developing countries to a maximum extent possible for improved service delivery.

Second, in order to build more effective and inclusive partnerships for development there is a need to reduce costly fragmentation of aid, increase aid's value for money, encourage a broad base of developing actors in recipient countries, deepen engagement with civil society organizations and adapt aid policies for countries in fragile situations.

Third, in order to move fast towards improved delivery and accounting for development results, there is a need to develop information systems which in turn should help in strengthening the quality of policy design. Cost-effective results management is important to assess the impact of developing policies. Donors need to align their monitoring with country information systems and incentives to improve aid effectiveness should be strengthened. In order to make aid more transparent, there still remains a need to make further improvements to public financial management and to further support ownership, the nature of conditionality should be reformed. Finally, greater predictability in aid flows is imperative so that developing countries are in a position to manage their own development strategies.

Pakistan in its draft Foreign Assistance Policy Framework[6] reinforces strengthened collaboration of all development actors in line with the principles outlined in the PD. The two basic principles governing the policy framework include: ensuring compatibility and convergence of foreign-aided development with national plans, and improve quality, effectiveness and efficiency of foreign assistance. The policy is based on principles of national ownership, alignment of national priorities, harmonization with national systems and procedures, results-oriented monitoring and evaluation, inclusive dialogue and information sharing.

The national budget streamlines the development priorities in the country. The draft policy therefore prefers budgetary support over other forms of assistance. This is intended to strengthen institutional capacity, reduce transaction costs, improve coordination, and make disbursement and delivery more flexible. The government will further prefer un-earmarked funding in order to avoid distortion in allocation of funds. Earmarking by donors reduces government's role in establishing development priorities. The budget support should also be complemented with technical assistance in order to ensure results in line with best practices. In various evaluations, project assistance was not found sustainable after a certain period. In order not to see this in future, project assistance should ideally be integrated into programmatic approaches and implemented through national institutional arrangements.

In order not to further add to the debt burden, the government will prefer grants and concessional (soft) loans. The latter will only be used where future cash flow is expected and pursuit of economic growth is helped. Loan assistance will be considered for infrastructure development and venues that help foreign exchange earnings. The feasibility study component of loan based programmes will be completed through grants which in turn will mean minimal expenditure on foreign consultants. The aid provided should be untied; however, goods and services equivalent to a certain proportion of total financial volume may be allowed if some specific project requires niche technology or expertise. Even in case of Technical Assistance (TA) (which should ideally be financed through grants) tying with source or origin of financial assistance will not be desired.

While maintaining the independence of NGOs, the government believes in sharing of information regarding funds and activities so that no duplication takes place at the national level. The government will work closely with NGOs in developing standard codes for NGO transparency and accountability.

A proper division of labour mechanism among development partners should be established in future. In order to avoid excessive fragmentation, the government will aim to ask donors to work in thematic areas outside of which all donors should support that development partner which is already active in other areas.

The proposals for financial assistance should follow aid prioritization criteria that includes: conformity with fiscal responsibility and debt limitation law, complementing domestic budgetary resources outlined in national plans, contribution towards achievement of regional balance by targeting underdeveloped areas.

FoDP

The PDF has served as a dialogue forum between various development partners. The forum allowed the donors to interact with the officials managing various socio-economic sectors in Pakistan. In the wake of heightened war in the region neighbouring with Afghanistan and a military operation that lasted for several months, followed by terror strikes in various cities, the US helped in forming a consortium of countries and organizations willing to assist Pakistan in successfully winning the war on terror and reconstruction of war-torn areas. The FoDP that has already met twice has asked Pakistan to make further efforts in eradicating terror elements inside its borders and plans to tie aid programme for Pakistan with security efforts. Many donors believe that this demand from the developed world may take a lot more time than currently being envisaged. Hence, many are of the view that replacing the PDF with the FoDP was a mistake and has disrupted the previous mechanism of structured dialogue.

Pakistan's present dialogue with donors under the FoDP focuses on: *(a)* security, *(b)* socio-economic recovery, *(c)* medium-term development programme, *(d)* integrated energy development and *(e)* institution building. The precise summary of proposals for the FoDP meeting in Tokyo focused on: *(a)* food security, *(b)* reducing cost of doing business in Pakistan, *(c)* poverty alleviation, empowerment and employment, and *(d)* Federally Administered Tribal Area (FATA) people empowerment.

In food security cluster, assistance is desired for: *(a)* water management and development and *(b)* development of agricultural resources on cost efficient lines. The proposed projects under water sector include the construction of Bhasha-Diamer dam, rehabilitation of irrigation infrastructure and 32 small dams. In the agriculture sector, proposed projects include the increasing of post-harvest efficiency, productivity enhancement, value addition and institutional development.

In order to reduce the cost of doing business, three specific sectors need attention. First, transport and communication sector will involve maintenance and development of roads, rail network and ports that can reduce the travel time and cost for merchandise goods and in turn increase the competitiveness of Pakistani goods. The mineral development strategy will focus on marble, granite and onyx value chain, iodized table salt plant and creating a quarry machine tool.

Projects focusing on poverty alleviation, empowerment and employment have been split into four main areas: *(a)* health and population, *(b)* education, *(c)* safety net for the vulnerable and *(d)* skills development and employment.

Under the health, education and livelihood cluster, proposed projects are aimed at: programme for access to health services, girls' secondary school education, safety net for vulnerable (which has also translated into Rs 70 million worth Benazir Income Support Programme), skills development, national employment programme and population welfare.

The ongoing energy crisis has meant rising costs for businesses and electricity shortages for both industry and household sector. The SME sector in Pakistan has been the worst hit due to unannounced electricity and gas stoppages. Three projects proposed in the Abu Dhabi meeting with FoDP included: Thar Coal development project, Bunji hydro power plant and Guddu thermal power. The total cost of developing these projects stands at US$8.5 billion in 2009 prices.

A lot of focus in future will be towards the rehabilitation of Internally Displaced Persons (IDPs). Pakistan faced two accounts of forced internal migration, namely: *(a)* earthquake of 2005 and *(b)* war operations in northern parts of the country that started in 2007. According to 2009 estimates, 310,000 people had migrated from their homes. In 12 relief camps approximately 61,180 IDPs were residing,[7] while 38,750 houses had been destroyed.[8] The daily expenditure per capita on food- and shelter-related facilities was around US$1.9. One of the key proposals includes empowerment of people in FATA of Pakistan who were displaced the most. A comprehensive package is required in the region that focuses on providing education, health, food security and infrastructure (including energy) to the people of this region. For social empowerment of people in this region, the government proposes scholarships for the FATA students, provision of missing facilities in schools, establishing the FATA Institute of Medical Sciences and establishing an Institute of Engineering and Technology.

The socio-economic revival and sustained growth will require help from the FoDP on mitigating cost of war on terror, market access and economic cooperation, securitization and debt swaps, and the establishment of the proposed FATA Pakistan Trust Fund.

Pakistan is seeking market access and expanded economic coop-eration with the US, the EU and Japan. With the US, plans focus on Reconstruction Opportunity Zones (ROZs) for FATA, Khyber Pakhtunkhwa province, earthquake affected areas and Baluchistan. Appropriate amendments should be made in rules of origin to maxi-mize gains for these zones. Pakistan, for a limited period should be allowed unilateral tariff concessions for exports particularly of textiles and garments sector. There should be early finalization of a bilateral investment treaty and there should be firm commitment to initiate the FTA negotiations. In case of the EU, Pakistan is seeking inclusion in Generalized System of Preferences Plus (GSP+) scheme and initiation of the FTA negotiations. In South Asia, the EU has already initiated talks with India towards the FTA arrangement. With Japan, Pakistan wishes increased market access for its agricultural commodities and an initiation of early negotiation on the FTA.

The FoDP have also been asked to enter into debt swap arrange-ments to ease the debt burden of Pakistan. The main item in this arrangement is the Paris Club debt which amounted to almost US$10.8 billion in 2009. A deferred oil facility has been requested from Saudi Arabia and the UAE. Pakistan has suggested the establishment of a multi-donor trust fund to administer the development in the FATA, Baluchistan, Khyber Pakhtunkhwa province and Azad Jammu and Kashmir (AJK).

The fundamental assumption behind productivity-led growth is security of assets and profits. Pakistan requires financial and technical assistance to substantially raise a trained police force in all four provinces. There is a need to provide the police force with forensic and surveillance equipment in order to improve their tracking ability. Women police units in every police station (1,200 in number) of Pakistan are desired. These should be autonomous and staffed by female employees.

The institution building cluster comprises of three main sub-sectors: e-governance, human resource development, gender empowerment and partnering with institutions. In case of e-governance, the focus should be on e-administration (computerization of urban and rural property records, systems and procedures), e-justice (computerization of judicial records) and e-security (computerization of records of law enforcement agencies). A key project towards improved gender em-powerment and HRD is the nursing sector initiative. Emphasis will be, on strengthening the quality and increasing quantity of nurses in Pakistan in order to produce a targeted number of nurses to meet both the domestic and international demand.

Pakistan also proposes strategies for partnering with institutions in the FoDP countries. Potential ways to collaborate include: 'adopt' an organization, public private partnership, exchange programmes, sponsorship schemes, technology transfer and endowment programmes. Two potential partnering arrangements may be with the Alternate Energy Development Board and the Pakistan Agriculture Research Council.

As a result of proposals submitted to the FoDP, it is estimated that an immediate incremental increase in the GDP will be around US$8 billion with an increase in employment of around 5.74 million labour. However, it is disappointing to note that after the first two meetings, the FoDP had pledged US$2.2 billion, which was later slashed to US$874 million. By April 2010, Pakistan had only received US$251 million (excluding US$325 million received from the Islamic Development Bank [IDB]). The contributors were Saudi Arabia, the US and the EU. The US also released the payment towards Coalition Support Fund after considerable delay.

Kerry-Lugar Programme for Pakistan

The interests of the US that revived in Pakistan after the 9/11 incident have translated more recently into expanded the USAID programmes. The assistance has focused on education, health and technical cooperation. The Kerry-Lugar Act 2010 aims to provide an annual US$1.5 billion civilian aid to Pakistan for the next five years. The advocates called this bill a move to rebuild trust with a critical ally.

The new US administration in 2009 framed its thinking in the new USAID Country Assistance Strategy for Pakistan (2010–14). It is realized that in order to meet Pakistan's development needs, assistance should flow from the public and private sector of the US in high impact projects that focus on energy, agriculture, education and health. In order to sustain these investments, complementary efforts should be undertaken to strengthen the human, financial, and institutional capacity. The funding mechanisms will be such that support for infrastructure projects will flow to the national government direct as budget support or public private partnership. Alongside, greater emphasis will be on relationship with Pakistani non-profit organizations and NGOs that are working in social sectors.

The US has formalized its contribution to the FoDP forum in the shape of the Kerry-Lugar Bill which was cleared by the US House of Representatives in September 2009. This aid programme is a step toward socio-economic development at civilian level population and will rejuvenate Pakistan's institutional capacity, developing tribal areas and encouraging multilateral solutions by engaging neighbouring countries such as India and Afghanistan. The programme proposed the use of NGOs rather than government ministries to disburse aid.

This aid arrangement will make Pakistan the second largest recipient of the US aid in the world. The assistance to be provided to Pakistan will mainly fall under categories[9] such as: *(a)* civil liberties, *(b)* political rights, *(c)* voice and accountability, *(d)* government effectiveness, *(e)* rule of law, *(f)* control of corruption, *(g)* immunization rates, *(h)* public expenditure on health, *(i)* girls' primary education, *(j)* public expenditure on primary education, *(k)* natural resource management, *(l)* business start-up, *(m)* land rights and access, *(n)* trade policy, *(o)* regulatory quality and *(p)* fiscal policy management.

Critics, while admitting that long-term non-military aid of US$7.5 billion over the next five years is a significant step initiated by the US for the socio-economic reforms in the country, argued that for economic growth in the country, increased market access for Pakistani goods should have been top on the agenda. The US has again designed a strategy that focuses on aid, not trade. The element of distrust between the two nations that originates from the US leaving Pakistan in the middle of an incomplete development agenda as soon as the Soviet Union retreated in late 1980s, still explains the apprehensions of people from all walks of life in Pakistan towards the Kerry-Lugar assistance (see Ashraf, 2009). Paris (2010) states, 'Pakistani opinion is so anti-American that sometimes it is hard to figure out what the US should do in Pakistan'. Kfir (2009) argues that the Kerry-Lugar strategy will not help substantially towards improving the socio-economic situation in Pakistan as it ignores the core problem in the region i.e., lack of strong democratic institutions. Nawaz (2010) argues that the war in Afghanistan could be lost if the US does not start helping Islamabad and discusses the need for the US to help

Pakistan in rebuilding its infrastructure that could knit the country together and create future employment and investments. The need for establishing education centres by the US has been stressed for its benefit in terms of upgrading human capital and strengthening civil society. O' Hanlon (2010) provides a way forward in promoting regional integration in the region that may well provide the much needed economic stability. The author suggests: the early passing of a bill that proposes free trade between Pakistan's tribal areas and the US, encouraging Pakistan and India in passing their own free trade accords, helping Pakistan–Afghanistan transit agreement to become a success, building fuel pipelines and electricity lines from Central Asia through Afghanistan and into Pakistan.

It has been repeatedly said that at the start of collective initiatives against global terror, coalitions usually are enthusiastic to help smaller partners. However, as the war prolongs it is these smaller partners that are left stranded with diminishing assistance. Table 5.14 indicates that this is precisely what happened in Pakistan more recently. The aid to death ratio (i.e., aid receipts per person killed) has been declining since 2003. Similarly, aid to economic loss ratio which was US$0.4 million in 2005 had fallen to half in 2008. Pakistan's war-related assistance has been one of the major factors in increased aid from non-DAC donors (see Figure 5.6).

Table 5.14
Aid, Loss of Life and Damage to the Economy

	ODA current (US$ million)	Aid to death ratio	Economic loss (US$ million)	Aid to economic loss ratio
2002	2,136	–	–	–
2003	1,071	3.5	–	–
2004	1,439	1.5	–	–
2005	1,607	1.9	4,400	0.37
2006	2,140	1.3	5,000	0.43
2007	2,244	0.6	6,000	0.37
2008	1,539	0.2	7,700	0.20

Source: Data on ODA from WDI (World Bank, 2010, 30 October 2010); data on number of deaths from SATP database (South Asia Terrorism Portal, 2010, 30 October 2010); data on economic loss (Government of Pakistan, n.d.a).

Figure 5.6
Major Recipients of Non-DAC Donor Humanitarian Aid, 2009

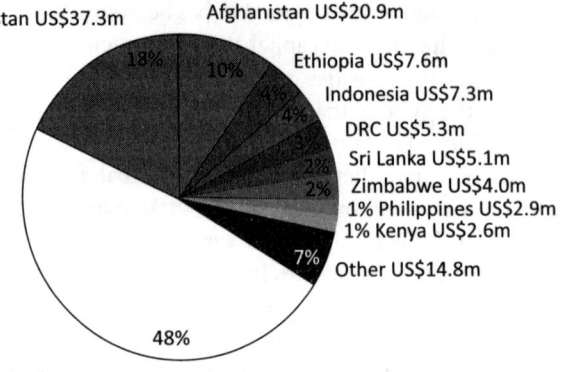

Pakistan US$37.3m   Afghanistan US$20.9m

Ethiopia US$7.6m
Indonesia US$7.3m
DRC US$5.3m
Sri Lanka US$5.1m
Zimbabwe US$4.0m
1% Philippines US$2.9m
1% Kenya US$2.6m
Other US$14.8m

18%   10%   4%   3%   2%   2%   7%   48%

Palestine/OPT US$99.7m

Source: The United Nations Office for the Coordination of Humanitarian Affairs (2010).

CONCLUSION

Pakistan being a frontline state in the war against terrorism has also remained one of the highest recipients of foreign aid. This chapter analyses foreign assistance through four main facets namely: the link between aid, security and growth with special reference to Pakistan, general equilibrium impact of foreign resource inflow on economic growth and poverty, aid effectiveness in Pakistan and priorities for aid policy reform in the country.

The empirical literature on the impact of aid on economic development in Pakistan is inconclusive due to aid being fragmented and volatile. The donors have remained poorly coordinated with a weak follow-up mechanism. Pakistan, for its part, has seen mixed experiences in aid absorption. While a decade long nationwide social action programme could not translate into improved social and welfare indicators, there are some success stories such as rural support networks, microfinance opportunities, cluster approach for earthquake relief and recovery.

While the economic implications of prolonged reliance on aid indicate Dutch disease effects at the macroeconomic level in Pakistan, there are more concerning effects at that micro level where society has started to perceive aid as a compensation (and not assistance) for Pakistan's involvement in wars led by developed nations. This behaviour besides corrupting the elite, also promotes rent seeking where agents gaining from war have a vested interest in keeping the conflict intensified. Pakistan along with its development partners has taken measures to move towards the directions indicated in the PD. The EAD is in the process of finalizing the Foreign Assistance Policy Framework which is governed by principles that ensure compatibility and convergence of aid with national plans and improve quality, effectiveness and efficiency of foreign assistance. Having a national aid policy is all the more important at this stage when Pakistan is in the process of seeking assistance from the FoDP consortium and Kerry-Lugar arrangement with the US. The improved mechanism should include appropriate amendments based upon the lessons learnt from past experiences.

Finally, as the reconstruction work takes off in the war-torn areas, there will be increased need for regular quantitative and qualitative analytical work by both government and donors. The research dissemination should then translate into a process of effective dialogue between all stakeholders.

ANNEXURE I

Table 5A.1
Total Bilateral Aid Disbursed (US$ Million)

Recipient(s)	2004	2005	2006	2007	2008	Total
Afghanistan	2,303	2,818	2,956	3,965	4,865	16,907
Bangladesh	1,414	1,318	1,220	1,515	2,061	7,528
Bhutan	78	90	102	90	87	447
China	1,716	1,814	1,248	1,487	1,489	7,754
India	774	1,851	1,383	1,384	2,108	7,500
Indonesia	127	2,509	1,311	896	1,225	6,068
Iraq	4,647	22,046	8,870	9,185	9,880	54,628
Maldives	28	76	38	37	54	233
Nepal	425	424	511	609	716	2,685
Pakistan	1,439	1,607	2,140	2,244	1,539	8,969
Palestinian Adm. Areas	1,115	1,116	1,450	1,872	2,593	8,146

(continued table 5A.1)

(continued table 5A.1)

Recipient(s)	2004	2005	2006	2007	2008	Total
Philippines	449	567	565	647	61	2,289
Rwanda	490	577	589	722	931	3,309
Sierra Leone	376	340	347	545	367	1,975
Somalia	199	237	391	384	758	1,969
Sri Lanka	506	1,155	786	613	730	3,790
Sudan	992	1,823	2,044	2,112	2,384	9,355
Turkey	285	396	566	792	2,024	4,063
Vietnam	1,846	1,913	1,845	2,511	2,552	10,667

Source: Economic Affairs Division, www.ead.gov.pk (accessed on 30 October 2010).

Table 5A.2
Aid Disbursed by United States (US$ Million)

Recipient(s)	2004	2005	2006	2007	2008	Total
Afghanistan	778	1,318	1,404	1,514	2,112	7,126
Bangladesh	63	49	42	49	93	296
India	51	57	97	85	52	342
Indonesia	69	156	190	117	115	647
Iraq	3,022	11,228	4,782	3,749	2,742	25,523
Nepal	35	52	62	54	78	281
Pakistan	77	323	478	434	351	1663
Palestinian Adm. Areas	274	181	206	212	491	1,364
Philippines	79	97	98	85	71	430
Rwanda	50	57	78	91	117	393
Sierra Leone	30	22	21	21	16	110
Somalia	32	37	95	59	243	466
Sri Lanka	–3	59	29	33	52	170
Sudan	378	759	739	710	848	3,434
Thailand	10	21	25	45	40	141
Vietnam	30	28	45	41	63	207

Source: Economic Affairs Division, www.ead.gov.pk (accessed on 30 October 2010).

NOTES

1. The authors are economists at the Planning Commission of Pakistan. Address for correspondence: vahmed@gmail.com. Acknowledgements are due to Mahmood Tufail, Muhammed Javed, Hamid Mahmood and Haroon Sarwar for their technical support and advice. The study also uses material provided by the Economic Affairs Division in Pakistan and International Monetary Fund (IMF) (Islamabad Resident Office) for which we are very grateful. The authors would like to acknowledge the comments provided on an earlier version of this chapter presented at the International Conference on 'Policy Priorities for Foreign Aid Reform in South Asia', 29–30 July 2010 at Colombo, organized by IPS, Sri Lanka, and Friedrich Ebert Stiftung. The usual disclaimer applies.
2. Average debt to export ratio between, 1986 and 1990 was 241.5 per cent and average debt to Gross National Product (GNP) ratio during the same period was 48.4 per cent.
3. For complete mathematical details see Ahmed and O' Donoghue (2010b).
4. This section draws from Ahmed and O' Donoghue (2010c).
5. This draws from material provided to us by the Economic Affairs Division.
6. Currently at consultative stage in the Economic Affairs Division.
7. Others were forced to find residence with friends and relative in other areas of Pakistan.
8. Approximate cost of repair is Rs 500,000 per house.
9. Categories as described in the annual 'Report on the Criteria and Methodology for Determining the Eligibility of Candidate Countries for Millennium Challenge Account Assistance'.

REFERENCES

Adams, R. H. (1995), 'Sources of Income Inequality and Poverty in Rural Pakistan', Research Report 102, IFPRI, Washington D.C.

Ahmed, Viqar and Rashid Amjad (1984), *The Management of Pakistan's Economy 1947–82*, Oxford University Press, Lahore.

Ahmed, Vaqar and Cathal O' Donoghue (2010a), 'Global Economic Crisis and Poverty in Pakistan', *International Journal of Microsimulation* (2010) 3(1): 127–29.

—— (2010b), 'Tariff Reduction in a Small Open Economy', *Seoul Journal of Economics*, 23(2) (Summer 2010): 461–89.

—— (2010c), 'Welfare Impact of External Balance in Pakistan: CGE – microsimulation Analysis', *The Lahore Journal of Economics*, 15(1) (Summer 2010): 45–90.

Alavi, H. and A. Khusro (1970), 'Pakistan: The Burden of US Aid', in *Imperialism and Under-development– A Reader*, in R. I. Rhodes (ed.), *Monthly Review Press*, Monthly Review Press, New York, pp. 65–6.

Alesina, A. and B. Weder (1999), 'Do Corrupt Governments Receive Less Foreign Aid?' NBER Working Paper Series, Working Paper 7108, May 1999.

Ashraf, S. (2009), *The Kerry-Lugar Bill: Difficult Choices for Pakistan*. Institute of South Asian Studies (ISAS) brief No. 131, date: 5 October 2009, National University of Singapore.

Baqai, M. (1973), 'The Role of Foreign Aid in Pakistan's Economic Planning', in M. Baqai and I. Brecher (eds) *Development Planning and Policy in Pakistan*, National Institute of Social and Economic Research, Karachi, Pakistan.

Boyce, J. K. (2002), 'Aid Conditionality as a Tool for Peacebuilding: Opportunities and Constraints', *Development and Change* 33(5): 1025–48.

Brecher, I. and S. A. Abbas (1972), *Foreign Aid and Industrial Development in Pakistan,* Cambridge University Press, New York.

Burnside, Craig and David Dollar (2000), 'Aid, Policies, and Growth', *American Economic Review,* 90(4): 847–68.

Carment, D., Y. Samy and S. Prest (2008), 'State Fragility and Implications for Aid Allocation: An Empirical Analysis', *Conflict Management and Peace Science*, 25(4): 349–73.

Chong A., M. Gradstein and C. Calderon (2009), 'Can Foreign Aid Reduce Income Inequality and Poverty?' *Public Choice* 140 (3–4): 59–84.

Chowdhury P. and A. Garonna (2007), 'Effective Foreign Aid, Economic Integration and Subsidiarity: Lessons From Europe', Discussion paper United Nations Economic Commission For Europe, Geneva, Switzerland No. 2007.2.

DAC (2008a), 'Service Delivery in Fragile Situations', *OECD Journal on Development 2008*, 9/3 OECD 2009.

DAC (2008b), 'Concepts and Dilemmas of State Building in Fragile Situations', *OECD Journal on Development 2008*, 9/3 OECD 2009.

De Spoelberch G. and Shaw R. D. (1987), 'A Model: The Aga Khan Rural Support Programme', *African Development Symposium*, 29 (6).

DFID (2000), 'The Sap Experience In Pakistan', Briefing Paper by IHSD Limited, London.

Ehrenfeld, D., S. Y. Kogut and H. Hove (2003), 'Aid Conditionality and the Peace Process: An Analysis of its Implementation', *International Journal of World Peace.* XX(4): 59–70.

Easterly, William, Ross Levine and David Roodman (Forthcoming), 'New Data, New Doubts: A Comment on Burnside and Dollar's 'Aid, Policies, and Growth' (2000).' *American Economic Review,* Forthcoming.

Easterly, William (2003), 'Can Aid Buy Growth?' *Journal of Economic Perspective*, 179(3): 23–48.

Easterly W. and T. Pfutze (2008), 'Where Does the Money Go? Best and Worst Practices in Foreign Aid', *Journal of Economic Perspectives*, 22 (2).

Faisal Cheema (2004), 'Macroeconomic Stability of Pakistan: The Role of the IMF and World Bank (1997–2003)', *ACDIS Occasional Paper* ACDIS CHE: 1.2004, Urbana-Champaign, USA.

Goodhand, J. and M. Sedra (2007), 'Bribes or Bargains? Peace Conditionalities and "Post-Conflict" Reconstruction in Afghanistan', *International Peacekeeping*, 14(1): 41–61, January 2007.

Government of Pakistan (n.d.a), *Economic Survey of Pakistan*, Government of Pakistan Islamabad.

Government of Pakistan (n.d.b), *Handbook of Statistics*, Government of Pakistan, Islamabad.

Guillaume De Spoelberch and Robert D' Arcy Shaw (1987), *A Model: The Aga Khan Rural Support Program*, Interview published in *Challenge*, January 1987.

Hamid, N. (1970), 'A Critical Appraisal of Foreign Aid Strategy', *Pakistan Economic and Social Review,* VIII (2): 149–51, December 1970.

Hansen, Ketil Fred and Axel Borchgrevink (2006), *The European Journal of Development Research*, 18(4): 622–641, December 2006.

Hilali A. Z. (2002), 'The Costs and Benefits of the Afghan War for Pakistan', *Contemporary South Asia*, 11(3): 291–310.

Husain, I. (2002), 'Pakistan and the IMF: 1988–2002', A case study. State Bank of Pakistan.

Husain, Ishrat (1992), 'External Debt and Foreign Aid to Pakistan', in Anjum Nasim (ed.), *Financing Pakistan's Development in the 1990s*, OUP and LUMS, Lahore.

Ishfaq, M. (2004), 'Aid Effectiveness Debt Capacity and Debt Management in Pakistan', *Department of Economics*, PHD thesis.

Ibrahim, A. (2010), 'United States Aid to Pakistan: United States Taxpayers have Funded Pakistani Corruption', *The DISAM Journal*, March 2010.

ILO (1996), 'Wage Workers in Agriculture: Conditions of Employment and Work', International Labour Office, Geneva, 1996.

Iqbal Z. (1997), 'Foreign Aid and the Public Sector: A Model of Fiscal Behaviour in Pakistan', *The Pakistan Development Review*, 36: 2 (Summer 1997): 115–29.

Jones, S.G. (2007), 'Pakistan's Dangerous Game', *Survival*, 49: 1(2007): 20.

Keefer, Philip E., Ambar Narayan and Tara Vishwanath (2005), 'Decentralization in Pakistan: Are Local Politicians Likely to be More Accountable?' http://siteresources.worldbank.org/INTINVTCLI/Resources/decentralizationinPakistan.pdf (accessed on 25 July 2010).

Kfir, I. (2009), 'U.S. Policy Toward Pakistan And Afghanistan Under The Obama Administration', *Middle East Review of International Affairs*, 13(4) (December 2009).

Khan, S. Rafi (1997), 'Has Aid Helped Pakistan', *Pakistan Development Review*, 36: 4 Part II: 947–57.

Khan and Ahmed (2007), 'Foreign Aid—Blessing or Curse: Evidence from Pakistan', *Pakistan Development Review*, 46 (3): 215–40.

Kole, J. W. (1971), 'House Votes to Knockout Aid for Pakistan, Greece', *The Milwaukee Journal*. 4 August 1971, p. 2.

MacLeod A. (2006), 'Early Recovery from Disaster: The Pakistan Earthquake: Humanitarian Reforms: Fullfilling its Promise?' UNCHR , FMR 29.

Malik A. (2009), 'Quality and Coordination of Official Development Aid in Pakistan', *The Brookings Global Economy and Development*, Working Paper 11.

Masud, N. and Yontcheva, B. (2005), 'Does Foreign Aid Reduce Poverty? Empirical Evidence from Nongovernmental and Bilateral Aid', IMF Working Paper C25, F35.

Ministry of Finance (2007), Pakistan Poverty Reduction Strategy Paper II (PRSP-II), Islamabad.

Muhammad, S. D. (2010), 'Microfinance Challenges and Opportunities in Pakistan', *European Journal of Social Sciences*, 14 (1).

Nawaz, S. (2010), 'A Formula to Fix America's Pakistan Policy', *The Wall Street Journal*, June 29, 2010.

O'Hanlon M. (2010), 'Building a Basis for Success in Afghanistan', www.brookings.edu.

OECD (2007), 'The Paris Declaration on Aid Effectiveness and the Accra Agenda for Action', OECD.

OECD (2010), 'OECD Statistics', www.oecd.org/dac/stats/qwids (accessed on 30 October 2010).

Pack, H. and Pack J. Rothenberg (1993), 'Foreign Aid and the Question of Fungibility', *The Review of Economics and Statistics*, 75 (2): 258–65.

Pasha, H. A. and A. F. Aisha Ghaus (1996), 'Sustainability of Public Debt in Pakistan', *Sustainable Policy Development Centre (SPDC)*, Conference Paper No. 21, Karachi.

Paris, J. (2010), *Prospects for Pakistan*, LEGATUM Institute, January 2010.

Padawangi, Rita (2010), 'Community-driven Development as a Driver of Change: Water Supply and Sanitation Projects in Rural Punjab, Pakistan', *Water Policy* 12 Supplement 1 (2010) 104–20.

Rabea M. (2007), 'Aid Effectiveness and the Role of Donor Intervention in the Education Sector in Pakistan—A Review of Issues and Literature', Mahbub Ul Haq Human Development Centre, *RECOUP Working Paper*, No. 6.

Rahim, E. and N. Z. Khan (1993), 'Foreign Aid, Domestic Saving and Economic Growth, 1960–1988', *The Pakistan Development Review*, 32(4): 1157–67.

Rodriguez, McGillivray and Morrissey (1998), 'Aid and the Public Sector in Pakistan: Evidence with Endogenous Aid', World Development, July 1998, 26(7): 1241–50.

Saeed K. A. (1995), *Economy of Pakistan*, Salam Publications, 4th Edition.

Shah, I. A. (2009), 'People's Participation in Rural Development Projects in the North-West Frontier Province of Pakistan: A Comparative Review and Analysis of Sarhad Rural Support Programme (SRSP) and Integrated Rural Development Project (IRDP)', *African and Asian Studies* 8 (2009): 175–84.

State Bank of Pakistan (n.d.), *State Bank of Pakistan, Annual Report*, State Bank of Pakistan, Karachi.

Svensson, J. (2000), 'Foreign Aid and Rent-seeking', *Journal of International Economics,* 51(2000): 437–61.

Suhrke, A. and J. Buckmaster (2005), 'Post-war Aid: Patterns and Purposes', *Development in Practice*, 15(6).

Tellis J. A. (2008), 'Pakistan's Record on Terrorism: Conflicted Goals, Compromised Performance', *The Washington Quarterly*, 31(2): 7–32.

The United Nations Office for the Coordination of Humanitarian Affairs (2010), 'Development Initiatives based on UN OCHA FTS data', www.unocha.org/ (accessed on 30 October 2010).

Vos, R. (1998), 'Aid Flows and "Dutch Disease" in a General Equilibrium Framework for Pakistan', *Journal of Policy Modeling*, 20(1): 77–109.

6

Afghanistan

ANNEKA DE SILVA

RECENT TRENDS IN FOREIGN AID RECEIPTS

Following events in 2001, foreign aid to Afghanistan has played an increasingly significant role in public expenditure. Given the conflict situation, domestic revenue has been particularly low, with the government only able to fund around 64 per cent of recurrent expenditure. Hence, donor aid has played a crucial role in funding both recurrent and development expenditures of the country (Ministry of Finance, 2009). Overall assistance to Afghanistan, from 2002, amounts to US$46 billion of which US$36 billion has been disbursed. Assistance into the country is largely made up of grants, with concessional loans accounting for only US$1.4 billion of total aid.

Afghanistan has been receiving aid from roughly 47 different development partners since 2002. Within this group, the US is by far the largest donor having contributed one-third of all aid since 2002. Following the US, the UK, the World Bank, the Asian Development Bank (ADB), European Commission (EC), Japan, Canada and Germany are also prominent donors within Afghanistan (see Figure 6.1).

Aid commitments have generally been secured during various international conferences on Afghanistan, such as those held in Tokyo (2002), Berlin (2004), London (2006) and Paris (2008). The 2009 *Donor Financial Review* (DFR), commissioned by the Afghan Ministry of Finance, reported that actual disbursements have fallen short of commitments, as illustrated in Figure 6.2. The disbursement rate

Anneka De Silva

Figure 6.1
International Assistance to Afghanistan, 2002–08

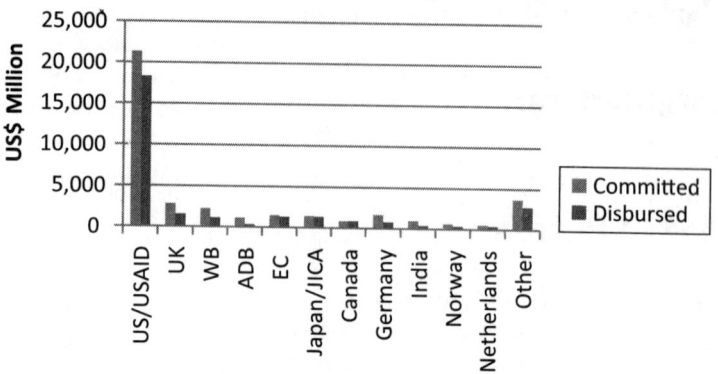

Source: Ministry of Finance, 2009.

over the period 2002–09 stood at 78 per cent. Whilst the USA has disbursed the largest amount of aid to the country, its disbursement rate is only 64 per cent of its original commitment. Likewise, the UK and the World Bank have disbursements of only 42 per cent and 28 per cent, respectively, with Germany and the EC disbursing less

Figure 6.2
Aid Committed and Disbursed, 2002–08

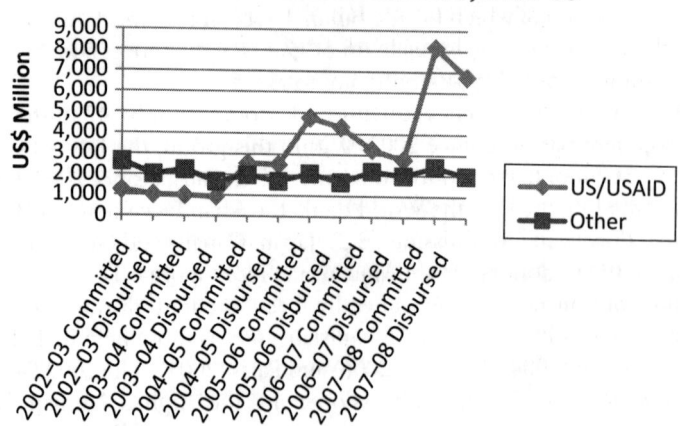

Source: Ministry of Finance (2009).

than two-thirds and the ADB and India disbursing only a third of their 2002–08 commitments.

This noted mismatch between commitments and disbursements is typical of most aid inflows and is usually related to time lags in project implementation and other bureaucracies. This is especially true of long-term projects wherein disbursements may take place many years after the initial commitments are made. Further constraints restricting disbursements in Afghanistan relate to lack of absorptive capacity, on behalf of the government, high levels of corruption and undesirable operating conditions. Whilst these discrepancies may stem from unavoidable practical obstacles, the lack of predictability with which aid is disbursed may have a number of negative implications on domestic financial management. This is especially true of a country such as Afghanistan wherein 36 per cent of recurrent expenditure and 100 per cent of development expenditure is funded by aid. The effects of this shall be discussed in greater detail later on in the chapter.

As can be seen, bilateral aid into the country makes up a much larger proportion of total aid flows than multilateral aid. A large proportion of this is made up of the inflows of aid from the USA. As seen in Figure 6.3, there is a steep increase in the inflow of aid from bilateral donors over the years 2002–08, with only two drops between the periods 2003–04 and 2006–07. Conversely, over the same period disbursements from multilateral donors have been much more stable with a slight peak in 2003–04 (see Figure 6.4 for trends in multilateral aid).

Figure 6.3
Trends in Foreign Aid, 2002–08 (Disbursed)

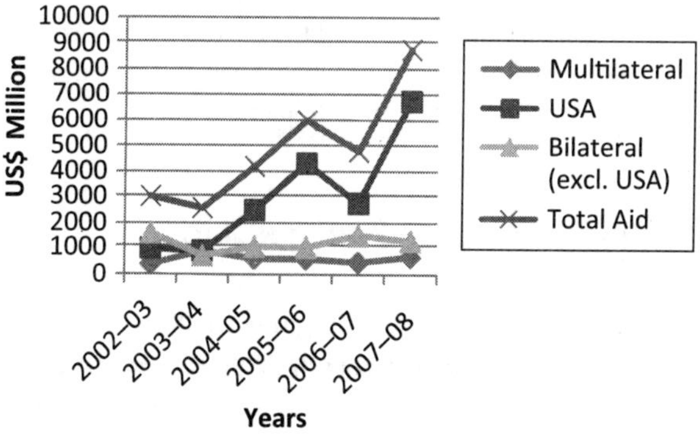

Source: Ministry of Finance, 2009.

Figure 6.4
Multilateral Aid, 2002–08

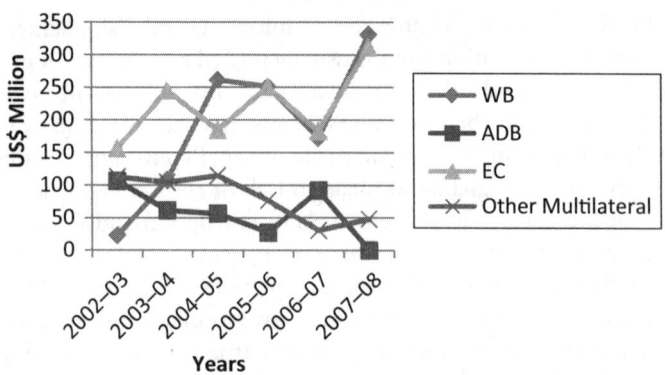

Source: Ministry of Finance (2009).

The significantly large increase in aid disbursed from the USA in the period 2007–08 follows the international conference held in Paris wherein the Afghanistan National Development Strategy (ANDS) (Afghanistan's poverty reduction strategy paper) was first presented to development partners. The subsequent increase in commitments is an indication of the support from the international community to the government of Afghanistan in implementing and executing the development strategy.

As previously mentioned, donor assistance plays a crucial role in funding government spending—this relates to both operating budget support and development support. Within the period of 2002–09, 77 per cent of total aid disbursements had been mobilized through donors whilst the remaining 23 per cent has been directed through and managed by the government, as outlined in Table 6.1.

CONTEMPORARY ROLE OF FOREIGN AID

Following the fall of the Taliban regime in 2001, foreign aid has played an increasingly prominent role in expenditures of the Government of Afghanistan. Due to the unstable security situation and subsequent weak institutional capacity, domestic revenues have continued to fall short of core budget and development expenditures.

Table 6.1
Modalities of Foreign Aid, 2002–09

Modality	Disbursement	Percentage of total
Donor-managed Assistance	**29,189.55**	**77**
Military	14,867.47	39
Non-military	14,322.08	38
Government-managed Assistance	**8,691.07**	**23**
General Budget Support	3,653.57	42
Development Support	1,495	17
Recurrent Expenditure Support	3,542.50	41
Total	**37,880.62**	**100**

Source: Ministry of Finance (2009).

The 2009 mid-year budget review indicated that the Government of Afghanistan was only able to finance 64 per cent of core budget expenditures, with the remaining expenditures being financed by foreign aid. Furthermore, development expenditures are solely financed by foreign donors. Hence, foreign aid plays a pivotal role in future development plans and sustaining economic growth. Given this heavy reliance on external funding, loans are offered at concessionary rates so as to increase the sustainability of donor-funded investments.

The aftermath of the conflict, following 2001, saw the country critically in need of humanitarian assistance and reconstruction of both physical and social infrastructure. Hence, much of the support from donors in the immediate period after 2001 was aligned towards achieving a state of stability within the country. Steps taken towards increasing security and reinstating the rule of law included the creation of the new Afghan National Army and reforming the Afghan National Police. Such priorities were reflected in the sectoral allocation of aid after 2002 with 45 per cent of aid being committed to security developments, 15 per cent for infrastructure, 9 per cent for both rural development and governance and 22 per cent for education, health, economic governance and social protection. The remaining aid allocations have been spent on programmes in cross-cutting issues such as gender, counter-narcotics, environmental protection and anti-corruption (Ministry of Finance, 2009). This disproportionately large investment in security has been supported and influenced by the US, Afghanistan's largest donor.

According to the 2009 DFR, 40 per cent (US$18.3 billion) of all development aid committed has been made by military agencies, with 98 per cent of that figure being committed by the US Department of Defense.

Domestic Revenue Collection

In 2008, the Government of Afghanistan released the ANDS which set out the national development plan for the period 2008–13. Whilst the ANDS promotes continued support in security, it also recognizes the need for greater development in other sectors of the economy, in order to relieve fiscal constraints of the government caused by factors such as weak revenue collection. Revenue collection has been notoriously poor in the country; this can largely be attributed to disruptions caused by the ongoing conflict arresting development in domestic institutions. Furthermore, the lack of capacity and law and order has subsequently allowed for opium production to flourish in the country, with Afghanistan being responsible for approximately 90 per cent of the world's opium production as of 2008 making it the largest economic activity in the country. The negative implications of the illicit trade on sustainable development and economic growth overwhelmingly outweigh the short-term economic benefits to the rural economy that accrue from the industry. In particular, given that production is illegal, the government is unable to collect revenues from the trade, further aggravating the low tax base constraint facing the government. Instead, such activity fuels corruption and stifles the development and credibility of domestic institutions which in turn fosters terrorism.

Revenue collection of the government has gradually improved over the years, with regard to both tax and non-tax revenues. Central Bank data shows that revenue collection was at a dismal 3.2 per cent of the GDP in the period 2002–03. In subsequent years, however, revenue collection has risen to around 7 per cent of the GDP in the period 2006–08. As can be seen in Table 6.2, year-on-year revenue collection has continued to rise. Despite the noted increments, however, Afghanistan still falls below the revenue-to-GDP ratio of other nations grouped within the same bracket of least developed countries, wherein revenues are typically around 20 per cent of GDP. Figure 6.5 illustrates trends in domestic revenue and expenditures over the period 2004–09. As can be seen, whilst domestic revenue is steadily rising it continues

Table 6.2
Revenue Collection, 2004–09 (AF Million)

	2004/05	*2005/06*	*2006/07*	*2007/08*	*2008/09*
Total Revenue	12,800	21,665	28,660	33,513	45,510
% Growth of Revenue	–	61.3	32	35.8	36

Source: Da Afghanistan Bank (2009).

to fall way below total budget expenditures (including both operating and development expenditures). Such figures indicate the extent of the fiscal constraints under which the government is operating and the subsequent inflated importance of foreign assistance in funding the operating budget.

Informal Sector Activity

Other causes of the low tax base include the dominance of the informal sector in economic activity. Informal activity extends beyond the illicit opium trade and is most dominant in the small holder industry. For example, electricity is provided largely by small holders operating in the informal sector. Informal activity is most prevalent in the rural areas of Afghanistan, especially given that most development tends to

Figure 6.5
Domestic Revenues and Expenditures, 2004–09

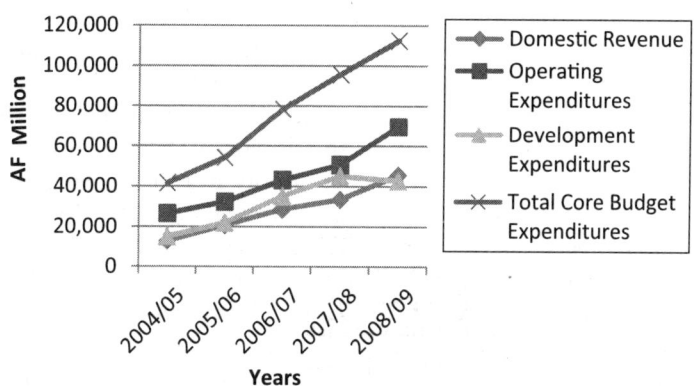

Source: Da Afghanistan Bank (2009).

be concentrated in the larger cities such as Kabul; hence, regulatory capacity in rural areas remains weak. It becomes very difficult to capture the extent of informal activity given that it takes many different forms ranging from casual rural workers to private sector entities which are registered but also engage in informal activities. Whilst the informal sector is imperative to the livelihoods of many in the rural communities, the inability of the government to obtain revenue from such activities is detrimental to long-term sustainability, especially when considering that such informal activity constitutes around 80–90 per cent of total economic activity.

National Development Priorities

Throughout the ANDS, there is great emphasis on encouraging private sector investment as a vehicle through which to overcome fiscal constraints and the accompanying aid dependence. Hence, the ANDS attempts to address many of the key areas negatively affecting the business environment such as, good governance, rule of law and human rights, security and economic and social development. Box 6.1 summarizes the development objectives as set out in the ANDS. Looking at Figure 6.6 we can see how the allocation of donor aid changes over the years. Post 2001, donor priorities were largely focused on investments in security, most of which came through the US, as mentioned earlier. However, following the release of the ANDS in 2008 we can see a vast shift in donor priorities, to an overall more balanced development effort. Expenditure in security has been considerably reduced with far greater emphasis on spending in infrastructure, education, agricultural development, health, economic governance and the rule of law.

Such drastic transition in donor spending clearly indicates a shift in-line with the Government of Afghanistan's development plan, as all aforementioned sectors fall under priority areas highlighted in the ANDS. However, we are unable to gauge from the available data where the aid has been directed within each general sector, and whether or not these fall in line with the specific areas outlined within the ANDS. For instance, within the ANDS there is heavy emphasis placed on donor assistance in increasing the provision of energy and water resources. Whilst the data shows that there is an increase in investment in infrastructure, we are unable to ascertain whether that has been

> ### Box 6.1
> ### Summary of the Afghanistan National
> ### Development Strategy 1397–91 (2008–13)
>
> The Afghanistan National Development Strategy (ANDS) was formally approved as the country's development plan by President Hamid Karzai on 21 April 2008. The document is a five-year development plan which outlines the national priorities for growth, governance, economic growth and poverty reduction for the period 2008–13.
>
> The 2008 ANDS serves as Afghanistan's Poverty Reduction Strategy Paper (PRSP) and was developed as a follow-up to the interim strategy released by the Government of Afghanistan in 2005. The main goals of the ANDS are:
>
> - Security—achieve nationwide stability, strengthen the enforcement of law and increase personal safety for citizens
> - Governance, Rule of Law and Human Rights—strengthen democratic processes and institutions, human rights, the rule of law, delivery of public services and government accountability
> - Economic and Social Development—reduce poverty, ensure sustainable development through a private-sector–led market economy, improve human development indicators and make significant progress towards the Millennium Development Goals (MDGs)
> - Cross-cutting areas—eliminating the narcotics industry
>
> *Source:* Government of Afghanistan (2008).

directed towards these two objectives or instead areas perceived to be of priority to the donors.

The Trade Deficit

Besides the importance of aid in supporting core budget expenditures, foreign aid also plays an important role in managing the balance of payments. Afghanistan has long battled with a relatively large trade deficit, caused by the volume of imports outstripping the volume of (legal) exports. In recent years, there has been a gradual reduction in the trade deficit. However, when considering that the Real Effective Exchange Rate (REER) has appreciated by more than 35 per cent over the period 2002–09, the outlook for increased competitiveness

Anneka De Silva

Figure 6.6
Aid Allocation by Sector, 2001–09

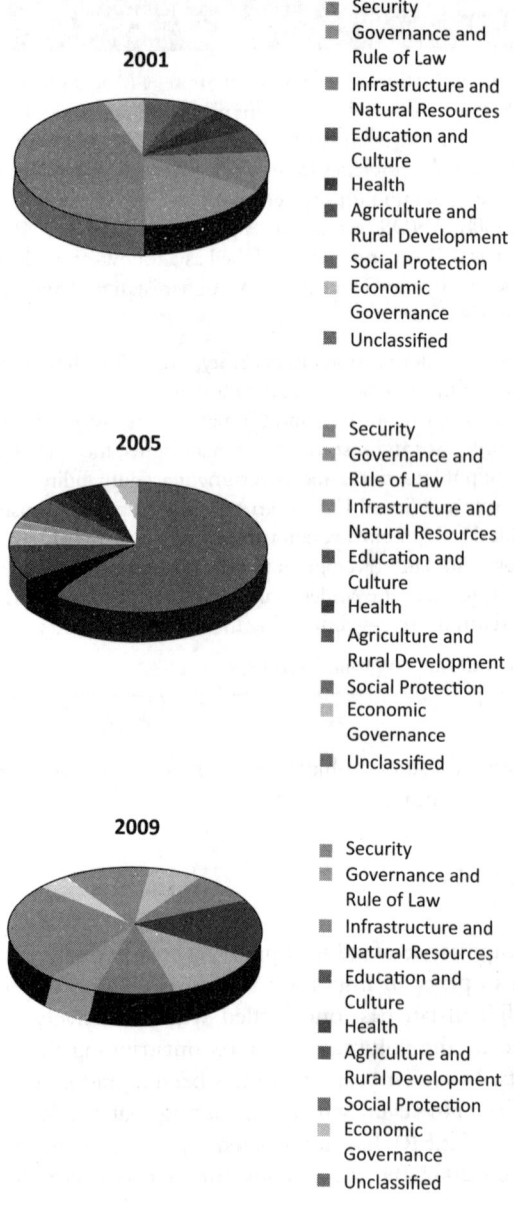

Source: Ministry of Finance (2009).

of exports is uncertain. This together with the limited regional export market faced by Afghanistan (due to neighbouring countries having subsidized production in key sectors) and rising commodity prices indicates that at least in the short run, managing a relatively large trade deficit will continue to be a feature of Afghanistan's external sector. Hence, in the short to medium term, foreign aid will continue to provide the country with the much needed foreign exchange to pay for imports and help in maintaining exchange rate stability. However, continued investment in the country's private sector should help to increase export competitiveness and import substitution in the long run.

CURRENT CHALLENGES OF EXTERNAL ASSISTANCE

Fiscal Management

Whilst external assistance is an essential source of public finances, continued reliance on aid flows can harbour inefficiencies within the existing Public Financial Management (PFM) system. One of the most pressing issues is the effect of donor assistance on fiscal sustainability. As previously discussed, low levels of domestic revenue mobilization has created a heavy reliance on incoming aid flows for funding recurrent and development expenditures within the core budget. By looking at the budget deficit before grants, we are able to gain some indication as to the extent of fiscal vulnerabilities (IMF, 2008). As of 2008, the before-grant core budget deficit was forecasted at 13 per cent of the Gross Domestic Product (GDP) over the period 2008 to 2013. When we consider that the official budget deficit (including grants) for 2008 was only 2.2 per cent of GDP, we can see the extent to which donor aid bridges the resource gap. Within the IMF's 2008 country report of Afghanistan, they point to such spending as being indicative of fiscal instability given that recurrent expenditure is the cost of running the government and, therefore, the government should be able to operate using sustainable (domestic) resources. This type of reliance increases the vulnerability of the whole economy to fluctuations in donor assistance, as cut backs in aid will force the government to make painful spending cuts. Indeed, as we have observed, donor disbursements have continued to fall below commitments, which validates the argument that dependence should be gradually reduced. Furthermore, the heavy composition of external funding in public expenditure directly ties the economy to external shocks that may be affecting donor countries. Whilst Afghanistan managed to pass through the global financial crisis relatively unscathed, such events potentially risk donors cutting down on assistance to recipient countries.

The problem of fiscal instability was addressed by the government and its respective development partners at the 2006 London conference. As a result, it was agreed and outlined in the Afghanistan Compact that by 2010/11 the ratio of domestic revenue to total estimated recurrent expenditure (in both core and external budgets) should stand at 58 per cent. However, in 2008 that ratio stood at roughly 15 per cent, with IMF estimations placing the 2010/11 ratio at approximately 24 per cent. Further targets have been set as part of the terms accompanying the current Poverty Reduction Growth Fund (PRGF) to close the operating budget deficit (covering operating expenditures with domestic revenue) by 2009/10; however, this date has since been revised to 2012/13. Such targets aim to place pressure on the government to restructure fiscal expenditures in the medium term, but the continued deviation from targets indicates the difficulty with which the government has in meeting these objectives.

Institutional Capacity

Afghanistan has been in a state of conflict for over 30 years. Given the sheer length of the conflict there are a number of deep-rooted structural obstacles which have been allowed to proliferate within the fragile state. These obstacles stand to hinder the speed with which development efforts take effect and regional disparities in poverty are overcome. Furthermore, if left unattended, these existent structural obstacles threaten to further aggravate the conflict situation.

Traditionally, Afghanistan was a decentralized state formed around tribal groups in the varying regions. Given this background, the contemporary centralized government structure has not gained much credibility amongst different stakeholders. This is made worse by the lack of legitimacy surrounding the state, with the government being renowned for harbouring a high degree of corruption. The lack of state capacity is the overarching factor affecting the ability of the state to change the negative perceptions surrounding it, given their restricted ability to independently lead development processes. The poor state capacity has been vitiated by the destruction of human capital throughout the war and the constant displacement of communities, which has facilitated the growth of competing power structures and warlords.

Sub-national Level Institutions

This lack of capacity is even more prominent at the sub-national level, which further magnifies the disconnect between civil society and the government. Sub-national level institutions can potentially be instrumental in bridging the gap between civil society and central-level government agents and donors. This in turn would allow for greater stakeholder consultation and the subsequent design, and implementation, of more inclusive policies. Stakeholder consultation is necessary in order to increase the efficacy of aid, as policymakers are better informed of the ground-level constraints which need to be addressed.

In the context of a fragile state, there is greater emphasis on the importance of strong sub-national level institutions in connecting different communities to the central system. Without this channel of communication there is room for (real or perceived) ethnic polarization, which may further fuel rebellion and conflict in the region. Currently, there is a lack of domestic ownership surrounding the state. The 2008 OPM/IDL Evaluation of the Paris Declaration (PD) in Fragile Situations reports that the state is perceived by society as being run by the international community and foreign firms. Such perceptions will allow for the proliferation of decentralized groups and further rebellion if these groups feel excluded from the activities of the government. Following 9/11, the global interest in Afghanistan increased tenfold. This interest began with the 'war on terror' but exposed other such issues in the country such as the opium production and the potential for Afghanistan to be a major trading centre in Asia due to its location. The global influence in decision-making of the central government works to further marginalize communities which are already cut off by the lack of downward accountability.

Provincial Reconstruction Teams (PRTs)

The PRTs are another factor that is affecting the ability of the state to develop strong sub-national level institutions. The PRTs are intended as an 'interim structure' deployed by the United Sates Agency for

International Development (USAID) in provinces where there is low security. There are currently 26 PRTs operating in Afghanistan, with the objective of creating a stable environment in which international and domestic civilian agencies can undertake development activities. A significant proportion of aid to the south and south-east regions is delivered through the PRTs. As a result, the PRTs have undertaken many development projects within these areas, which have been of varying quality and impact (Waldman, 2008). Whilst in some instances it has been necessary for PRTs to become involved in development, due to the highly unsecure environment, projects are often of an ad hoc nature which increases the difficulty with which they can be aligned with government priorities. Furthermore, the presence of the PRTs takes away the opportunity for sub-national level institutions to develop. This can be especially harmful in areas where insurgency is strongest, as it is important to establish a government presence which is well informed of development constraints at the grassroots level.

Marginalized Communities

As highlighted by the OPM/ILD Evaluation, there are a number of risk factors that if left unattended threaten to further destabilize the country. Firstly, the pace of reconstruction and development has been relatively slow, which has caused discontent amongst stakeholders. The slow pace of development observed may be due to the concentration of aid in central locations, with a noticeable lack of development in the exteriors of the country. This has further fuelled the persistence of poverty in Afghanistan. Such a backdrop is ideal for illicit trades such as the opium industry to flourish. The lack of state outreach and authority has enabled the opium industry to proliferate in the country, with underprivileged communities that are excluded from the growth in Kabul and other such urban centres being easily targeted for involvement in production. The spread of illicit trades is particularly harmful to the conflict situation, as it stimulates the growth of corruption which further undermines the development of law and order in the country. In turn, such an environment harbours and encourages terrorist activity.

The lack of national ownership of the central government has been fuelled by the high number of civilian deaths caused by military action. This highly unsecure environment has led to a reduced sense of trust and guardianship of the state. It is in such an environment that competing power structures are formed which once again slows the progress of development due to a lack of cooperation between the central government and varying social segments. This segregation further hinders the capacity of the government as the pool of human resources becomes smaller.

State-building

Strengthening the function and credibility of the state is imperative to facilitating country-led development. As previously discussed, social perceptions of the central government seriously affect the ability of the state to implement policies for inclusive growth; given that both civil society and regional authorities must be willing to cooperate with the development efforts of the central government. The effects of a 30-year-long conflict on governance can be seen, with high levels of corruption creating regional disparities and disenfranchised rural communities. However, of late the state of governance has improved to some extent due to initiatives that have been undertaken following the implementation of the PD in 2005.

Volume of Aid

As discussed by Nixon (2007) state-building is highly sensitive to the amount of aid that is flowing into the country and the activities of development partners in the country. Nixon assesses the different aspects of aid that affect the progress of state-building in Afghanistan: the volume of aid and the delivery of aid. With regards to the volume of aid, there are two opposing arguments surrounding the quantity of aid flows; too little and too much. The former argument compares the aid that has been disbursed in Afghanistan with that of other post-conflict countries. In the first two years following the fall of the Taliban regime, Afghanistan received US$57 per capita, whereas other post-conflict countries such as Bosnia, East Timor and Haiti received US$679, US$233 and US$73 per capita, respectively (Dobbins et al., 2005). This is believed to hinder the ability of the state to fully implement development initiatives which, in turn, undermines the credibility of the state amongst the intended beneficiaries of the development.

The opposing argument is that too much aid is received by the state. This argument focuses on the high degree of aid dependence in public spending—with external aid flows constituting approximately 40 per cent of the core budget and 100 per cent of development expenditures. The unavoidable donor presence that accompanies public spending may negatively affect the state-building process, as activities of the government become associated with donors. Hence, donors become credited with development efforts and the ability of the state is undermined.

Modality of Aid

The modality of aid is another factor that can be potentially very harmful to the state-building process. Aid that is channelled through the external budget, bypassing the government system, reduces the state control over both resources and development activities. This, in turn, hinders the ability of the state to fully develop mechanisms to improve upon monitoring and accountability—both crucial components of gaining legitimacy and credibility. For the period 2009–12, it has been predicted that only 30 per cent of total aid flows will be passed through the core budget, with the remaining 70 per cent being managed by donors (Ministry of Finance, 2009).[1]

Development activities undertaken independently by donors, as part of the external budget, run the risk of being unsustainable in the long-term. This relates to structures created by donors which are intended to be taken over by the government in the future, however, the government may not have the sufficient capacity required for operating the donor established structures. This can damage the progression of state building, especially where the government is unable to successfully manage donor-built programmes which have a large number of beneficiaries.

Activities falling under the external budget also carry problems of accountability. Many donor-led projects have long time spans over which they are implemented, in such instances it becomes difficult to keep a track of the activities of the different agents involved in implementing the project and, hence, upward accountability to donors and downward accountability to beneficiaries is poor (Nixon, 2007). Downward accountability has been a particular issue amongst infrastructure developments taking place under the external budget. Whilst, in such cases, it is the responsibility of the donors to increase the account-ability of their activities, ultimately it is the state that is held answerable to the beneficiaries.

However, despite the harmful aspects of aid flowing through the external budget there are certain practical constraints that lessen the benefits of passing aid through the core budget. One such example is the community-driven development project, the National Solidarity Programme (NSP) which is run by the Ministry of Rural Reconstruction and Development (MRRD) and implemented by a number of NGOs. The NSP is funded by both bilateral and multilateral donors, with funds for the project reaching the core budget through the Afghanistan Reconstruction Trust Fund (ARTF). Problems with the project arose when the disbursement of funds to beneficiaries were delayed. It was found that in five provinces, where the NSP was being implemented, disbursements were delayed to half of the community driven councils (established by the project) in some cases by up to a year. The delay in funds saw half-finished developments resulting in discontented communities and increasing distrust in the MRRD, international donors and NGOs involved in the project. The experienced delays were a result of a number of factors, such as poor accounting of the NSP cash-flow requirements which increased the difficulty with which donors were able to plan and disburse cash to the project. However, the biggest factor causing the delayed disburse-ments was due to the procedures of the ARTF. Whilst donors are able to express their preference for the expenditure of aid that they deposit in the trust, funds are primarily used to cover recurrent expenditure. Hence, money that was intended to be spent on the NSP was used to cover gaps in recurrent expenditure, leaving the project short of funds.

Geographical Disparities in Aid Distribution

The heavy focus on reinstating security and combating terrorist activity within the country has led to a large proportion of aid, from some of Afghanistan's biggest donors, being concentrated in those provinces that are believed to be the worst affected by the conflict. The US concentrates over half of its budget in just four of the least stable provinces. Similarly, both DFID and Canada demonstrate biases in allocations of aid to fragile provinces, with 20 per cent of all DFID aid going to Helmand and over 25 per cent of Canadian aid being allocated to Kandahar. The available data indicates that overall spending is greater in provinces where rebellion is stronger; with the most unsecure provinces of Nimroz, Helmand, Zabul, Kandhar and Uruzgan being allocated US$200 per capita, whilst other provinces receive less than half this amount (Waldman, 2008). Figure 6.7 illustrates the provincial disparities in aid committed.

Whilst greater spending in the country's capital city, Kabul, can be understood given the probable location of ministries and donor offices there, the large disparity between spending in Kabul and in other provinces reflects the highly centralized system. Further to this, Kabul is the province experiencing the highest levels of development. Much of the increments in tax revenues are a result of advances in tax collection in Kabul. Hence, whilst investments into the province are producing a return, it is important that spending does not continue to favour the highly urbanized locations in order to cut down on persistent income inequality and future reliance on urban centres for government expenditure.

Figure 6.7
Provincial Disparities in Total Planned/Committed
Government and Donor Aid, 2007–08

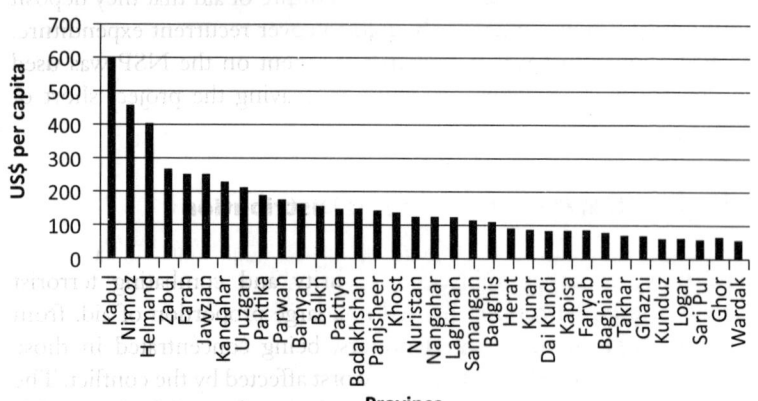

Source: Waldman (2008).

As noted by Waldman (2008), concentrating aid flows where the conflict is strongest creates opportunities for insurgency to develop elsewhere. Such noticeable disparities between development spending of both the government and donors can harbour animosity towards the state, especially in areas suffering from persistent poverty. This can in turn allow for competing political structures to emerge, which will increase the difficulty with which the government can execute policies in varying regions. Furthermore, a seemingly neglected province with high levels of poverty and a disenfranchised community is an ideal environment in which terrorist and illegal trades (such as opium production) can take place.

MEASURING AID EFFECTIVENESS IN AFGHANISTAN: THE PD

The following section draws upon the results of the 2008 OECD survey on Monitoring the PD.

Box 6.2
Summary of the 2005 PD on Aid Effectiveness

The PD on Aid Effectiveness is the result of the second High Level Forum (HLF) held in Paris, France, in 2005. The agreement recognised the need for reforms in aid deliverance so as to increase the likelihood of achieving the Millennium Development Goals by 2015.

The Declaration consisted of five principles which, if satisfied, were believed to enhance the effectiveness of aid. These principles are:

- *Ownership*—partner countries take greater control over development activities with a clear agenda.
- *Alignment*—donors align their development priorities to the priorities of the government as specified in their development plan.
- *Harmonization*—donors use common arrangements for planning, disbursement and reporting so as to reduce transaction costs.
- *Managing for Results*—improving the country assessment and monitoring of national development strategies.
- *Mutual accountability*—increasing the transparency of both countries and their development partners roles in aid decisions.

Source: OECD (2005).

Ownership

Indicator 1: Do Countries Have Operational Development Strategies?

Ownership of development processes is one of the central objectives outlined within the PD on Aid Effectiveness (2005) which aims to promote the ability of a country to lead its own development policies and strategies. The PD target for 2010 is to raise the proportion of recipient countries having operational development strategies to at least 75 per cent. The movement towards promoting domestic ownership of development is motivated by the ability to achieve more sustainable development results through domestically derived policies. This is subject to a number of assumptions, such as adequate stakeholder consultation in designing policies and absorptive capacity of government institutions.

Attempts to achieve domestic ownership of development can be assessed by the strength of the national development plan. A strong development plan is necessary in order to signal commitment and direction on behalf of the government, which should in turn encourage donors to disburse funds through the government. The joint World Bank and IMF assessment of the ANDS indicates that within the document there is good poverty analysis, costing and prioritization. However, potential challenges discussed in the assessment related to implementation of the overall strategy. This comments mainly on the existing absorptive capacity of government institutions and their ability to oversee and implement policies falling under the ANDS. In 2008, the World Bank gave Afghanistan's national development strategy a rating of D out of a score of A (highest) to E (lowest), which indicates that there is much needed improvements to be made.

A lack of government capacity may be one of the factors contributing to the low levels of aid directed through the national budget. According to the 2009 DFR, only 23 per cent of aid was channelled through the government's core budget, whilst the remaining 77 per cent fell under the external budget, with funds being disbursed directly to donor projects. Such circumvention of the government in development activities restricts the opportunity for further capacity building and increases the likelihood that ongoing development will fall out of line with national priorities.

There are a number of reasons for the continued deviation away from government-led development. As mentioned before, the lack of absorptive capacity may be a contributing factor, with government institutions not having the correct resources and systems to absorb and implement the aid. Another contributing factor may be the high levels of corruption that exist within government bodies (Waldman, 2008). Such corruption is a direct deterrent to utilizing government systems, due to fear of resources being leaked away from the intended development. Whilst there remains to be a strong movement towards tackling corruption levels within the government, other measures have been introduced to try and overcome problems of asymmetric information that may cause donors to divert funds away from the government. The donor trust funds, namely the ARTF, the Law and Order Trust Fund for Afghanistan (LOTFA) and the Counter Narcotics Trust Fund (CNTF), have been externally created by the World Bank (ARTF) and the United Nations Development Programme (UNDP) (LOTFA and CNTF) to act as mediums through which donor funds can be pooled and used by the government to finance its priority programmes. The endorsement of the funds by international organizations (and in the case of the ARTF, its management by the World Bank, Islamic Development Bank [IDB], ADB, United Nations Assistance Mission in Afghanistan [UNAM] and UNDP) is intended to reduce the perceived risk associated with channelling aid through the government, thus encouraging donors to support government-led development.

Despite the noted strengths of the ANDS, as reported by the World Bank and the IMF, its use in encouraging domestic ownership of development is questionable as not all of the priorities are fully incorporated into the core budget. Therefore, the ability of the ANDS to draw aid through the core budget is limited given that the priorities are not reflected in the budget.

Alignment

Indicator 2a: How Reliable Are Country Public Financial Management Systems?

Utilizing the domestic PFM system is essential to capacity building and sustainable development. Whilst reforms of the PFM system are primarily the responsibility of the recipient country, growth of the system can only ensue given sufficient utilization. The large volume of aid, required for recurrent and development expenditures, holds the potential to be a tool through which reforms in domestic PFM systems can be honed. Therefore, it becomes the responsibility of donors to support such reforms in this manner, by allowing aid to pass through country PFM systems. Furthermore, using domestic systems enables donors to better align their programmes with national (inclusively derived) priorities.

Whilst, in theory, the utilization of domestic systems is important for increasing the effectiveness of aid, given a lack of active reforms of the system such utilization is redundant. Hence, the extent and effectiveness of reforms employed by the country is important in encouraging donors to deliver aid through domestic PFM systems. In the 2008 survey on Monitoring the PD, Afghanistan received a rating of 3.0 for its PFM system, using the World Bank's Country Policy and Institutional Analysis (CPIA) score from 1 (very weak) to 6 (very strong). Although this score is relatively low, when we consider that in 2005 Afghanistan was not included in the CPIA scoring, due to formal institutions having just been set up, we can infer that sufficient progress has been made towards improving domestic capacity and the strengthening the legal framework.

Despite the advancements in the PFM system, the 2008 survey on the PD notes that reforms have mainly been concentrated at the national level. However, at the sub-national level, capacity of financial systems are still very much constrained. Future reforms must support development of sub-national level institutions so that these systems can also be utilized, which will in turn augment the extent with which the country can claim ownership of development processes.

Indicator 2b: How Reliable Are Country Procurement Systems?

The 2008 survey measured Afghanistan's procurement system based on the Methodology for the Assessment of National Procurement Systems which assess the national system based on internationally accepted good practices, the overall performance of the system and compliance with national legislation and standards. Afghanistan received a rating of C, out of a scoring of A (highest) to D (lowest). The low rating was due to serious weaknesses related to: the inadequate legal framework; the absence of a common set of procurement manuals and standard bidding documents; and a general low level of institutional capacity. However, measures have been taken to improve the system, namely the World Bank assisted procurement reform which focused on capacity building and strengthening institutions. Furthermore, in 2005 the procurement law was approved and following this the Procurement Policy Unit was established under the Ministry of Finance in 2006 and the Special Procurement Committee was set up in 2007.

Indicator 3: Aligning Aid Flows on National Priorities

Indicator 3 assess how much of the total aid flows to the country are disbursed through the national budgets. This provides a proxy for measuring alignment, as it signals donor cooperation with government priorities and programmes. The measurement used within the 2008 survey looks at the discrepancy between the government's budget estimates and actual disbursements by donors. In 2006, only 55 per cent of the aid included in the budget estimate was disbursed. By 2008, this figure had increased to 69 per cent; this is mainly due to increased utilization of the three main trust funds (ARTF, LOTFA and ANTF) and increased dialogue between the government and development partners. As outlined in the 2008 survey, the discrepancies experienced may be due to the lack of capacity amongst line ministries reducing the accuracy with which aid flows are recorded and delays in procurement systems and contracting systems slowing disbursements.

Indicator 4: Coordinating Support to Strengthen Capacity

Indicator 4 measures the degree to which donor technical assistance (TA) meets the requirements of the domestic capacity building strategies. The 2006 survey revealed that only 37 per cent of TA was aligned with national development strategies in this manner. However, advancements have been made in this respect, with the 2008 survey reporting that 54 per cent of TA is coordinated with country programmes—which is beyond the PD 2010 target of 50 per cent.

One of the biggest constraints affecting the low levels of capacity is a lack of human resources. In overcoming this constraint, the country requires a significant amount of TA. The 2008 survey reports that whilst indicators on coordinating support have improved since the 2006 survey, the technical support is over a short-term gap-filling nature as opposed to assessing which human resources are needed in the long term.

Indicator 5: Using Country Systems

Indicator 5 is directly linked to 2a and 2b, measuring the quantity of aid that is allowed to pass through domestic PFM and procurement systems. In the 2006 survey, 44 per cent of aid flows to the government utilized the country's PFM system in budget execution, financial reporting and auditing. As reported by the 2008 survey, reforms have continued to encourage donors to make use of the domestic system, with the utilization rate increasing to 48 per cent of total aid flows (with the actual volume of aid passing through the system having doubled). The main challenges to significantly increasing the use of country systems relate to absorptive capacity and corruption which in turn reduces donor confidence.

Usage of procurement systems have, between the years 2006 and 2008, fallen from 44 per cent to 18 per cent. However, as pointed out in the 2008 survey, this decline may be caused by improved administration and reporting which has tackled some of the problems caused by double counting of funds passing through the trusts. In order to increase use of the procurement systems, donors must be made aware of its new legal framework and the capacity should be strengthened in terms of implementation and enforcement.

Indicator 6: Avoiding Parallel Implementation Structures

Parallel Implementation Units (PIUs) are often established and used by donors so as to support and manage a specific project being implemented. The motivation for relying on PIUs is greater where domestic capacity is low, given that domestic systems may not be equipped to handle the requirements of the project. However, such structures can be potentially very harmful to sustainable development as they take away the opportunity for local institutions to benefit from the development ensuing within the country. Furthermore, PIUs often drive up the cost of human resources in the country, given the higher wages offered by donors, to levels that local institutions cannot afford—further limiting the pool of resources available to them.

Given the security situation and the serious lack of capacity at the sub-national level, most donors have taken steps to create PIUs in implementing their projects. The 2006 survey reported 28 PIUs operating in Afghanistan; whilst the 2008 survey reported 26 (the survey notes that donors most likely under report their use of PIUs). There has been a large amount of headway made in the way of improving the capacity of public administrative systems, such as the donor-funded management capacity programme which aims to bring skilled nationals to the government. Other initiatives have been the UNDP supported Capacity for Afghan Public Services programme, which is being implemented by the Capacity Development Secretariat of Independent Administrative Reforms and the Civil Service Commission. The project trains civil servants working in ministries and government agencies, with the ultimate goal of strengthening leaderships and policymaking skills creating a degree of self-sufficiency amongst civil servants; skills which can be transferred in the future.

Indicator 7: Providing More Predictable Aid

The predictability of aid has been noted in the PD as an important factor in enabling aid-reliant countries to efficiently plan and allocate resources and make medium- to long-term plans. Indicator 7 measures both the ability of donors to disburse aid in a predictable fashion and the ability of donors and the government in accurately recording disbursements. The accurate recording of disbursements is an important facet in achieving ownership, alignment and transparency. Given the dominance of aid in both core and development expenditures, the ability of the government to keep checks on aid flows is essential for development and reliability of the PFM system.

Figures reveal that predictability of disbursements had fallen between the years 2006 and 2007 from 84 per cent to 70 per cent, respectively. Conversely, predictability of aid from the average donor increased between the two years, from 39 per cent in 2006 to 45 per cent in 2007. More recent figures from the 2009 DFR reveal that between the months of January and November 2009 there was a reduction of US$3.9 billion of committed donor aid. However, this reduction in commitments was not accompanied by a formal notification from donors.

The main source of poor predictability reported by the survey is believed to be surrounding aid used in the external budget. In contrast, aid provided in support of the core budget is much more predictable, which validates the argument for government-led aid management. Reforms for improving the predictability of aid have been initiated by the government, such as the Harmonising Reporting Format and the DFR.

Indicator 8: How Much Aid Is Untied?

Tied aid refers to the conditions attached to incoming aid, such as use of suppliers in donor countries. Such conditions are believed to reduce the effectiveness of aid as they drive up costs of projects (due to higher input costs from suppliers of donor countries) and limit the ability of domestic suppliers to benefit from the development ensuing from the aid.

The 2006 survey reported that only 44 per cent of aid to Afghanistan was untied, based on self-reporting of donors who are members of the OECD Development Assistance Committee. In contrast, the average rate of untied aid amongst donors operating in other countries is 75 per cent. However, the 2008 survey reports a vast improvement in delivering untied aid to 94 per cent. This has largely been attributed to reforms in aid provided by the US, who are Afghanistan's largest donors.

Harmonization

Indicator 9: How Much Aid Is Programme Based?

The coordination of aid is believed to improve aid efficiency, due to the reduced likelihood that efforts will be duplicated and the resultant overall lower costs of aid management. Using common arrangements, such as pooling money into the same programme, is one method of achieving harmonization. Indicator 9 measures the proportion of total assistance that is disbursed within programmes. In 2006, figures stood at 43 per cent of aid being disbursed in a programme-based approach, with 54 per cent of this being delivered directly through the government budget. However, the 2008 survey reported a fall in programme-based support with only 40 per cent of aid being coordinated through donor programmes. However, these figures were recorded prior to the full implementation of the ANDS in which sector prioritizations was defined. A lack of sector prioritization on behalf of the government was noted as one of the constraints affecting the spread of programme-based development; hence, following the ANDS there is greater clarity and incentive for donors to invest in harmonizing their activities.

Indicator 10: Conducting Joint Missions and Sharing Analysis

Sharing the responsibility of both the mission and analytical work conducted between donors or with a country authority is an efficient way in which donors can increase the pool of resources required for such activities. The 2008 survey reveals that 43 per cent of missions were conducted jointly, causing a reduction in the total number of missions from 2006 where only 26 per cent of missions were conducted jointly. Missions between bilateral and multilateral donors were conducted jointly in the areas of appraisal, revenue and public expenditure management. Furthermore, 32 per cent of country analytical work was conducted jointly in 2008. However, this figure falls short of the 2010 target of 66 per cent.

Managing for Results

Indicator 11: Do Countries Have Results-based Monitoring Frameworks?

The PD emphasizes the importance of allocating resources based on desired results. This requires that both countries and donors are well informed of desired results and measure their progress of achieving these results. In 2007, Afghanistan was given a D rating for their monitoring framework out of a score of A (highest) to E (lowest). The assessment indicated that due to a lack of capacity in monitoring and tracking of development activities the quality and coverage of monitoring is limited.

Mutual Accountability

Indicator 12: Do Countries Have Reviews of Mutual Accountability?

The PD recognizes the importance of both donors and partner countries being accountable to each other and the various stakeholders of their development activities. The PD requires donors and partner countries to jointly assess, using existing country-level mechanisms, progress in achieving commitments made on aid effectiveness.

Currently in Afghanistan, there are a number of mechanisms which assess such progress. The Afghanistan Compact provided a mechanism through which commitments made by donors and the governments are assessed through regular reports and meetings held by the Joint Coordination Monitoring Board (JCMB). The ARTF also contains an assessment mechanism to monitor performance, through a performance assessment matrix. Lastly, assistance to the security sector is monitored through the Combined Security Transition Council.

DOMESTIC REFORM PRIORITIES

Supporting Development of Domestic Institutional Capacity

Low levels of domestic institutional capacity are one of the major constraints to enhancing aid effectiveness. Poor institutional capacity hinders the ability of the government to effectively claim ownership of development through the ANDS and other such government plans, due to structural bottlenecks restricting absorptive capacity and their ability to implement policies. Furthermore, capacity constraints at the sub-national level (where capacity is lowest) restricts the ability of the government and its development partners to fully align priorities and coordinate development, given that donors are unable to utilize country systems for implementation of projects. Increasing institutional capacity will enable the government and its respective development partners to undertake other measures to enhance aid effectiveness such as, monitoring and coordinating development projects.

More training schemes for capacity development, such as the UNDP initiated Capacity for Afghan Public Service Programme, should be initiated by the government. It is important for such schemes to be developed by the government as they are better informed of the human resource constraints affecting capacity. The government-led initiatives signal strong commitment to reforming domestic institutions which should help to better encourage donors to utilize domestic systems. Furthermore, capacity development of sub-national institutions should be prioritized, in order to extend the outreach of the government to rural areas and reduce geographical disparities in development.

TA provided to the government by donors should focus on long-term capacity building, instead of just assisting with short-term project implementation. This would require donors to consult heavily with the government and other stakeholders in order to identify which skills are lacking from the labour pool. Further to this, donors should continue to support and work with government bodies investing in capacity, such as the Capacity Development Secretariat of Independent Administrative Reforms and the Civil Service Commission, and deliver TA to capacity development schemes administrated by these authorities.

Increasing the Predictability of Aid

Given the heavy reliance on aid for core budget expenditures, aid predictability is an important determinant of the Government of Afghanistan's ability to design and implement long term plans. The record of aid predictability in Afghanistan has varied, with what was a relatively strong rate in 2006 of 84 per cent falling to 70 per cent in 2007. Informal changes in aid disbursements are more commonly associated with aid allocated for use in the external budget, as external budget developments are solely controlled by donors and, hence, disbursements are less transparent. This supports the premise that a larger proportion of aid should be directed through the core budget. Increasing allocations to the core budget would also help the government to develop domestic systems (in particularly the PFM system) and increase the alignment of donor and government priorities.

The government must take steps towards enhancing absorptive capacity and their ability to implement policies outlined in the ANDS. Management of existing systems, such as the donor trust funds, should be honed so as to cut back on time lags and other issues that increase the risk with which donors utilize country systems. Donors should aim to align a greater proportion of their development priorities with those outlined in the national development strategy, so as to support more core budget activities.

Domestic Revenue Mobilization

Poor domestic revenue collection has been a key issue contributing to the state of aid dependency in the country. The restricted resources available for execution of recurrent and development expenditures is largely caused by the dominance of the informal sector in economic activity, of which the government is unable to tax. Informal sector employment is most common amongst the rural poor, where alternative sources of income are scarce. In order to widen the tax base both the government and donors must focus on establishing alternative, sustainable livelihoods for those rural communities most susceptible to involvement in the informal sector. This would cut back on the economic and social losses caused by simply eradicating informal sector activity, such as the opium trade, and strengthen the credibility of the government especially amongst rural communities wherein there is often insufficient contact with central government authorities. To maximize the benefits accruing to both governance and the local communities, such development should aim to adequately consult stakeholders and, where possible, take the form of a community driven development model. This would enhance ownership amongst local communities and sustainability of projects.

Coordination of Development Activities

PRTs and NGOs play an important role in aiding communities suffering from low security and those which are largely neglected by the state. It is important, however, to integrate the activities of both PRTs and NGOs with those of the government. Such coordination of development will help to avoid the mismatch of development priorities that is common, especially amongst PRTs. Furthermore, it can facilitate the establishment of sub-national level institutions that work directly with the local communities, avoiding the growth of parallel institutions. Both donors and the government should actively work to cooperate in delivering assistance to rural communities. Furthermore, greater coordination between donors would help to reduce transaction costs and instances of conflicting development priorities.

CONCLUSIONS

The issues highlighted in this chapter have brought to light the unavoidable reliance on aid in Afghanistan at present. Such aid dependence is a result of the long-lasting conflict which has stifled development and subsequently reduced the ability of the government to earn revenues. Given the sheer scale of required reconstruction and development, dependence on aid can be expected to be a feature of expenditure in development activities in the medium term. However, in the interim period, dependence on aid for recurrent expenditures must be curbed. Recurrent expenditures reflect the cost of running the government; therefore, self-sufficiency is important for fiscal stability, as a reduction in funds from donors may lead to painful cuts in public spending having to be made. In the context of a fragile state, ensuring stability of the government is imperative given that insurgencies may be highly reactive to changes in government behaviour.

Within this chapter a number of issues affecting the effectiveness of aid have been highlighted. In order to overcome these constraints and increase the ability with which aid can maximize stable growth and development, both donors and the government need to align their priorities towards achieving common goals on aid effectiveness. The priorities that have been identified relating to fiscal management include: increasing the predictability of aid, augmenting domestic revenue mobilization and enhancing domestic institutional capacity. These priorities should help in creating the conditions for long-term fiscal sustainability, wherein the country is able to at least support recurrent expenditures. This chapter also examines the role of both the government and donors in increasing the effectiveness of aid within a low security state. The focus of this discussion has surrounded the limited outreach of the government to rural areas and the subsequent need for the government to develop strong sub-national level institutions. It is important that these sub-national institutions coordinate development activities with the international agents (such as PRTs and NGOs) who commonly have a greater presence in undertaking development activities within low security, rural regions. Creating this direct channel of communication between the central government and rural communities will help to enhance the creation of more inclusive policies, thus reducing the regional disparities in development and the subsequent opportunities for insurgencies to materialize.

NOTE

1. This figure from the 2009 DFR should be interpreted with caution given that larger donors who do not channel funds through the government were not included in this report. Hence, the figure for government managed aid is actually expected to be much lower than the stated 30 per cent.

REFERENCES

Afghanistan Compact (2006), *Proceedings of the International Conference,* 'Building on Success: The London Conference on Afghanistan', London.

Afghanistan National Development Strategy (2005), 'An Interim Strategy for Security, Governance, Economic Growth and Poverty Reduction', Islamic Republic of Afghanistan.

Afghanistan Public Financial Management Performance Assessment (2008), World Bank, May. Available at: http://www.worldbank.org/ (accessed on 5 October 2010).

Da Afghanistan Bank (2009), *Annual Economic and Statistics Bulletin, 1387 (2008–2009)* Available at: http://www.centralbank.gov.af (accessed on 5 October 2010).

Dobbins, J., S. G. Jones, K. Crane, A. Rathmell, B. Steele, R. Teltschik and A. Timilsina (2005), *The UN's Role in Nation-Building: From the Congo to Iraq,* RAND Corporation: Santa Monica, CA.

Government of Afghanistan (2008), 'Afghanistan National Development Strategy 1397–1391 (2008–2013)', Islamic Republic of Afghanistan.

IMF (2008), 'Islamic Republic of Afghanistan: Selected Issues', IMF Country Report No. 08/71, February.

Ministry of Finance (2007), 'Prioritizing Aid Effectiveness: Taking Forward the Afghanistan Compact and Paris Declaration Commitments', Islamic Republic of Afghanistan.

——— (2009), *Donor Financial Review 2009.* Available at: http://www.budget mof.gov.af/units/Aid_Coord_Effectiveness/Aid_Coord_Effectiveness.html (accessed on 10 October 2010).

Nixon, H. (2007), 'Aiding the State? International Assistance and the Statebuilding Paradox in Afghanistan', Afghanistan Research and Evaluation Unit Briefing Paper series, http://www.areu.org.af/index.php?option=com_content&task=view&id=39 &Itemid=73 (accessed on 6 November 2010).

OECD (2009), *Managing Development Resources: The Use of Country Systems in Public Financial Management,* OECD Publishing, France.

——— (2008), 'Afghanistan' in *2008 Survey on Monitoring the Paris Declaration: Making Aid More Effective by* 2010, http://www.oecd.org/document/18/0,3746,en_2649_3236398_41395474_1_1_1_1,00.html (accessed on 10 October 2010).

——— (2005), 'Paris Declaration of Aid Effectiveness, Ownership, Harmonisation, Alignment, Results and Mutual Accountability', Paris.

OPM/IDL (2008), 'Evaluation of the Implementation of the Paris Declaration: Thematic Study—The Applicability of the Paris Declaration in Fragile and Conflict-affected Situations', http://www.oecd.org/dac/evaluationnetwork (accessed on 1 June 2010).

Saikal, M. (2010),' Afghanistan and Economic Regionalism: A Decade of Opportunities and Challenges (2001–2010)', The World Bank, Washington D.C.

Waldman, M. (2008), 'Falling Short: Aid Effectiveness in Afghanistan', *ACBAR* Advocacy Series, ACBAR, Kabul.

POLICY PRIORITIES AND ROLE OF AID IN POST-CONFLICT ECONOMIES

7

Sri Lanka

DESHAL DE MEL AND ANNEKA DE SILVA

TRENDS IN FOREIGN AID IN SRI LANKA

Foreign aid has played an important role in Sri Lanka's development process, particularly in terms of financing large scale infrastructure projects and also social services such as education and health, poverty reduction programmes such as Gemidiriya, sectors such as agriculture and in emergency situations such as post-tsunami reconstruction and more recently post-conflict reconstruction. Aid has been vital in Sri Lanka in terms of financing capital intensive government expenditure, since Sri Lankan governments have continuously failed to generate sufficient revenue to meet recurrent expenditure. In recent years, the contribution of foreign aid to Sri Lanka has increased in support of post-conflict reconstruction activities as indicated in Table 7.1.

Table 7.1
Contribution of Foreign Aid in Sri Lanka, 2005–09

	2005	2006	2007	2008	2009
Public Debt % of GDP	90.6	87.9	85	81.4	86.2
Foreign Debt % of GDP	39	37.5	37	32.8	36.5
Foreign Aid % of GDP	3.1	3.3	5.4	2.9	7.4
Foreign Aid % of Government Expenditure	9	9.4	16.2	9.2	20.3

Source: Central Bank of Sri Lanka (various issues).

Historically, approximately 80 per cent of Sri Lanka's foreign aid has been disbursed by Japan, the Asian Development Bank (ADB) and the World Bank. This has been associated with long repayment periods and concessional rates of interest. The ADB Special Fund Resources, for instance, had 30 year maturity and interest rates of 0.5 per cent, and many of Sri Lanka's early World Bank loans had maturity of up to 40 years with 0.75 per cent service charge (Kelegama and de Mel, 2007). In recent years, however, Sri Lanka's access to concessional finance from multilateral donors has declined (see Figure 7.1) since the country has reached higher levels of per capita income and is now classified as a lower middle income country. A greater share of Sri Lanka's ADB loans are now from Ordinary Capital Resources financing (which is usually LIBOR plus a small premium) and World Bank loans have shorter repayment periods of around 20 years.

As can be seen from Figure 7.1, there has been a general downward trend in multilateral aid receipts since 2003. Multilateral aid picked up again in 2008 and 2009 due to increased support for post-conflict assistance to Sri Lanka's Eastern and Northern Provinces in 2008 and 2009, respectively. Aid from Japan has also declined from US\$262 million in 2004 to US\$200 million in 2007 before picking up again in 2008 and 2009.

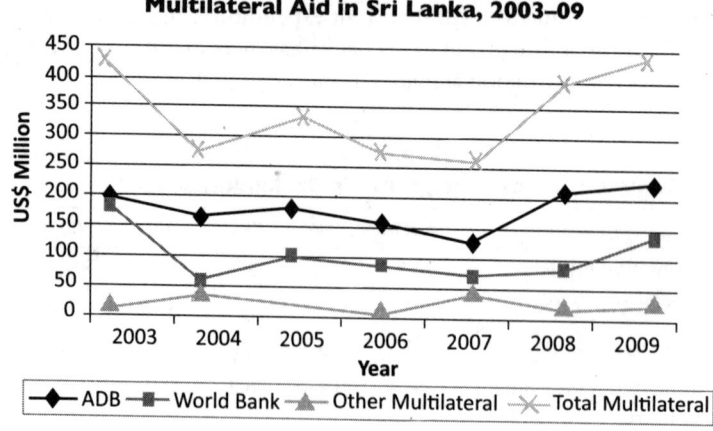

Figure 7.1
Multilateral Aid in Sri Lanka, 2003–09

Source: Central Bank of Sri Lanka (various issues).

Along with the decline in access to finance from the country's traditional donors, Sri Lanka also faced a decline in aid due to certain western bilateral donors withdrawing support as a result of an intensification of the conflict in the country (Kelegama and de Mel, 2007). In fact, one of the major aid packages pledged during the Tokyo donor conference in 2003 which included the Poverty Reduction Growth Facility (PRGF) financed by the International Monetary Fund (IMF) and the World Bank, was also halted due to a lack of progress in the peace process that broke down in July 2003 (Kelegama and de Mel, 2007). In this context, Sri Lanka looked to non-traditional donors such as China and other eastern bilateral donors.

Lending from China was negligible prior to 2007 when it reached US$163.5 million. In 2009, China was the highest lender to Sri Lanka with aid amounting to US$292.8 million. Lending from India has changed its nature in recent years. Whilst Indian aid prior to 2009 was almost exclusively through the Indian line of credit (non-project based), since 2009 project based lending has taken place as India has taken more interest in financing development projects in Sri Lanka. In 2009, India disbursed US$27.4 million in project financing. Unlike western bilateral donors who withdrew due to concerns relating to alleged human rights violations during the final stages of the conflict in Sri Lanka, donors such as China have placed less emphasis on such non-economic issues. This has made non-traditional bilateral donors more attractive to the Sri Lankan government in recent years, resulting in higher flows of bilateral aid into Sri Lanka, as demonstrated in Figure 7.2.

A more pronounced difference in Sri Lanka's external borrowing trends has been the spike in commercial borrowing in recent years. With declining access to concessional borrowing and the withdrawal of certain donors due to concerns relating to the conflict in Sri Lanka, the government resorted to increased commercial borrowing to roll over existing debt and to finance other development activities as depicted in Figure 7.3. However, the problem here is that commercial borrowing entails far higher rates of interest and has far shorter repayment windows. Using this type of borrowing to finance development projects, whose benefits will only be realized in the long term, is not a sustainable means of development finance. In fact, one of the terms of Sri Lanka's recent Stand By Arrangement (SBA) with the IMF was to adopt a ceiling on foreign commercial borrowing.

Figure 7.2
Bilateral Aid in Sri Lanka (Excluding Japan), 2005–09

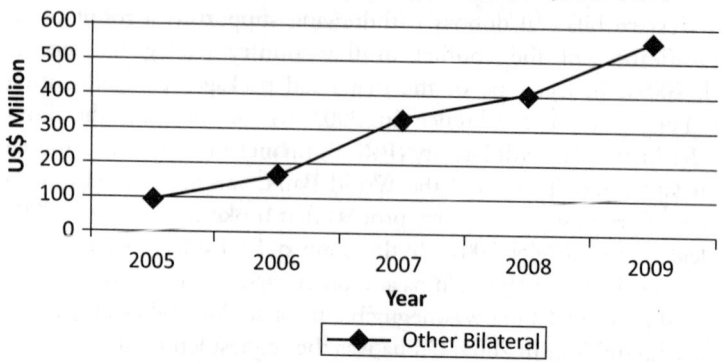

Source: Central Bank of Sri Lanka (various issues).

Figure 7.3
Trends in External Finance, 2005–09

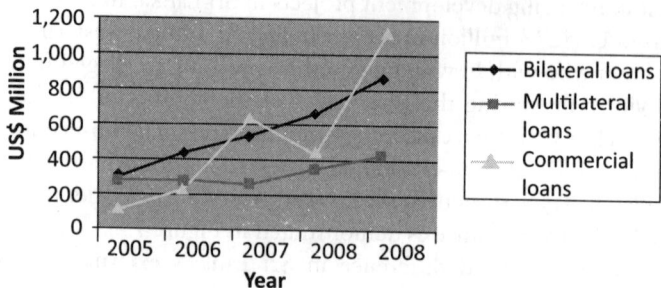

Source: Central Bank of Sri Lanka (various issues).

CONTEMPORARY ROLE OF FOREIGN AID IN SRI LANKA

Sri Lanka has long been a recipient of foreign aid which has played an important role in contributing to the capital expenditure of the budget (since 1990 Sri Lankan governments have failed to balance the current account of the budget, requiring all capital expenditure and part of recurrent expenditure to be financed through borrowing). The access to concessionary Overseas Development Assistance (ODA) from international donors, primarily Japan, the ADB and the World Bank, has enabled the country to carry out developmental activity without placing excess burden on short-term debt financing, since these loans have traditionally been characterized by low interest and long repayment horizons. As a result, even today the bulk of Sri Lanka's foreign debt stock has long repayment horizons and therefore does not place substantial pressure on short-term repayment (though this trend is gradually changing as depicted in Figure 7.4). Nonetheless, fiscal management in Sri Lanka has over the years been weak, often manifesting in unstable macroeconomic outcomes.

Figure 7.4
Outstanding Foreign Debt, 2005–09

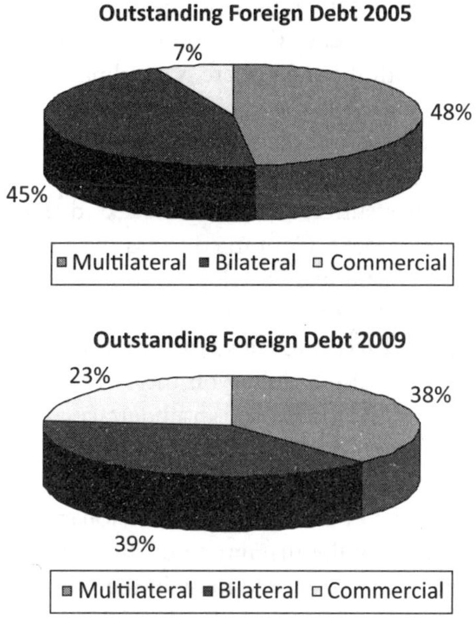

Outstanding Foreign Debt 2005

7%

48%

45%

▣ Multilateral ■ Bilateral □ Commercial

Outstanding Foreign Debt 2009

23%

38%

39%

▣ Multilateral ■ Bilateral □ Commercial

Source: Central Bank of Sri Lanka (various issues).

It is in such an unstable macroeconomic position that Sri Lanka found itself through much of 2009 and early 2010—particularly in terms of its fiscal situation. As a result of the global economic crisis of 2008–09, Sri Lanka faced significant downturns in government revenue (due to falling import prices and volumes) and increases in expenditure (higher interest payments, military and humanitarian expenditure and higher salaries due to cost of living allowances) in 2009, resulting in the end of year budget deficit reaching 9.7 per cent of the Gross Domestic Product (GDP). An important additional constraint is the fact that the government entered an SBA with the IMF in July 2009 which stipulated that the budget deficit for 2007 should be maintained at 7–7.5 per cent of the GDP.

It is clear from this backdrop that the spending power of the Sri Lankan government is to a great extent curtailed by the constrained fiscal environment. In such a situation, borrowing becomes a necessity and two options could be pursued. Domestic borrowing could be problematic since it could create upward pressure on interest rates (which have declined but continue to remain relatively high), thereby stifling private investment. Furthermore, according to Sri Lanka's Technical MoU with the IMF, there is a ceiling on domestic borrowing. Foreign borrowing is the alternative and this could be achieved either through commercial markets or concessionary borrowing from donors. The recovery in global financial markets following the economic crisis has suffered further setbacks due to the turmoil in European sovereign debt. Continued stress in this market is likely to make investors demand higher risk premiums to compensate for this risk, pushing up interest rates. This would make it more challenging for Sri Lanka to find access to affordable commercial borrowing in the short term. There is also a ceiling on the level of international commercial borrowing that Sri Lanka can undertake as per the agreement with the IMF.

Therefore, the most suitable form of financing government expenditure gaps would be in the form of concessionary borrowing. This is further exemplified by the magnitude of the expenditure required in resurrecting the post-conflict economy in the North and East (NE) of the country. The economic, physical and social infrastructure in the two provinces was severely affected during the conflict and reconstruction would require a very substantial degree of financial resources. Given the government's fiscal constraints, the contribution of donors to reconstruction in the NE has already taken on significant proportions as outlined in Table 7.2.

When examining the existing disbursements to the NE during 2009 and leading up to June 2010, it is clear that the bulk of concessionary

Table 7.2
ODA Disbursed by Sector for NE Specific Projects, 2009

Sector	US$ million	Percentage
Roads	8.74	6.74
Bridges	8.12	6.26
Ports	13.44	10.36
Other Infrastructure[1]	29.4	22.67
Agriculture	11.14	8.59
SMEs	0.19	0.15
Housing	18.45	14.22
Local Services	2.01	1.55
IDPs	0.35	0.27
Community Support	18.37	14.16
Education	0.1	0.08
Other[2]	19.4	14.96
Total	129.71	100.00

Source: External Resources Department (various years).
Note: This table does not include national level projects which may have some NE components.

external financing has gone into the cost-heavy infrastructure sector, along with urgent needs of housing and resettlement as demonstrated in Table 7.3. There has also been support for the priority livelihood sectors, agriculture and fisheries (one of the community support projects of the ADB targets coastal communities). The aid that has gone into the NE reflects the short-term priorities in the region. With time, however, one could expect more support to filter into social services sectors, such as health and education, along with increased support to small and medium enterprises (SMEs) and entrepreneurs to ensure sustainability of economic recovery.

The other factor that influences the potential necessity of foreign aid in a post-conflict economy is the gap between the foreign exchange requirements for post-conflict reconstruction and foreign exchange earnings. With recovery in global commodity prices, the import intensity of reconstruction measures could be substantial. This may

Table 7.3
ODA Disbursed by Sector for NE Specific Projects,
January–June 2010

Sector	US$ million	Percentage
Roads	2.07	3.86
Bridges	0.71	1.32
Ports	9.08	16.92
Power	0.17	0.32
Other Infrastructure[3]	15.94	29.71
Agriculture	3.56	6.64
SMEs	0.13	0.24
Housing	3.75	6.99
Local Services	0.3	0.56
IDPs	1.44	2.68
Community Support	4.11	7.66
Other[4]	12.39	23.09
Total	53.65	100.00

Source: External Resources Department (various issues).
Note: This table does not include national level projects which may have some NE components.

not, however, be a major short-term concern in Sri Lanka, as despite the fact that prospects for export earnings in the short term are not optimal, foreign exchange inflows due to remittances and short term capital inflows (particularly in government securities and equity) have supported Sri Lanka's foreign exchange reserve position. At the same time, it should be kept in mind that such a situation was made possible due to the increased investor confidence in the Sri Lankan economy that was influenced by the SBA with the IMF.

POTENTIAL COSTS OF FOREIGN AID

The fiscal situation and the needs of post-conflict reconstruction make it clear that there is an important role for concessional foreign aid in Sri Lanka's short- to medium-term development agenda. However, excessive reliance on foreign aid has costs, and these will be examined in the next section.

Impacts on Long-term Fiscal Management

Whilst foreign aid has played an important role in contributing to development activities in Sri Lanka, it could be argued that the easy access to low cost finance undermined the discipline in financial management in Sri Lanka and made the country aid dependent to an extent. Successive Sri Lankan governments were able to spend the entirety (and more) of government revenue on recurrent consumption (see Figure 7.5), knowing that foreign finances would be available to finance capital intensive investment. The long time horizons of this external finance ensure that governments need not be too concerned about repayment during the political cycle.

Macroeconomic imbalances and volatility have been a frequent repercussion of this fiscal indiscipline. In times of economic prosperity these imbalances are not pronounced, however in times of economic distress, underlying macroeconomic imbalances manifest in highly

Figure 7.5
Fiscal Imbalances in Sri Lanka, 1990–2009

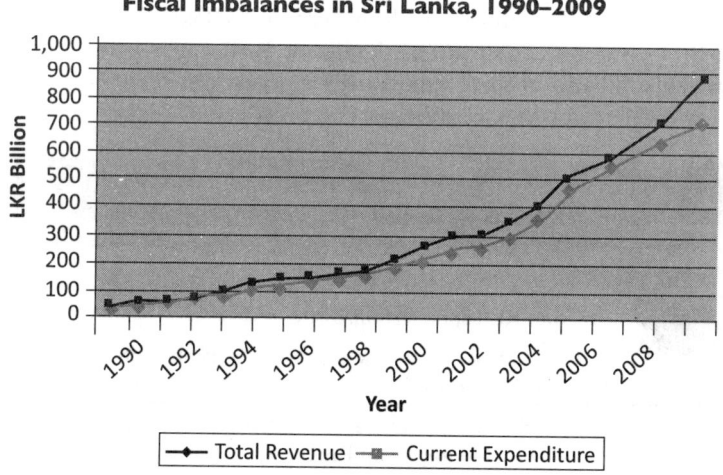

Source: Central Bank of Sri Lanka (various issues).

unstable outcomes. Furthermore, in Sri Lanka's case it can be seen that fiscal indiscipline can become entrenched, particularly in terms of current expenditure. Successive governments have liberally expanded the size of public service cadres and extended numerous welfare support programmes, which are very difficult to roll back at times when austerity is required. As a country's income levels increase, access to concessionary finance from donors diminishes, as has been experienced in Sri Lanka. In this context, it is essential that countries enhance fiscal management practices and pre-empt a situation where access to concessionary finance falls whilst fiscal deficits remain high due to lags in curtailing current expenditure.

Challenges for Short-term Macroeconomic Management

Along with the implications of aid dependence for long-term fiscal management, large inflows of aid create challenges for short-term macroeconomic management as well, particularly in terms of managing the exchange rate, monetary base and inflation. Significant capital inflows in the form of aid can result in an appreciation of the Real Exchange Rate (RER), which in turn will undermine the net export position and thereby reduce incomes through the Dutch Disease Effect. The manifestation of Dutch Disease Effect is contingent on how aid inflows are utilized by the government (Box 7.1).

In a post-conflict situation, significant RER appreciation can be particularly harmful since export market access can prove important

Box: 7.1	
Exchange Rate Management Policy Options	
Spend All	Spend all on non-trade sector—Complete aid absorption but RER appreciation.
	Spend all on tradable sector—No aid absorption but no RER appreciation.
Save All	Build up international reserves or use aid to repay foreign debt—No impact on RER.
	Use aid to repay local debt—RER appreciation.
Source: Authors.	

for post-conflict recovery, particularly in a trade dependent country such as Sri Lanka. However, as can be seen, governments have sufficient tools to prevent exchange rate appreciation in the event of foreign aid inflows. It has been found that 30 out of 36 countries studied did not demonstrate significant correlation between aid and real exchange rate. It is not just aid inflows that can influence the RER but also capital inflows, such as remittances, and short-term inflows into equity and bond markets. In a post-conflict situation, increased confidence in the economy could attract significant capital inflows into equity and debt markets and remittances also tend to spike in support of relief and rehabilitation measures.

Capital inflows could also be inflationary or could affect interest rates depending on the policy framework of the monetary authority. If the monetary authority attempts to prevent an appreciation of the exchange rate as a result of capital inflows by building up foreign reserves, this would result in an expansion of the domestic monetary base, creating inflationary pressure. However, in such a situation, the monetary authority could also mop up excess domestic liquidity by selling government securities. This could place upward pressure on domestic interest rates which may result in an upward spiral of sorts, as higher interest rates could attract further capital inflows, repeating this cycle.

In Sri Lanka's context, the post-war situation saw a substantial spike in foreign capital inflows due to remittances and emergency relief measures. This occurred during the mid-2009 as the global economy was in the midst of a significant downturn and, therefore, Sri Lanka's export sector was under some pressure. As a result, a priority was to not allow significant appreciation of the domestic currency, as this would have placed further stress on the export sector. Accordingly, capital inflows were used to build up foreign reserves and at the same time, excess domestic liquidity was mopped up by the sale of treasury bills, in order to contain domestic monetary expansion. However, domestic interest rates were not to a great extent affected by this action, since private demand for credit had remained sluggish in the aftermath of an economic slowdown in 2009. As private demand for credit increases in line with economic recovery, upward pressure on interest rates could manifest in due course. It should be noted, however, that the sensitivity of capital flows to domestic interest rates in Sri Lanka is limited since only 10 per cent of government securities are open for foreign purchase (after late 2011, the limit was increased to 12.5 per cent). It is clear that aid and associated capital inflows create a variety of challenges for domestic macroeconomic management, and these are even more pronounced in post-conflict situations.

Conditionality

Political Conditionality

It was earlier mentioned that Sri Lanka's increasing affinity towards bilateral donors is a reflection of reduced access to concessionary finance from traditional donors due the country's increased per capita income. However, increased per capita income alone does not fully explain the change in Sri Lanka's recent aid relationships. During the final decade of the NE war in Sri Lanka, international engagement in the peace process and the final stages of the war increased significantly. The Tokyo Conference on Reconstruction and Development of Sri Lanka in June 2003 saw US$4.5 billion pledged to the country by different donors. However, it was noted in the declaration that the continued disbursement of this money was conditional on progress in the peace process. As the peace process came to a halt in 2003, with the unilateral withdrawal of the Liberation Tigers of Tamil Eelam (LTTE) from the process, Sri Lanka failed to receive the bulk of the pledged aid.

At the same time, many European bilateral donors withdrew or reduced aid to Sri Lanka during the final years of the NE war. Many donors overestimated their capacity to influence domestic political issues in Sri Lanka, particularly in an environment where alternative sources of finance, such as lending from Eastern bilateral donors and commercial borrowing, reduced the leverage of traditional donors. The problem with tying aid to progress in the peace process was that there are two parties required to ensure progress in a peace process, and one of those parties (the separatist LTTE) had a vested interest in the government not receiving donor financing. Donors such as China did not place significant weight on political conditionalities and, therefore, the Sri Lankan government felt more comfortable working with them.

The predictability of aid (a key theme in the Paris Declaration [PD] on Aid Effectiveness) is severely undermined when implicit or explicit political conditionalities are associated with aid agreements. For instance, the discontinuation of the aid pledged in the Tokyo Conference would have significantly undermined the then government's development plans. The excessive internationalization of the peace process could also undermine the credibility of the government amongst domestic stakeholders, particularly regarding issues of ownership of the domestic political and development agenda. It would be therefore better for donors to be more realistic about their ability to affect domestic political issues and to avoid such political conditionalities that serve neither to achieve objectives of creating peace nor achieving development.

Economic Conditionality

Conditionality can, however, be used in an effective manner that is in the interests of the partner country. Economic conditionality, unlike during periods of structural adjustment policies in the 1980s and 1990s, no longer permeates the relationship between developing nations and donors. The nature of economic policy conditionality has changed to a great extent and is no longer characterised by rigid frameworks set down by donor agencies. Instead, most loan agreements now include loan covenants, which detail jointly agreed actions and safeguards to be carried out along with projects. These include environmental safeguards, resettlement and compensation plans and any requisite reforms that both parties agree to. The majority of aid programmes that Sri Lanka enters into are project based and therefore macroeconomic conditionality does not play a major role. However, more recently, macroeconomic conditionality has been a central focus of public debate as Sri Lanka obtained an SBA from the IMF in July 2009.

Sri Lanka obtained the SBA due to the macroeconomic crisis that was triggered by the global economic crisis coupled with domestic economic stresses which resulted in a fall in external reserves to approximately six weeks' worth of imports in March 2009. In fact, at this point, the SBA was delayed (possibly influenced by opposition from certain voting members relating to the conduct of the final stages of the NE war in Sri Lanka).[5] Given the strained external financial situation in Sri Lanka at the time, the government approached other sources of finance including the government of Libya. The SBA eventually came through in July 2009. The terms of the Agreement demonstrate the increased flexibility of IMF lending in recent times (see boxes 7.2 and 7.3).

The nature of the commitments in the LoI is in line with the macroeconomic policy priorities of the country, that is, enhancement of revenue, curtailment of expenditure through transfers to state enterprises and containment of short-term public debt by

Box 7.2

Summary of Technical Memorandum of Understanding (MoU) between Government of Sri Lanka and the IMF, July 2009

Level of central government borrowing from domestic financial institutions would be subject to a ceiling.	The ceiling would be flexible depending on the availability of external borrowing (loans/grants), privatization proceeds and external debt service payments.
Performance criteria on Central Bank reserve money.	Contingent on commercial banks' reserve requirements compliance.
Floor on net international reserves.	Floor flexible based on foreign programme financing and foreign holdings of government securities and debt service repayments.

Source: http://www.cbsl.gov.lk/pics_n_docs/02_prs/_docs/notices/imf_sba_tmu.pdf (accessed in August 2010).

limiting commercial borrowing. The LoI and the technical MoU provide a suitable degree of flexibility that creates a broad agreed upon policy framework, whilst enabling the government to identify economically and politically feasible mechanisms to implement these. In the past, Sri Lanka's loan agreements had gone into specific details of reform, such as privatization processes or restructuring of specific institutions. In many such cases, political challenges made the specific commitments impossible to meet, thereby resulting in failure to implement the conditions and termination of the agreements. Examples include the reforms to the People's Bank as part of the IMF Poverty Reduction and Growth Facility (PRGF) in 2003.

Another manifestation of the increased flexibility inherent in the current agreement with the IMF, is the continuation of the programme after a three-month hiatus during which Sri Lanka was unable to meet the domestic borrowing criteria as specified in the MoU. Despite Sri Lanka failing to meet the 7 per cent budget deficit target in 2009 (budget deficit for 2009 was 9.7 per cent), the programme targets were revised to provide flexibility to the government to take into account

---

Box 7.3

**Summary of the Letter of Intent of Government
of Sri Lanka to the IMF, July 2009**

- Recognizing the pivotal significance of fiscal challenges the government refers to the Fiscal Management Responsibility Act and the need for reducing the budget deficit. The initial target was to maintain a budget deficit of 7 per cent in 2009 and to reduce it to 5 per cent by 2011.
- Recognizes the importance of revenue enhancement, mentioning the appointment of the Presidential Taxation Commission, and expenditure rationalization, without specific details of expenditure rationalization.
- Commitment to limiting government commercial borrowing to US$1,750 million during the programme period.
- Outlines objective of making key loss-making state run institutions return to a break even position by 2011.
- The government also expresses commitment to limiting intervention in foreign exchange markets and to not introduce new exchange control mechanism.

Source: http://www.cbsl.gov.lk/pics_n_docs/02_prs/_docs/notices/imf_sba_tmu.pdf (accessed in August 2010).

---

increased costs of reconstruction expenditure and the constrained external environment which has affected the revenue position. Accordingly, new targets are 8 per cent budget deficit for 2010, 6.8 per cent for 2011 and 5 per cent for 2012.

What can be drawn from Sri Lanka's latest agreement with the IMF is that a programme containing conditionalities that are in line with domestic priorities, has sufficient flexibility to enable the government to adopt economically and politically feasible approaches (nuances which are often beyond the grasp of development partners), and yet entrenches a degree of discipline that enables a government to tie its hands to implement necessary economic reform. Political stability of the government is also necessary in order to enable tough reforms to go through without risk of political upheaval in such circumstances. In the early stages of the 2009 IMF SBA, it seems that a suitable balance has been struck; however, it remains to be seen whether this would continue through till the end of the programme period.

Loan Covenants

Loan covenants are considered to be an improvement from the more strict conditionality system that was attached to loans in the past. As explained earlier, these are agreements between the state and the donor on what processes need to be carried out alongside the project in question. Covenants and safeguards too have their drawbacks, particularly relating to the extent of bureaucratic processes in dealing with them. As a result, large amounts of time and resources are spent in understanding and implementing the agreements in question. This contributes to delays in project implementation. Development partners are reluctant to compromise on safeguards to the environment and social issues, and this also reflects in most cases the priorities of the government; however, what could be expected is for joint efforts to streamline covenants in order to minimize delays and capacity utilization that results from them.

Implications for Domestic Capacity

Implications for Domestic Institutions

The existence of domestic capacity constraints has raised many questions as to the effect that development partners have on institutional development. Donor dominance in the implementation of projects has often been criticized as excluding domestic bodies from involvement in development. This in turn, leads to the creation of dual institutions—the government and development partners—as opposed to a combined effort with ample transfers from donors to domestic institutions and vice versa (the role of Parallel Implementation Units [PIUs] are discussed in the next section). In a post-conflict context, there is great opportunity for state-building which can only be realized given that domestic institutions are actively involved in the reconstruction process, enabling them to expand and strengthen their capacity. To achieve this, the responsibility of development must be shared evenly between the state and its respective development partners.

Sri Lanka's past experience with NGOs in the post-tsunami recovery period was a prime example of poorly coordinated development activities which lacked sufficient incorporation of domestic institutions into donor-funded projects. Whilst the effort exerted by donor bodies was imperative to the reconstruction of the affected areas, reports suggested that there were serious issues with efficiency. One such example cited was the employment of 183 expatriate workers by the International Red Cross, with per worker remittances exceeding US$120,000. Foreign workers were chosen over local country experts, despite their lack of local knowledge and technical expertise (Kelegama and de Mel, 2007). Hence, a large proportion of domestic human resources were underutilized, leaking potential income out of the country and dampening efficient implementation.

The presence of donors may serve to create a number of distortions in the economy, which in turn hinder the growth of domestic capacity. One such distortion is experienced in the labour market wherein the externally determined wages offered by donors are much higher than the wages that the government can afford. This can lead to competition for resources between donors and the government, with the higher wages offered by donors attracting local skilled labour and consequently reducing the labour pool available to the government—an internal brain drain of sorts. Local labour utilization by international organizations is more commonly recognized as a fundamental feature of encouraging national ownership of development. From the country perspective, the economy can benefit from the transfer of skills from foreign institutions to the recipient country. Likewise, donors can benefit from the local knowledge brought in by domestic employees. However, the issue of wage distortions created by donors may in fact exclude the government from future utilization of local skilled labour, who instead seek employment with international agencies. Matching the higher wages offered by international organizations may, in many cases, be an unsustainable strategy for the government, which would in turn further arrest institutional development.

Implementation of donor-funded projects is associated with an increased administrative burden for the government's implementing institutions. The reporting requirements, donor mission visits, dealing with loan covenants and safeguards are all resource intensive, and occupy significant amounts of time of the employees of the state apparatus. In many cases, particularly related to dealing with social and environmental safeguards, domestic capacity is not always available and therefore special resources have to be employed in order to fulfil the requirements in dealing with such issues. These are costly both in terms of time and in terms of financial burden. This would be particularly felt at the sub-national level, and even more severely in post-conflict situations.

Implications for Local Private Sector Capacity

At present, there is much attention surrounding the use of externally sourced resources in donor-funded projects. Donors face a dilemma in terms of striking a balance between ensuring the most efficient use of resources to implement projects, usually achieved by calling for internationally competitive tenders, and for enabling local entrepreneurs to benefit from donor-financed activity. The latter objective may require some positive discrimination in tendering procedures, which is in most cases against the regulations of development partners.

This issue is particularly pertinent in post conflict situations. Employing locally sourced resources in reconstruction can work to strengthen industry in the area and encourage the growth of industrial clusters, thus diminishing supply constraints. The employment of local resources and firms in development activity can also create livelihoods and kick start local economic activity, which is essential for supporting sustainable peace. This will help in making the region self-sufficient so that, in the medium term, the area will be able to support the growth ensuing from the initial projects, creating a multiplier effect. Of course, this could also have negative implications in terms of driving up costs of resources. This was experienced during the post-tsunami re-construction efforts where domestic prices, of non-tradable items in particular, increased due to high demand for reconstruction activities. The higher costs of material could make it difficult for households and firms to finance their own construction activities.

This is not necessarily a problem related to donor-funded reconstruction and would be experienced in any large scale reconstruction effort, however, in cases where there is high competition for resources amongst different donors, the impact on prices could be more pronounced. Selecting inexperienced domestic contractors could potentially result in another negative outcome; project implementation may be delayed due to capacity weaknesses in domestic firms. Such issues have in the past been experienced in Sri Lanka as is evident in the Department of Foreign Aid and Budget Monitoring project evaluation reports.

In the Sri Lankan case, the utilization of southern contractors in development work in the North has been a matter of debate. Capacity constraints—in terms of labour, material and other resources—in the north have made it implausible for local firms to successfully bid for re-construction projects. However, as pointed out by an international donor during interviews, such outsourcing is not necessarily bad for rehabilitation of the north. Assuming that there is a sufficient transfer of skills to the local communities from the external workers, such initiatives can work to stimulate both growth in the north and the south. However, once again this is contingent on whether or not the government chooses to prioritize this. Some of the concerns expressed by different development partners interviewed for this study related to the lack of transparency of both government and donor projects. For instance, whilst a project may promise to use a fixed percentage of local workers in construction, quite often the majority of those will be low skilled labour, whilst high skilled labour is outsourced. In a transitional economy with strong growth, such as Sri Lanka, there exists a good opportunity to capitalize on the growth through supporting local suppliers in markets which they have previously had limited exposure. Expanding the capacity of industry in this way will help to create employment and raise national income; thus, reducing the likelihood of future conflict grounded in economic disparities.

Furthermore, using domestic resources in donor-funded projects is a good way in which to normalize outwardly designed development. This normalization of projects is imperative in order for successful implementation. Therefore, a heavier reliance on local resources in the design and implementation of projects can help to maximize effectiveness due to their knowledge of local markets and communities. In addition to this, the responsiveness of local communities to reconstruction will be greater, knowing that they are being directly involved in the effort and, hence, there is national ownership of development.

PRIORITIES FOR ENHANCING AID EFFECTIVENESS IN SRI LANKA

Effectiveness of the PD in Sri Lanka

The PD on Aid Effectiveness is an attempt to prioritize joint commitments and obligations of donors and partner countries in order to enhance the developmental impact of aid. The PD and the follow up Accra Agenda for Action (AAA) have to a great extent defined the global aid effectiveness agenda. The key principles include:

- ownership (partner countries set the development agenda);
- alignment (donors align programmes with this development agenda and partner country financial systems);

- harmonization (donors to use common arrangements for planning, disbursement and reporting to reduce transaction costs);
- managing for results (improving management of aid to ensure better results—such as performance based budgeting); and
- mutual accountability (increasing the role of parliaments in aid decisions and participatory approaches to national development strategies).

The PD is, however, largely the Organisation for Economic Co-operation and Development (OECD) driven agenda which donors and partner countries have signed on to. Therefore, it is important for individual countries to independently identify challenges in enhancing aid effectiveness and evaluate the relevance and effectiveness of the PD in enhancing aid effectiveness in their countries. Sri Lanka was one of the countries which provided a formal evaluation of the PD as an input into the preparation for the Third High Level (HLF) Forum in Accra. Drawing from this report and other available literature on aid effectiveness in Sri Lanka (IPS 2008; Kelegama and de Mel, 2007) it is clear that there is some disconnect between the PD and Sri Lanka's priorities for aid reform. However, the AAA goes some way in bridging this disconnect.

Ownership

With regard to ownership, Sri Lanka's recent governments have spearheaded strong national development frameworks, around which the major donors have aligned programmes. The current framework is the 10 Year Development Framework of the *Mahinda Chinthanaya* (MC) 2006–16 (Ministry of Finance, 2006). The Annual Development Forum acts as a pledging conference where the government presents development plans and donors commit financial support. Therefore, enhancing country ownership of the development agenda is not really a priority in Sri Lanka as the government quite clearly identifies which donors should engage in which area of development. In fact, some donors who were interviewed as part of this research were of the view that one flaw in the current structure in Sri Lanka is that in some cases, the government's selection of donors is not always in line with donor comparative advantages and expertise and, therefore, more coordination would be warranted in this selection process.

Nonetheless, there is room for reform in terms of enhancement of ownership in Sri Lanka. Ownership as outlined above refers largely to ownership of the overarching planning process, whereas ownership should also extend to more micro-level planning and implementation as well. In the case of the latter, there is room for improvement in ownership of some donor-funded development activities. Ownership of implementation is largely contingent on the capacity of relevant implementing agencies in the partner country. In Sri Lanka, whilst capacity is relatively strong, there are still a number of parallel implementation units in operation along with a high number of external consultants drawn into the implementation process.

Also, in terms of ownership, there is a difference between formal structures and informal realities. Formal systems indicate strong domestic ownership of donor-funded projects, where line ministries take the lead in identification and conceptualization of issues and activities which are then put forward for donor funding via the External Resources Department. Whereas in reality, often donors identify bottlenecks and suggest projects to line ministries, which in turn would conceptualize projects that are to a great extent reflective of donor structures and priorities. This is again a reflection of capacity gaps in domestic line ministries.

The other important factor with regard to the issue of ownership is the breadth of ownership that is being referred to. In Sri Lanka, ownership of the broad development agenda by the state is beyond question; however, there is some doubt regarding the extent of ownership of the development agenda amongst a broader group of stakeholders. Sri Lanka's PD evaluation report highlights the fact that sub-national governments and civil society groups lack the same level of input into the formulation of the development agenda as the central government institutions.

The AAA correctly identifies the fact that a broader level of engagement in the formulation of the national development agenda is a priority. This would ensure that there is greater stakeholder voice in defining the agenda for donor supported interventions. This is particularly important in post-conflict situations where a potential disconnect between central government perspectives of development priorities and priorities and expectations of local populations, could fuel further conflict. Therefore, broader consultations on development priorities, engaging populations affected by conflict, would be essential to ensure sustainable peace and development.

Alignment

As mentioned above, alignment of donor programmes with the national development strategy occurs to a large extent in Sri Lanka. According to the Sri Lanka country evaluation of the PD, 89 per cent of aid was to the public sector with 77.6 per cent of aid going through the national budget. The balance largely reflects bilateral aid going through non-budget channels into non-state organizations and activities. Only 40 per cent of bilateral aid (excluding Japan) was to the public sector. The extent of donor alignment to partner country procurement and financial management systems has been mixed in Sri Lanka. National procurement systems were utilized 50.7 per cent of the time with 40 per cent of donors interviewed for the PD evaluation not using National Procurement Agency guidelines, all of which were bilateral donors. 70.5 per cent of aid used national accounting systems and 65.9 per cent used national audit systems. Notably, Sri Lanka's major donors (historically) like the World Bank, ADB and Japan all use the standard Public Financial Management (PFM) systems. Bilateral donors have in general shown less faith in national systems.

Half the donors interviewed in Sri Lanka's PD evaluation used PIUs amounting to 50 such project units, including both bilaterals and multilaterals. However, 72 per cent of all PIUs were in ADB projects. Japan on the other hand, used none. The PIUs were utilized largely due to donor reporting requirements (as much as to fill capacity gaps in domestic implementation agencies). Most PIUs are governed by government procedures on recruitment and remuneration. Whilst PIUs can be seen as useful interim arrangements to meet capacity gaps, particularly in large projects, in the medium term steps must be taken to absorb them into standard implementing agencies due to the capacity drainage from government agencies and the potential friction that results between the PIUs and the permanent government entities.

The other principle under the theme of alignment, is the issue of tied aid. In Sri Lanka, the bulk of foreign aid (approximately 80 per cent) has historically been from the World Bank, ADB and Japan. At present, none of these institutions and countries utilize tied aid. Details on the extent to which aid from bilateral donors is tied are difficult to gauge accurately; however, the Sri Lanka PD evaluation estimates that only 25 per cent of non-Japanese bilateral aid is untied (Japanese aid is entirely untied). In cases such as the Indian line of credit, there are clear examples of tied aid where material utilized in implementation of projects financed by the line of credit must be sourced from India. This material could be more expensive than other alternatives, thus, pushing up the cost of implementation (keeping in mind the fact that the line of credit is a loan and must be re-paid). In other cases such as American support to enhancing competitiveness of Sri Lankan export industries, the garment sector was excluded from such support, despite accounting for 40 per cent of Sri Lanka's export earnings, due to pressure from domestic lobbies in the United States. In other cases of bilateral support, the quid pro quo could take various forms such as expectations of diplomatic support on the global political stage and preferential treatment for lucrative commercial deals.

In a post-conflict context, a lack of alignment between donor and government priorities can weaken the relationship between the two parties, hindering the progress of post-conflict development. Thus, it is important that the government and its respective development partners show unison in their activities. If a perception is created among domestic stakeholders that relief and rehabilitation in particular are dominated by donors, it could undermine the government's credibility in post-conflict resolution. This in turn could undermine peace building efforts in the long term.

Whilst there are many multilateral, and some bilateral, donors that have managed to align their activities well with the government's development plan in Sri Lanka, there are a number of donors who fall out of sync. This tends to occur with the donors that are focused more on the immediate rehabilitation effort, as opposed to developments of which the benefits are realized in the medium term, such as infrastructure investments. The importance of the donor effort in the aftermath of the war cannot be denied; however, the predominant donor presence in this relief process significantly affects domestic perceptions, and this could lead to animosity towards the government within certain communities. Therefore, it should be a priority of both the government and its development partners to work together and particularly to demonstrate ownership and collaboration as opposed to donor dominance, so as to reduce the risk of donor-funded activities inadvertently harming the peace process.

Harmonization

The rationale for harmonization of donor planning, activities and reporting is to reduce transaction costs of aid delivery and to enhance efficiency by ensuring that donors occupy niches according to their respective comparative advantages. The Sri Lankan PD evaluation report finds that donors fell short of meeting PD targets in 2005, with only 16.5 per cent of 236 donor missions that year being coordinated amongst donors (PD target 40 per cent), and 52.3 per cent of donor analytic works were coordinated, short of the 66 per cent PD target. Considering the fact that the implementation of the PD took place after 2005, one could expect these ratios to have improved in the last five years. Nonetheless, harmonization has not been an identified priority of the Sri Lankan government (Kelegama and de Mel, 2007). By avoiding donor-led coordination, the government can maintain choices amongst different donors, and is thus able to strengthen its own bargaining position with regard to channelling donor funds and select donors according to its own preferences.

However, government-led harmonization of donors could achieve both ends of maintaining government prerogative of donor selection, whilst contributing to the reduction of transaction costs associated with multiple missions, systems and reporting procedures. In order to achieve the highest degree of efficiency in this endeavour, it is important to establish institutionalized two way communication channels between the government and donors to ensure that the correct choices are made regarding donor selection based on comparative advantages of donors, coupled with government priorities and needs. The existing annual development forum is not a sufficient framework to achieve this end, and forums such as the National Council for Economic Development (NCED—which includes a cluster on donors), which also has scope for private sector and CSO participation, could be utilized more effectively to create this institutionalized channel.

There have been cases of donor harmonization at a sectoral level. The Sector Wide Approach (SWAP) in the education sector development programme (ESDP) has helped channel aid into the appropriate areas, but there has been only limited harmonization on donor procedures, therefore transaction costs remain. Another challenge is the limitation in capacity for project planning and design by domestic agencies in this kind of complex endeavour. Such harmonization could also be counter-productive since donors have to work with harmonized arrangements and still adhere to its own reporting and other requirements.

Managing for Development Results and Mutual Accountability

These areas identified in the PD are certainly in line with priorities for enhancing aid effectiveness in Sri Lanka. Whilst Sri Lanka has had strong national development plans that cement ownership of the development framework, more work is needed to help translate these more effectively into developmental outcomes. These include measures such as the incorporation of broader stakeholder perspectives into formulation of development strategies (both at the parliamentary level and through forums that engage civil society groups and sub-national governments and the private sector), results-based budgeting, enhanced review mechanisms, and evaluations of performance. Donors in turn, should support government attempts at strengthening capacity to implement these agendas. It is encouraging to note that the Department of Foreign Aid and Budget Monitoring, under the Ministry of Finance, has taken steps to make public through their websites the reviews of PD goals and reviews identifying shortcomings and lessons learned of various donor funded projects in Sri Lanka. A continuation of this practice will be of great value. It is also important to provide avenues for the beneficiaries of donor funded projects to participate in review and evaluation mechanisms in an open and transparent manner. Such efforts should be led by the government with the cooperation of development partners.

Other Priorities for Reform

Improved Targeting of Aid

The poor targeting of aid projects is one of the major factors reducing effectiveness. One such example is the over-provision of fishing boats and tools by donors to households affected by the tsunami of 2004. As a result of poor targeting, boats were allocated to households that were not previously employed in the fishery sector. Further to this, 52 per cent of fishing households that lost their boats in the disaster did not receive the boat aid transfers that they were eligible for. The inclusion of non-fishing households into the fishery sector put downwards pressure on domestic prices, due to over-fishing, hurting local producers in the process. This was the result of poor targeting on behalf of the donors, due to deficient micro-level data. Targeting is an important prerequisite to aid, helping to increase effectiveness by distributing resources only where they are most needed. Conversely, universal transfers can often create distortions in the economy, such as the distribution of food that can indirectly place upwards pressure on local food prices hurting domestic production in the process. Such was the experience in the post-tsunami recovery period, which saw the over-fishing of fish stocks due to the inflow of new fishermen facilitated by the aid transfers.

The redistribution of wealth is an issue that demands great sensitivity at the best of times; where there has been a history of social conflict this need becomes even greater. Hence, the importance of well thought-out, inclusive policies, which have adequately consulted stakeholders in their design, is essential to avoiding further aggravating social tensions. In addition to this benefit, increasing the targeting of aid projects increases the need for the government to be more prudent in their allocation of funds; strengthening fiscal management in the process.

Despite the obvious benefits of selective aid distribution, there are a number of practical issues which may put into question the feasibility of accurate targeting. Targeting relies heavily on the availability of reliable micro-level data so that policymakers can observe trends in the distribution of wealth, enabling them to best determine where to direct resources. As in the post-tsunami experience, this data may not always be available. With regard to areas in the Northern and Eastern provinces there may be serious gaps in data due to the inability of the government to keep a record of the communities that were previously living within LTTE controlled regions. Failing this, the next best option would be for policymakers to consult directly with the local communities wherein the development is set to take place. This can be done through a house-by-house process or alternatively conducted through a civil society organization (CSO).

However, there are certain drawbacks associated with both of these approaches. The former is very time consuming making it impractical especially where assistance is needed in the immediate aftermath of a crisis, such as the cessation of the war. In this sense, using a medium such as CSOs, through which to consult with society can cut down on the time lag and high costs associated with data collection. However, there remain certain caveats with CSOs that, within the context of a society with a history of ethnic and political conflict, risks disrupting social cohesion. Given issues of migration and displacement that would have occurred during the war, the social capital in some of the areas lacking data may have been negatively harmed. Social capital is a key component to forming strong CSOs that provide an accurate representation of society. In regions where people previously displaced by the war are returning back, this social capital may be lacking. Hence, it may be difficult to form CSOs which are completely inclusive, as members of the community which are returning to the area may not have developed the trust to consult with CSOs. Furthermore, the CSOs may not be fully aware of the existence of some of those returning to the area. In such instances, CSOs that are relied on for designing policies related to redistribution risk excluding people from reconstruction and, hence, thwarting the growth of social capital whilst threatening the peace process.

Despite the obvious benefits with increasing stakeholder consultation in the design of development policies, it may not be a feasible option. An interview with a donor working largely in development in the Northern and the Eastern regions of the country, revealed that there often is an ad hoc approach to designing policies, due to the unavoidable obstacles to consultation such as displacement. Similarly, the situation on the ground may not give the government and its development partners the time with which they can devise ways to overcome the impediments to stakeholder consultation.

Furthermore, consultation may not always be a robust method to forming inclusive policies. Beneficiaries may change their behaviour in order to make themselves more eligible for the transfers. This may be more of an issue with newly resettled communities and where donors and the government are working in regions which they have previously had limited exposure to. With regard to the post-conflict regions of the NE, an improvised approach is often the most feasible and advisable. Given the duration of the war, there is no real knowledge of what the social norm is for these regions. Such communities would have been subjected to many varying rules of authority and relocation such that the social stratification that existed prior to the war is no longer relevant within these regions. Therefore, it may be largely redundant to try and formulate a plan of what policy should be trying to reconstruct.

Distributional Effects of Aid: Lessons from the Past

In the context of post-conflict reconstruction in Sri Lanka, donors would have to be sensitive to potential negative externalities of developmental activities on maintenance of peace and social harmony. It is important to draw on lessons from past experiences in order to inform future activities. The distributional effects of aid, particularly perceptions thereof, can be a potential obstacle to long-term development and, within a post-conflict context, detrimental to social reconciliation. The experience of the Mahaweli Development Project (MDP) is one such example wherein development was perceived to have aggravated social tensions.

The MDP was implemented in the 1970s with funding from international donors including the World Bank, Britain, Germany, Sweden and Canada. The project intended to provide jobs and land for the landless through irrigating surplus land in the dry zones of the North-Central, Northern and Eastern provinces. This newly irrigated land was to be allocated between approximately 18,500 families with each receiving 0.2ha, on which they could live and cultivate paddy and other crops.[6] The movement of Sinhalese communities into areas of the Northern and Eastern provinces that were labelled as 'Tamil homelands' by Tamil political groups was a controversial aspect of the MDP. Such demographic changes refer to the shift in ethnic ratios in districts such as Trincomalee, where in 1946 Tamils and Sinhalese made up 40 per cent and 21 per cent of the population, respectively, but by the 1970s both groups accounted for 34 per cent each. Such changes in land distribution further fuelled grievances of Tamil communities. Whilst these perceptions are the outcome of many years of irrigation schemes during the post-independence era, many authors point out the fact that donor funded projects such as the MDP of the late 1970s and 1980s failed to take cognizance of the ethnic dimensions of developmental activities (see Warnapala, 1994; Silva, 2005; Gunatilake, 2001). The actual impacts on populations during the early stages of the MDP in the Eastern Province are less pronounced than the differences observed between 1946 and 1970 (as demonstrated in Table 7.4), nonetheless, perceptions are often more influential in ethnic conflict and political reality than actual outcomes.

As argued by Peiris (1994), much of the criticism that the government received over their implementation of the MDP was the result

Table 7.4

Population by Ethnicity in the Eastern Province, 1971 and 1981

District	Ethnicity	1971	1981
Ampara	Sinhalese	30%	38%
	Tamil	22%	20%
	Muslim	46%	42%
Batticaloa	Sinhalese	4%	3%
	Tamil	69%	71%
	Muslim	24%	24%
Trincomalee	Sinhalese	29%	30%
	Tamil	35%	22%
	Muslim	32%	46%

Source: Department of Census and Statistics (1973, 1983).

of misinterpreted data and the coincidental concentration of greater development in the Sinhalese-dominated regions, as opposed to a policy favouring Sinhalese communities.

The experience of the MDP illustrates the susceptibility of development projects to scrutiny from domestic stakeholders, and hence, the role of perceptions is essential in donor engagement in post conflict areas. Therefore, so as to ensure that policy cannot be misconstrued as favouring any one ethnic group, projects must be sensitive to the ethnic composition of the regions concerned. Restructuring social capital is a vital prerequisite to post-conflict development; hence, whilst a degree of redistribution may be unavoidable, policy should aim to minimize such disturbances and ensure maximum transparency regarding project objectives and modalities so as to prevent undue inferences being made. Such measures would require greater engagement with domestic stakeholders on behalf of both the government and donors.

Domestic Reform Priorities

1. Institutional Capacity Building: The enhancement of domestic institutional capacity to manage aid is a key priority to improve overall aid effectiveness in Sri Lanka. Institutional constraints occur at all levels. At the national level, the coordination of

donors and prioritization of aid, monitoring and evaluation of projects will require substantial resources and policy emphasis, particularly the latter issue. At the sub-national level and at line ministries, the extent of domestic ownership of donor-funded project conceptualization and implementation is contingent on capacity to do so in these institutions. Therefore, it will be important to invest significant resources in the development of capacity of domestic institutions dealing with donor-funded projects at both national and sub-national levels. This is an area which donors themselves could support, under the overall leadership and coordination of the government.

2.   Coordination of Government Agencies: One factor that adds to transaction costs in aid delivery is the fact that responsibilities of the government are often dispersed across several different agencies, be it at the provincial or national level. This is a problem that affects many aspects of economic activity in the country. Whilst the External Resources Department (ERD) and the Department of Foreign Aid and Budget Monitoring (Ministry of Finance) are involved in coordination of aid mobilization and monitoring and evaluation respectively, there is no clear system of streamlining aid delivery. One of the major stumbling blocks that has delayed projects in the past has been the issue of land acquisition. Streamlining processes such as these will ensure that disbursement of aid occurs more effectively and benefits accrue in a faster manner.

3.   Clarity in Responsibilities of Sub-national Governments: One particular case of coordination failure in the post-conflict situation in Sri Lanka relates to the demarcation of responsibilities of the sub-national governments and central government. Donors interviewed were of the view that whilst sub-national institutional capacity is an important constraint to the effective delivery of aid, an equally important challenge is the lack of clarity between the roles of the central government agencies and the sub-national government agencies in project implementation. The capacity issue creates a dilemma in terms of the responsibilities for different arms of government. The principle of subsidiarity suggests that sub-national governments should play an important role in the implementation of donor-funded projects since they would have better knowledge of local issues and realities. However,

capacity constraints at the local level would limit the extent of the role played by sub-national governments. One way out would be for more resources to be released to sub-national governments in order to enhance capacity for implementation. This again, should be led by the government and supported by development partners.

4. Counterpart Funding: Another important domestic issue that has contributed to weaknesses in aid disbursement and effectiveness is the delay in provision of counterpart funding for certain projects. This has largely been reflective of fiscal constraints in Sri Lanka which has inhibited timely cash flows from the government. One would expect the proposed fiscal reform, under the FMRA and the IMF Agreement, if it is followed through, would address this problem. A related weakness has been the lack of emphasis on maintenance and continuity of donor funded activities. This again is an issue that needs to be tackled jointly by donors and governments by committing sustainable finances and other resources to longer term maintenance of donor funded developmental projects, particularly by investing in the resources of institutions in charge of maintenance.

5. Transparency: Many of Sri Lanka's larger multilateral development partners place a significant degree of emphasis on transparency. Therefore, details of funded projects in terms of inputs, conceptualization and independent evaluation reports are to a great extent, available for public scrutiny. This is, however, not always the case for other development partners. The government should take measures to enhance transparency of all donor funded projects, building on the work done so far by the Department for Foreign Aid and Budget Monitoring to develop public access to evaluations of a selection of donor funded projects. This would entail making public the inputs into projects, the time frames and objectives, and these could be benchmarked against results and outcomes. Such subjection to public scrutiny would create strong incentives for both donors and the government to enhance aid effectiveness and will also help identify gaps in aid effectiveness and provide easy access for lessons for future projects.

Conclusion

It is clear from the arguments put forward in this chapter that whilst foreign aid plays an important role in Sri Lanka's short-term development objectives, in the long run it is important for countries like Sri Lanka to reduce reliance on concessional aid to finance developmental objectives. In Sri Lanka's experience, the country has long relied on concessional aid with long repayment horizons to finance the entirety of capital expenditure. However, as the country experiences income growth, the access to such concessional aid diminishes. This has forced the country to resort to expensive commercial borrowing with short repayment horizons to finance long-term development objectives. Given this unsustainable position, it becomes important to enhance domestic resource mobilization through rationalization of fiscal positions. This becomes a medium term policy priority in Sri Lanka.

In the interim period, concessional aid will play an important role in Sri Lanka's post-conflict development. Therefore, domestic policies in terms of managing this aid and donor policies in aid delivery will be an important determinant of the effectiveness of aid in delivering positive developmental outcomes. In this chapter, we have pointed out a number of issues relating to the enhancement of aid effectiveness, both from the perspective of donors and from the perspective of the recipient government. The major priorities identified include support for domestic institutions dealing with foreign aid funded projects, enhanced targeting of aid, institutionalizing stakeholder consultations at all stages—planning, implementation, monitoring and evaluation. The chapter also identifies specific issues that need to be addressed in post-conflict situations, particularly relating to the need for donors to be sensitive to the capacity constraints of domestic institutions and the potential detrimental impacts of donor dominance in projects, impacts of projects on domestic resources, and the importance of including local actors in development projects whilst being sensitive to the potential negative externalities that development activities could have on social cohesion and harmony.

Notes

1. Other infrastructure refers to general infrastructure rehabilitation programmes, such as the French Trincomalee Integrated Infrastructure Project and the Japanese Pro-poor Eastern Infrastructure Project.

2. Other refers to general projects in the NE—specifically referring to the ADB Conflict Areas Rehabilitation Project (US$15.81 million) and the United Nations Development Programme (UNDP) Transition Recovery Program (US$3.59 million).

3. Other infrastructure refers to general infrastructure rehabilitation programmes such as the French Trincomalee Integrated Infrastructure Project and the Japanese Pro-Poor Eastern Infrastructure Project.

4. Other refers to general projects in the NE, specifically the ADB Conflict Areas Rehabilitation Project (US$3.3 million) and the World Bank Emergency NE Recovery Project (US$9.05 million).

5. Britain, the US, France and Germany abstained from voting when the Executive Board was deciding upon the SBA to Sri Lanka.

6. World Bank Independent Evaluators Report on Mahaweli Ganga Development, http://lnweb90.worldbank.org/oed/oeddoclib.nsf/DocUNIDViewForJavaSearch/0D869807701D1EEE852567F5005D8903.

REFERENCES

Central Bank of Sri Lanka (various issues), *Annual Report*, Colombo.

Collier, P. and A. Hoeffler (2002), 'Aid, Policy and Growth in Post-Conflict Societies', World Bank Policy Research Working Paper 2902.

Culpeper, R. and B. Morton (2008), 'The International Development System: Southern Perspectives on Reform', The North-South Institute, Ottawa.

Department of Census and Statistics (1973), *Census 1971*, Department of Census and Statistics, Sri Lanka.

———— (1983), *Census 1981*, Department of Census and Statistics, Sri Lanka.

External Resources Department (various years), 'Disbursements of Foreign Funded Loan/Grant Agreements', www.erd.gov.lk (accessed on 20 June 2010).

Goodhand, Jonathan, Bart Klem et al. (2005), *Aid, conflict and Peacebuilding in Sri Lanka, 2000–2005,* Six part series Volume 1, The Asia Foundation, Colombo.

Government of Sri Lanka, 'Letter of Intent to the IMF', www.cbsl.gov.lk (accessed on 24 June 2010).

Gunatilake, G. (2001), 'The Ethnic Dimension of Socio-Economic Development', Marga Institute. Independent Evaluation Group (2004),'Sri Lanka—Third Mahaweli Ganga Development Project', World Bank, Report Number: 29489, Colombo.

International Crisis Group (2010), 'Sri Lanka: A Bitter Peace', International Crisis Group, Asia Briefing No. 99.

———— (2009), 'Development Assistance and Conflict in Sri Lanka: Lessons from the Eastern Province', International Crisis Group, Asia Report No. 165.

IPS (2008), *IPS State of the Economy Report*, IPS.

Keefer, P. (2008), 'Foreign Assistance and the Political Economy of Post-Conflict Countries', Development Research Group, The World Bank, Washington D.C.

Kelegama, S. and D. de Mel (2007), 'Southern Perspectives on Reform of the International Development Architecture: Sri Lanka Country Study', The North-South Institute, Ottawa.

Ministry of Finance (2006), *Mahinda Chinthanaya*, Ten Year Developmental Framework, Government of Sri Lanka.

OECD (2008), 'Sri Lanka Paris Declaration Evaluation Report' OECD, Paris.

——— (2005), 'Paris Declaration of Aid Effectiveness: Ownership, Harmonisation, Alignment, Results and Mutual Accountability', OECD, Paris.

Peiris, G.H. (1994), 'Irrigation, Land Distribution and Ethnic Conflict in Sri Lanka: An Evaluation of Criticisms', *Ethnic Studies Report*, 12(1): 43–88.

Shanmugaratnam, N. and K. Stokke (2004), 'Development as a Precursor to Conflict Resolution: A Critical Review of the Fifth Peace Process in Sri Lanka', Agricultural University of Norway (mimeo).

Shastri, A. (1990), 'The Material Basis for Separatism: The Tamil Eelam Movement in Sri Lanka', *The Journal of Asian Studies*, 49(1): 56–77.

Silva, K.T. (2005), 'Politicisation of Ethnicity, Ethnification of the Stage and Challenges for Post Conflict Transformation in Sri Lanka', in V. Raghavan and K. Fischer (eds), *Conflict Resolution and Peace Building in Sri Lanka*, Tata, McGraw-Hill, New Delhi.

Warnapala, W. (1994), *Ethnic Strife and Politics in Sri Lanka*, Lake House Publications, Colombo.

World Bank (2008), 'Sri Lanka: Country Assistance Strategy 2009–2012', South Asia Country Report, Washington D.C.

8

Nepal

BISHWAMBHER PYAKURYAL

BACKGROUND

Overview

Policy priorities for receiving and managing external assistance have been the central theme of foreign aid administration in developing countries. External assistance has helped countries to achieve greatest human progress in the last few decades. The Marshall Plan of the US for example, rebuilt Europe's economy after the Second World War. The assistance by addressing the Green Revolution in agriculture helped Asia to drive for long-term growth in the 1960s and 1970s. The aid has raised immunization rates from 15 per cent to nearly 80 per cent in the 1980s, and efforts to save millions from HIV/AIDS especially in Africa are one of the several outcomes of Foreign Aid Policy (FAP) (Beckman, 2010).

However, several policies on foreign aid followed by the development partners are quite old and outdated. It needs to be re-visited since there has been a massive change in the political economy of both the developed and developing countries. Beckman (2010) observes that in Bangladesh, the United States was found to collect several times the amount in tariffs that it offered in assistance. In Afghanistan, United Sates Agency for International Development (USAID)-related two separate contractors were found doing the same project in the same town (Beckman, 2010). Afghanistan has asked international partners to align at least 80 per cent of development and governance assistance over the next two years (2010–12) in a list of recently brought out 23 national priority programmes and projects. This is important in pulling the country out of poverty and turmoil instead of financing in temporary and unsustainable programmes, which cannot make the life of Afghans better in the long term (http://www.msnbc.msn.com/id/ 38209650/). These events raise important questions: is achieving broad-based development a distinct goal of the development partners in global engagement or is it merely a tool to serve diplomatic or defence objectives?

The accumulated debt burden of developed countries doesn't give any hope sooner to revive pre-crisis export-led growth in the region. It suggests the need to explore new sources of domestic and regional demand as a compensation for the weakened Western demand for their exports. The Economic and Social Survey of Asia and the Pacific 2010 recommends,

> parts of the solution could be to develop a more consumer-centric economy in the region—one in which rising consumption is increasingly fed by production from within the region. By allocating financial capital more efficiently within the region, more jobs could be generated and the benefits of economic growth could be spread more equitably, in turn stimulating increases in private consumption. (ESCAP, 2010)

The policy for standard reform programmes includes *(a)* an improvement in the performance of public sector economic institutions, and *(b)* macroeconomic and sectoral economic policy measures. Under institutional reforms, strengthening of the public expenditure programmes needs to be addressed and under macroeconomic measures, attempts should be made to reduce fiscal and balance of payments (BoP) deficits by restraining public expenditure growth, tightening monetary policy, and adjusting the exchange rates (Berg, 1988). As a public expenditure reform programme, the Government of Nepal constituted three important committees in the past, which include Public Expenditure Review Commission (2000), Fiscal Reform Task Force (2002) and High-level Public Expenditure Commission (2004). After the completion of these reports, some reforms in the public expenditure front were visualize;, however, the impact on managing macroeconomic difficulties by reducing BOP deficits remained minimal.

During 1980s, the World Bank, International Monetary Fund (IMF) and bilateral donors tied up economic assistance on policy-based lending. Structural Adjustment Programme of the International Financial Institutions and Economic Support Fund and other food aid programmes by the USAID can also be presented as an example. During these years, most of the reform measures were focused on 'liberalization' and market-oriented policy without much emphasis given to the policies for satisfying basic human needs (Beckman, 2010).

The policy issues often linked in foreign aid reform programmes include, significance of foreign aid, priority based assistance, possibility of replacing external assistance through domestic resource mobilization, opportunity costs, impact on inflation/exchange rates, elimination of donor-driven assistance, linking governance with aid effectiveness, the possibility of 'new donors', and long-term exit strategy for aid. These indicators should revolve around the question of equity implications, impact on poverty and income distribution and managing and sustaining the concept of inclusive growth. This chapter intends to cover these areas briefly to recommend policy changes in both the recipient and donor countries for making the aid programme as effective as possible.

Foreign Aid in Nepal

The history of aid begins modestly since the nineteenth century and has grown through various stages. End of the Second World War, Cold War and independence movements during 1940s and 1950s, rise of multilaterals in 1970s and non-governmental organizations (NGOs) in the 1980s are important sequences for the growth of aid in different forms. After joining the Colombo Plan for Cooperative, Economic, and Social Development in Asia and the Pacific in 1952, Nepal started receiving various scholarships in technical and professional areas. This was the time when all other aid was received as a grant. The priorities in external aid were focused in agriculture, transportation infrastructure, and power generation. Equally important areas identified were communications, industry, education and health.

During 1950s, India and the US contributed more than one-third of all grants, followed by China, the then the Soviet Union, Britain, Switzerland, Australia, Japan, and New Zealand. The US aid concentrated on agriculture and rural development and basic infrastructure during the 1950s and added health and education in the 1960s. Indian aid concentrated on administrative reforms, transportation and communication in the 1950s and was extended to irrigation, education and drinking water in the 1960s. The period 1960s was dominated by bilateral assistance mostly as a grant for development projects. With the establishment of 'Nepal Aid Group' in 1976, the quantum of foreign aid increased more significantly.

During 1970s, multilateral donors also come into the picture noticeably and played a significant role in financing development activities of Nepal. During the same period, more than 70 per cent of development expenditure of Nepal was financed through multilateral assistance. The major multilateral donors included the International Development Association of the World Bank and the Asian Development Bank (ADB). Interestingly, loan share on total foreign aid also increased significantly after the advent of multilateral donors in Nepal. By the 1990s, a lot of changes were setting in. Japan emerged as the biggest aid contributor to Nepal followed by the US, the UK and Germany. During this period, 'small' European countries like Denmark, Netherlands, Finland and Norway as a group and international non-governmental organizations (INGOs) became important donors.

The foreign policy of Nepal is guided by its geographical reality, socio-cultural settings and the state of the economy. Nepal's geo-physical setting and time zone location assume strategic significance in South Asia. Nepal is surrounded by rapidly growing two neighbourhood economic giants, India and China, the Elephant and Dragon economies. Maintaining economic interests with these countries should be the country's priority in economic diplomacy. Figure 8.1 exhibits trends in foreign aid in Nepal.

Figure 8.1 shows that both grants and loans in absolute figures have been increasing over the years. Nepal received Rs 1.01 million in FY 1950–51 as grant. This amount significantly increased after FY 1958–59 and reached as high as Rs 86.42 million. Since then, total aid flow in Nepal continued to show an upward trend over the years, except for a few years. The amount further increased and Nepal received an average of Rs 466 million in 1970s, while the figure reached an average of Rs 3,705 million in 1980s. The significant increase in foreign aid in the 1980s was attributed to substantial amount of borrowing from donors. During 1990s when Nepal escalated the reform process, average figure for the 1990s increased to as high as Rs 12, 989 million. Nepal received total aid of Rs 18, 787 million in FY 2001/02 which has reached to a total

Figure 8.1
Trends in Foreign Aid in Nepal, 1950/51–2008/09

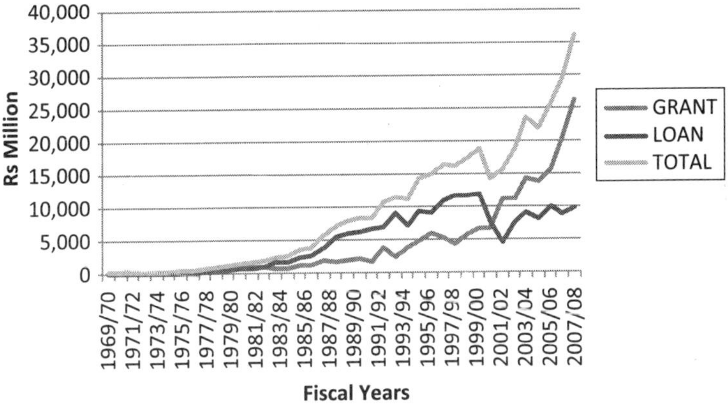

Fiscal Years

Source: Pyakuryal, Adhikari and Dhakal (2008); MOF (2009).

of Rs 36, 351.7 million in 2008–09 with a significant share of grant on total aid (Figure 8.1).

The distribution of the foreign aid between grant and loan, however, shows a mix picture. In early years, the grant has been the dominating component of foreign aid. Up to 1982–83, the grant component was higher than the loan on total foreign aid flow. During the 1960s and 1970s, the share of grant used to be around three fourth of total aid. But the share of grant started to decline gradually. After FY 1983–84, loan started to be higher than grant up to FY 2002–03. During this period, the grant component on an average decreased to nearly 32 per cent leading to a significant increase of loan component to as high of 68 per cent on average. However in recent years, after FY 2002–03, the grant component again started to outweigh loan. For instance, the grant component for the period 2002–03 to 2007–08 has remained at 64 per cent on average, while the loan has decreased to 36 per cent. The figures are similar for the recent years of 2008–09 with the share of grant recording almost 72 per cent share in total aid received (Figure 8.2).

Table 8.1 shows that multilateral donors have been significant contributors on providing foreign aid in Nepal. During the period 1980s, nearly 65 per cent of total aid was received from bilateral donors. This distribution nominally changed during 1990s consisting 67 per cent of total aid received from the bilateral donors. In recent years, except in FY 2006–07, multilateral donors continued to be the

Figure 8.2

Composition of Foreign Aid by Grant and Loan, 1969/70–2008/09

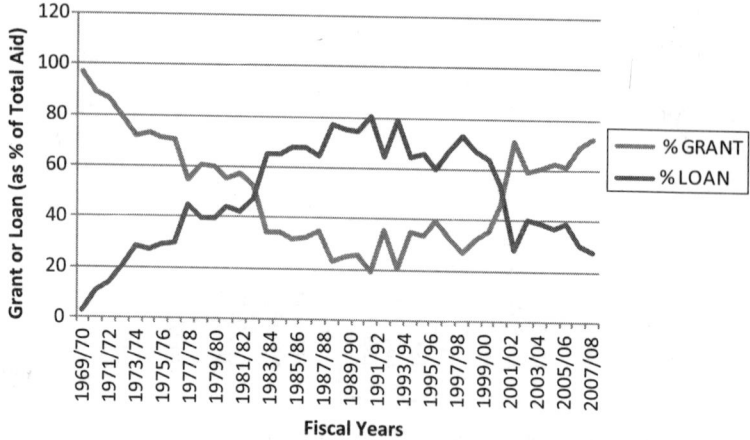

Source: Pyakuryal, Adhikari and Dhakal (2008); MOF (2009).

dominant contributor. If we do not account for FY 2006–07, multilateral donors' contribution still stands as high as 60 per cent of total aid received. In FY 2006–07, however, Nepal received almost 67 per cent of its aid from bilateral sources.

During 1990s, the average share of loan on total assistance by multilateral donors stands as high as 90 per cent, while the same for bilateral donors is just 20 per cent. The trend however shows that share of loan on multilateral donors', aid had decreased to an average of 57 per cent after FY 2000–01. Likewise, loan from bilateral donors has also decreased to an average of 12 per cent during the same period (Table 8.1).

Nepal Development Forum (NDF)

The NDF, previously known as 'Nepal Aid Group Meetings', started from 1976. Building understanding between Government of Nepal and its development partners on the adequate availability and effective mobilization of aid has been the central theme of NDF.

The NDF in general has the following objectives:

- Charting Nepal's development roadmap along the path of sustained peace and resulting socio-economic transformation with support from the development partners

Table 8.1
Foreign Aid by Donors' Type

Source		1986–90	1991–95	1996–2000	2001–05	2005–06	2006–07	2007–08	2008–09
Bilateral	Total	1,812.70	3,358.30	4,988.08	7,146.98	7,658.40	16,406.43	10,207.75	9,333.10
	% bilateral	37.80	36.64	31.37	39.43	34.74	63.46	34.84	25.67
	Grant	1,258.80	2,038.20	4,194.66	6,842.3	7,617.80	7,401.84	9,575.64	8,720.20
	% Grant	69.44	60.69	84.51	93.66	99.47	45.12	93.81	93.43
	Loan	553.90	1,320.10	793.42	304.68	40.60	9,004.59	632.11	612.90
	% Loan	30.56	39.31	15.49	6.34	0.53	54.88	6.19	6.57
Multilateral	Total	2,983.00	5,808.20	1,0910.10	1,1180.50	14,383.40	9,447.94	19,092.85	27,018.60
	% Multilateral	62.20	63.36	68.63	60.57	65.26	36.54	65.16	74.33
	Grant	208.00	514.90	1,058.20	3,248.36	6,209.70	8,399.01	10,745.09	17,662.60
	% Grant	6.97	8.87	9.61	28.76	43.17	88.90	56.28	65.37
	Loan	2,775.00	5,293.30	9,851.90	7,932.14	8,173.70	1,048.93	8,347.77	9,356.00
	% Loan	93.03	91.13	90.39	71.24	56.83	11.10	43.72	34.63
Total	Total	4,795.70	9,166.50	1,5898.18	1,8327.48	2,2041.80	25,854.37	29,300.60	3,6351.70
	Grant	1,466.90	2,553.10	5,252.86	1,0090.66	1,3827.50	15,800.85	20,320.73	2,6382.80
	Loan	3,328.80	6,613.40	1,0645.32	8,236.82	8214.30	10,053.52	8,979.88	9,968.90

Source: Pyakuryal, Adhikari and Dhakal (2008); MOF (2009).

- Committing to create reforms agenda through reviewing the progress made and challenges encountered during the implementation of high priority projects
- Developing a new FAP of Nepal and the National Action Plan for Aid Effectiveness in consultation with the development partners
- Building roadmap for trade, investment and private sector development through creating a conducive environment and increasing competitiveness

Altogether 15 meetings have been held to date, including Nepal Donor Consultation Meeting (NDCM) held in 2008 in the form of mini-NDF. Twelve meetings from 1976 to 2000 were held abroad and the subsequent meetings have been conducted in Nepal. The 13th NDF was the first to have been convened in and co-chaired by Nepal, while the 14th was the first to have been led solely by Nepal. Table 8.2 shows the chronology of these meetings.

The outcome of NDF is Government's proposal for a National Action Plan comprising a three-tier framework—overall programme, individual programme and financial modality levels. For harmonization, donors were expected to align their assistance with the Poverty Reduction Strategy (PRS), sector strategies, and the Medium-term Expenditure Framework (MTEF). Harmonization at the external financing modality level, proposes a shift from the traditional project financing to more budget and programme support.

Given that the deep-seated economic, social, regional and ethnic inequalities are the underlying causes of the insurgency, it should be recognized that peace building and development and reform initiatives are mutually reinforcing and need to be pursued simultaneously. The peace accord of November 2006 between the Maoists and Nepal's seven major political parties has made several commitments to reconstruct and repair damaged buildings and other infrastructural facilities and rehabilitate and settle displaced citizens. The country is facing severe macroeconomic difficulties. The savings-investment gap is alarmingly high. This necessitates increased foreign assistance especially to support the peace process and the country's recovery from 10 years of violent conflict. There has been overwhelming external support to help Nepal restoring peace and security as early as possible. For example, the US$514 million of official development assistance received in 2006 financed 81 per cent of 2007–08 capital expenditure and 26.5 per cent of all government expenditure (UNDP, 2010).

Table 8.2
Meetings of Nepal Aid Group/Nepal Development Forum, 1976–2009

Date	Type	Country	Date	Type	Country
Dec 1976	Nepal Aid Group Meetings	Japan	Oct 1990	Nepal Aid Group Meetings	France
May 1978	Nepal Aid Group Meetings	France	Apr 1992	Nepal Aid Group Meetings	France
Jan 1980	Nepal Aid Group Meetings	France	Apr 1996	Nepal Aid Group Meetings	France
Dec 1981	Nepal Aid Group Meetings	France	Apr 2000	Nepal Aid Group Meetings	France
Dec 1983	Nepal Aid Group Meetings	France	Feb 2002	NDF	Nepal
Jan 1986	Nepal Aid Group Meetings	Japan	May 2004	NDF	Nepal
Apr 1987	Nepal Aid Group Meetings	France	Feb 2008	NDCM	Nepal
Nov 1988	Nepal Aid Group Meetings	France	May 2009 (Cancelled)	NDF	Nepal

Source: http://www.mof.gov.np, http://www.http://www.mof.gov.np/ndf2009/ aboutndfndf2009.php (accessed on 20 September 2011).

Significance of Foreign Aid in Budgets and Fiscal Policy

Foreign aid has been a critical component of development agenda in Nepal since its early effort of planned development. As foreign aid is a function of both demand and supply factors, the ever increasing flow of foreign aid can be attributed to both increase in developmental activities and increase in number of donors over the years.

Nepal has historically been practising deficit budgets as a part of its fiscal policy. The fiscal deficit, which is defined as difference between total expenditure and total revenue, shared nearly 50 per cent of total expenditure in early 1990s. With reform in public expenditure and the revenue front under the Enhanced Structural Adjustment Programme (ESAP) during early 1990s, the trend, however, shows a decreasing fiscal deficit in Nepal. The figure decreased to nearly 35 per cent in FY 2000–01 and has further decreased to nearly 33 per cent in FY 2007–08.

The budget deficit, when added foreign grant to fiscal deficit, also shows a similar trend. The budget deficit, as a percentage of total expenditure, which used to be as high as of 45 per cent in FY 1990–91 decreased to nearly 30 per cent in FY 2000–01. In recent years, the budget deficit shares around 20 per cent of total expenditure in Nepal. Moreover, Nepal has not been able to meet the saving-investment gap through domestic sources of financing its expenditure. The total consumption is seen growing over the years accounting nearly 88 per cent of total Gross Domestic Product (GDP) in recent years.

Given high fiscal deficits, high saving-investment gap and low share of domestic borrowing on meeting its expenditure, the role of foreign aid has been crucial in the Nepalese case. With its low per capita income, even if resources are effectively mobilized and directed to the productive sector, the required level of development may not be substantially achieved and, therefore, the need of foreign aid is compelling. Foreign Aid has been a significant component of budget and periodic plans on meeting the expenditure in Nepal. The share of foreign aid in total expenditure of Nepal (grant and loan) is shown in Figure 8.3.

The role of external sources in financing the Budget deficit in Nepal is also crucial. For example, Nepal financed almost 75 per cent of its fiscal deficit by external sources in FY 1999–2000. It was the time when Nepal was just opting for the structural adjustment programme and, therefore, recorded higher fiscal deficits due to increasing national expenditure. Since the flow of foreign aid cannot be attributed to receipts demand due to increasing developmental activities, the supply side might have also played a significant role in having such a higher share due to the commitments of donor partners in the new democratic Nepal. Nevertheless, over the years the dependence on foreign aid seems decreasing.

Available figures show that the share has decreased by almost a quarter accounting for half of the share by foreign aid on fiscal deficits in recent years. Figures show that loan component was substantial during 1990s; however, it has decreased in recent years sharing nearly 17 per cent

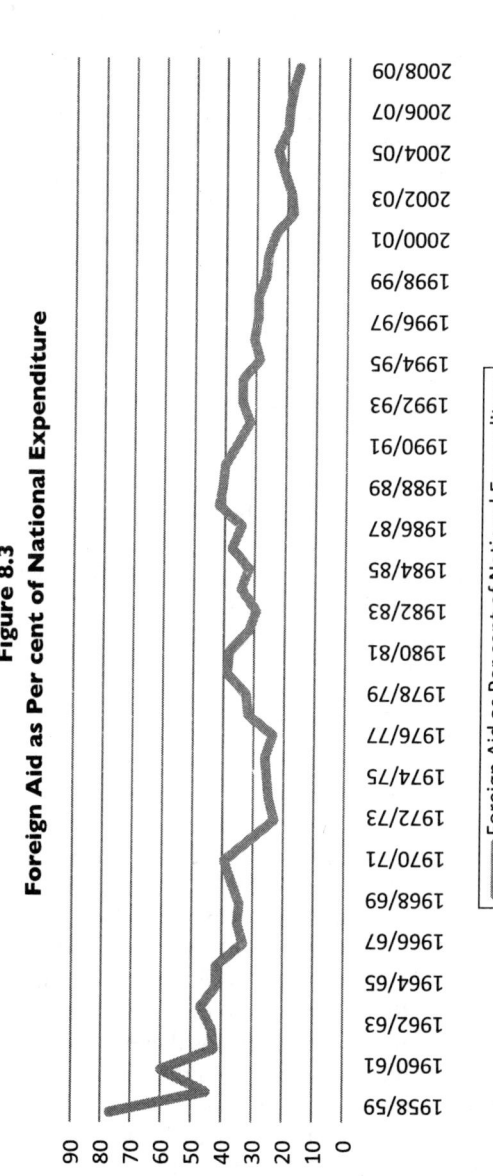

Figure 8.3
Foreign Aid as Per cent of National Expenditure

— Foreign Aid as Per cent of National Expenditure

Source: Pyakuryal, Adhikari and Dhakal (2008); MOF (2009).

of total deficit. As foreign aid is primarily meant to finance developmental activities (except in a few cases of consumption expenditure), it is natural to seek the relationship between development (capital) expenditure and foreign aid. Available statistics show Nepal's dependence on foreign aid to finance its development expenditure. For example, Nepal met its development expenditure fully through foreign aid during the first period plan (1956–61). These figures have, however, decreased over the years; still the share stands at nearly half of development expenditure (Pyakuryal, Adhikari and Dhakal, 2008).

FOREIGN ASSISTANCE AND DEVELOPMENT

Review of Development Priorities

Since 1956 to date, a total of 11 plans have been implemented. The First Plan (1956–61) was followed by the Second (1962–65), Third (1965–70), Fourth (1970–75), Fifth (1975–80), Sixth (1980–85), Seventh (1985–90), Eighth (1992–97), Ninth (1997–2002), 10th Plan (2002–07), and Interim Plan (2007–10) covering a period of over five decades. The second Three Year Plan (2010–13) has recently been endorsed by the Government.

Compared to the four consecutive Plans whose main emphasis was on the establishment of basic infrastructure, the Fifth Plan acknowledged people-oriented development and egalitarian distribution built in the production process. The underlying principle in the Fifth Plan was significantly different since its objective was not only to maximize the output but also to make output consistent with the minimum felt needs of the people (NPC, 1975). The basic objective emphasizes mass-oriented production and maximum utilization of the labour force. The Sixth Plan (1975–80) spelt more loudly on meeting minimum basic needs of the people by giving a new dimension in the planning objectives. Reduction in income inequality, by increasing alternative employment opportunities was therefore the priority of the Sixth Plan. Specific objectives were to increase production at a higher rate by increasing opportunities for productive employment. In view of this, the Seventh Plan attempted to narrow down the gulf between planning and implementation. To achieve this goal, it aimed at building up the productive capacity of the economy by focusing on conserving and expanding the physical resources.

The Eighth Plan, after the restoration of democracy in 1990, was meant to address the aspiration of the people raised during the movements. With the inclusion of a few popular programmes, this Plan gave special focus on sustainable development, poverty reduction and on reducing regional disparities. Despite the fact that Nepal continues to adopt reform programmes, it was realized later that the programme should be tied up with sectoral priorities. The Ninth Plan was tied up with prospective planning and accordingly priority areas were identified. These were, agriculture and forestry; water resources; human resource and social development; industrialization, tourism development and international trade; and physical infrastructure.

The 10th Plan came as Nepal's Poverty Reduction Strategy Paper (PRSP) with a main objective of poverty alleviation. The other objectives, closely tied up with poverty alleviation, were to achieve broad-based sustainable economic growth, social sector development, rural infrastructure and targeted programmes for targeted people. This Plan acknowledged the need for special treatment of marginalized and vulnerable groups of the society, as they failed to reap the benefit of urban sector development.

The three-year Interim Plan came after the end of a decade-long Maoist insurgency in Nepal. Therefore, the prime focus of the Plan was for relief, reconstruction, rehabilitation, reintegration and revival of the economy. Special focus was placed for inclusive growth to accommodate marginalized groups on developmental activities. The overall objective as usual, was to alleviate poverty through pro-poor broad-based economic growth. It also gave emphasis on promoting good governance and effective service delivery, increase in investment in physical infrastructure, social development and inclusive development process.

Sectoral Allocation of Foreign Aid and Policy Priorities in Nepal

While Nepal had experienced major shifts in development priorities over the years, so is the case for foreign financing with regard to these priorities. When Nepal was influenced by democratic socialism, the priorities were on the establishments of public enterprises. Later, Nepal received aid for industrialization along with transport, communication and other physical infrastructure (see Box 8.1).

Box 8.1

Policy Priorities in National Plans

Periods	*Policy Priorities in National Plans*
From 1950 to the 1960s (First to Third Plans)	Emphasis was placed on 'infrastructure development' (roads, communications, power supply etc.) based on the need for national integration.
During the 1970s Period (Fourth to Fifth Plans)	The concept of 'regional development' was introduced through these plans. The country was divided into four Development Regions. A north–south axis for development was established in each of these regions that linked the Terai and the Hills. Development bases were planned along these axes. In addition, Nepal went ahead with the construction of an east–west road that would link these districts, and pursued national economic integration and development.
During the 1980s (Sixth to Seventh Plans)	Top priority was given to the 'production sector', particularly agriculture, rather than infrastructure development in the past. It aimed at maximum use of the labour force.
Eighth Plan (1992–97)	The Eighth Five Year Plan was formulated during the initiation of institutionalizing the process of democratization by promulgating the new constitution in 1990 and the re-emergence of a parliamentary system in 1991. The major objectives were sustainable economic development, poverty reduction and reduction of regional disparities through decentralization. Prioritized areas were the promotion of agriculture, energy development,

(continued box 8.1)

(continued box 8.1)

	infrastructure development in rural areas, job creation, population control, the promotion of industry and tourism, export promotion, macroeconomic stability and civil service reform.
Ninth Plan (1998–2002)	The priorities of the Plan were tied up with prospective plans and areas of focus were agriculture and forestry; water resources; human resource and social development; industrialization, tourism development and international trade and physical infrastructure. Other initiatives included science and technology, power sector development; utilization of ecological and biological diversity; regional balance; development of disadvantaged sectors; productivity enhancement and quality management; decentralization and strengthening local self-government and administrative reform.
10th Plan (2002–07)	The 10th Plan came as the Nepal PRSP with the main objective of poverty reduction. The other objectives, closely linked with its major objective, was to achieve broad based sustainable economic growth, social sector development, rural infrastructure and a few targeted programs. As such, Nepal started MTEF, Immediate Action Plan (IAP) and the development of policy matrix. National Planning Commission prioritized development projects into P1, P2 and P3 categories and 100 per cent funding was guaranteed for P1 projects.

(continued box 8.1)

(continued box 8.1)

Three Year Interim Plan (2007/08–2009/10)	This plan had given special emphasis on increasing the public investment to provide relief, increase employment opportunities and peace establishment as well as reconstruction, rehabilitation and reintegration and the revival of the economy. Special attention has been given to the woman, Dalit, Adibasi, Janajati, the Madhesi community, low income groups, and those excluded from the economic, social and regional development processes of the country. The main objective of this plan is to generate an experience of a direct feeling of change in the lives of the general public by supporting in the establishment of peace and reducing the existing unemployment, poverty and inequality in the country.

Source: NPC (various plans).

The sectoral allocation of foreign aid (Figure 8.4) shows that Nepal has been receiving aid in the areas of agriculture including irrigation and forestry sector; transport, power and communication; industry and commerce sector; social services sector.

During early 1990s, Nepal received a higher quantum of foreign aid in transport, power and communication followed by industry and commerce; and agriculture. A year after Nepal implemented the Eighth Five Year Plan in 1992, the agriculture sector received the highest share of foreign aid. However, this trend was aborted in the following year and again, transport, power and communication sector continued to receive the highest share of foreign aid flow in Nepal. This shows a divergence between National plan's priority and actual areas of funding. Nepal continued to receive a larger share, though declining, on transport, power and communication up to FY 2003–04. Trend reveals that the social sector has been financed with an increasing share over the years right from early 1990s to recent years. After 2003–04, the social sector has been receiving the highest share of foreign aid in

Figure 8.4
Sectoral Allocation of Foreign Aid, 1990–2009

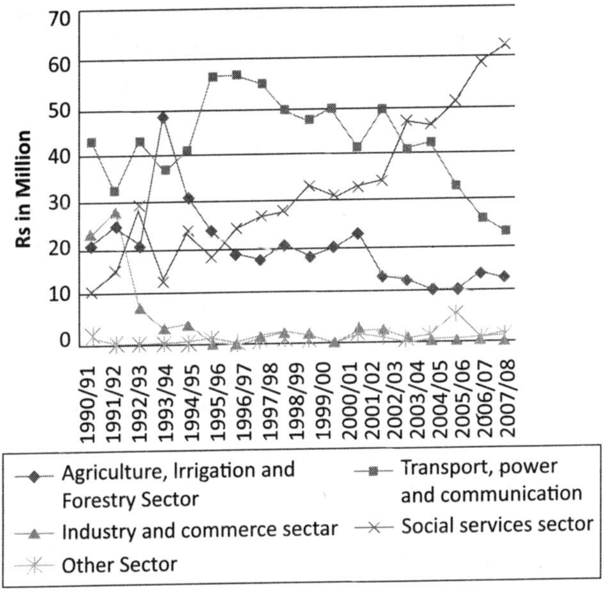

Legend:
- Agriculture, Irrigation and Forestry Sector
- Industry and commerce sectar
- Other Sector
- Transport, power and communication
- Social services sector

Source: MOF (2009).

· Nepal. The industry and commerce sector has been receiving a nominal share of foreign aid in recent years.

While Nepal had different policy priorities at different National Plans, there are no one-to-one correspondence between policy priorities and areas with higher investment. This is not only a case of national expenditure on less prioritized areas through domestic source of financing expenditure; rather the same story is experienced in case of foreign aid. For example, despite a major poverty thrust given during the Eighth and Ninth Plan period, the external resource allocation as outlined above does not demonstrate a strong linkage between focused priority and resource allocation. The total resource flow during the period of 1990 to 1998 in the basic social services sectors, which includes primary schooling, drinking water and sanitation, primary health, and family planning, has increased on an average annual rate of 11.4 per cent.

However, the total volume of aid is found to be inadequate to address the poverty reduction objective. During the same period, the average annual rate of increase in the education sector remained at 5.3 per cent. In the year 1998, the total disbursement from all external sources to basic social services amounted to US$59.4 million. Similarly, the disbursement in the education sector amounted to US$27.8 million, representing 6 per cent of the total disbursement. The education sector suffered a decline of 37.3 per cent in 1998 as compared to 1997. Although before 2002 the inflow of aid did not show proper matching with the need and priority of the nation, the situation has improved after that period. The main reason behind that is the implementation of FAP and the 10th Plan based on the PRSP. If we take development expenditure as a measuring rod of prioritization of the sectors, then estimated development expenditure during the first MTEF period (2002/03–2004/05) is highest for energy sector (23,164 million), followed by agriculture, forestry and fisheries (19,268 million), and transport (13,189 million). The aid received by Nepal during 1998–2005, as mentioned above, also follows the same ranking. This is the indication of the donor group's consistency with priority of the country (Pyakuryal, Adhikari and Dhakal, 2008).

There is no doubt that foreign aid has contributed to the development of Nepal. In his study, (Bhattarai, 2009) found that aid is positively related to per capita real GDP in the long run. He also concludes that aid effectiveness increases with the increase in good policy environment in the long run. Therefore, the prime issue here is not whether foreign aid has contributed to the GDP and development of Nepal; rather the issue is whether foreign aid has been used effectively? Has it been able to channelize to the most productive sectors so that development activities can be accelerated? Is there scope for improving the allocative efficiency of foreign aid?

External assistance is not value free. The aid targeted for developmental projects is often alleged to have been directed towards the political and strategic interests. However, if the key objective of Overseas Development Assistance (ODA) is to promote development, it should be a measure to link aid to the priorities of the recipient countries. Therefore, managing foreign assistance has usually been quite poor to access aid to needy countries in general and targeted beneficiaries in the recipient countries in particular.

Contribution of Foreign Assistance to Development Goals

The criticism that aid has actually hampered development goals of the poor countries is drawing attention to the majority of aid practitioners. Easterly (2006) is of the view that foreign aid has not achieved much to achieving development goals. He states,

> A tragedy of the world's poor has been that the West spent US$2.3 trillion on foreign aid over the last five decades and still had not managed to get 12-cent medicines to children to prevent half of malaria deaths. The West spent US$2.3 trillion and still had not managed to get four-dollar bed nets to poor families. The West spent US$ 2.3 trillion and still had not managed to get three dollars to each new mother to prevent five million deaths.

It is indeed a tragedy that so much well-meaning compassion did not bring expected results for needy people. Willingly or unwillingly, the donors' approach has merely been to de-link sizeable amount of assistance with need-based priority.

This section elaborates the reasons for declining of the volume of foreign aid; the conditionality imposed by the donors and its implications; and difficulties created by inadequate access of the grant to poor countries. Such elaboration is helpful to find out why foreign aid has not supported development goals of the recipient countries.

The conditional aid loans based on policy reforms provided to Africa and many other countries including Latin America just remained discouraging. Easterly says the evidence is stark: US$568 billion were spent on aid to Africa, and yet the typical African country is no richer today than 40 years ago. The structural adjustment failed linking policy reforms and economic growth.

The rich donors are always behind their commitment to offer 0.7 per cent of their gross national income as official development aid. The OECD reveals, when aid is broken down by regions over time, the poorest countries get less of the foreign aid. For example, of the aid that has been delivered, roughly a quarter seems to have gone to the poorest regions from all Development Assistance Committee (DAC) aid since 1970. The figures show net ODA in US dollars terms is not discouraging. However, net ODA as a per cent of Gross National Income (GNI) is still below the commitments (OECD, 2010) (Figure 8.5). The level

Figure 8.5
Net ODA 2009 as Per cent of GNI

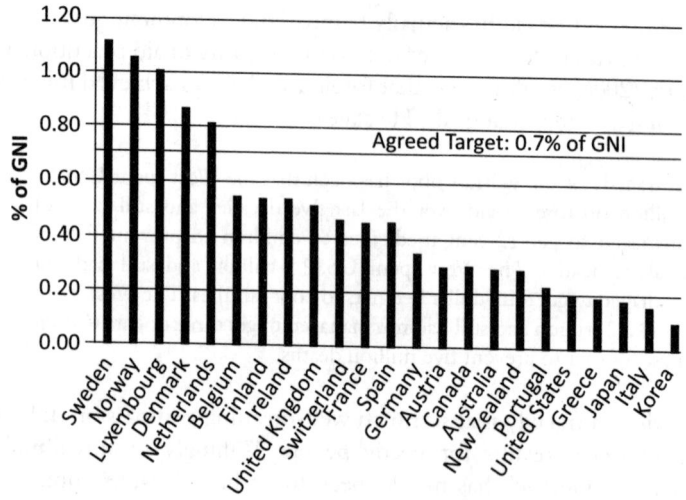

Source: OECD (2010).

of aid did not increase when GNI of rich countries increased. Instead of 0.7 per cent, the amount of aid has been around 0.2 to 0.4 per cent, some US$100 billion short during 1990–2009 (Figure 8.6).

There are a number of factors that have led to the decline in aid. Some of the reasons include an ideology shift on governments and markets; increasing number of countries competing for development funds; and donors' differing interpretation on what constitutes development assistance. Similarly, there have been significant increases in non-development aid. The expanded categories of ODA involve debt relief; administrative costs; grants to NGOs and domestic agencies to support emergency relief operations; provision of surplus commodities of little economic value; and technical cooperation grants to pay for the services of nationals of the donor countries.

However, some recent findings on the contribution of foreign aid to a nation's development goals show some positive results. The findings show developmental aid is satisfactory but not enough. For example, the 2008 Survey on Monitoring the Paris Declaration (PD) covering close to US$45 billion of development aid in altogether 55 countries

Figure 8.6
Official Aid, 1990–2009

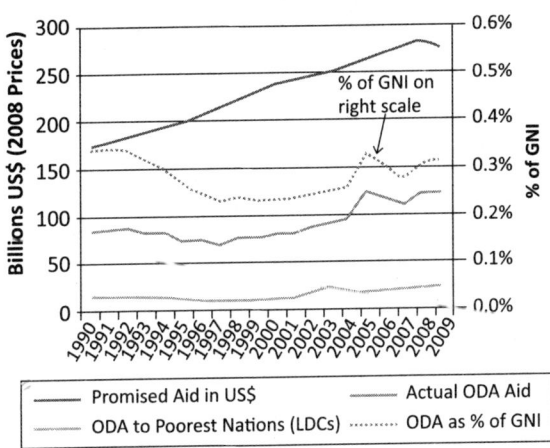

Source: OECD (2010).

shows that both the donors and recipient countries have made some progress towards achieving the international commitments. The early implementation of the PD also shows that there has been a significant and tangible strengthening of national development policies and strategies (Deutscher and Fyson, 2009).

The Nepalese experience too reveals the same concerns. There has been, indeed, a large discrepancy between aid commitment and disbursement. The trend shows that the problem has even been more serious during the last decade (Table 8.3). Since flow of foreign aid is also the function of governance, such high discrepancy is attributed to political instability in the country during those time periods. Such variations between commitment and disbursement, has implications for budgetary practices in Nepal.

The budget is prepared on the basis of commitment. The reduction in the commitment inevitably will have the negative impact on the achievement of development goals. The reasons for the differences between the commitment and disbursements have been attributed to lack of matching funds; weaknesses on making the claims for reimbursement; and inability to fulfill the agreed grants and loan conditionality.

Table 8.3

Foreign Aid: Commitment and Disbursement (Rs Million)

	1997–2000	2000–01	2001–02	2002–03	2003–04	2004–05	2005–06	2006–07	2007–08	2008–09
Bilateral Commitment	12,959.53	17,495.90	18,438.70	15,312.40	8,223.60	21,225.40	14,755.50	17,706.10	13,106.40	22,355.50
Bilateral Disbursement	5,131.47	2,771.20	4,675.30	10,044.40	9,013.20	9,230.80	7,658.40	16,406.43	10,207.75	9,333.10
Share of Disbursement in Commitment (%)	39.84	15.84	25.36	65.60	109.60	43.49	51.90	92.66	77.88	41.75
Multilateral Commitment	10,647.97	13,791.00	14,789.00	27,890.30	15,514.40	16,926.90	6,168.70	19,316.80	36,079.80	20,778.80
Multilateral Disbursement	11,591.87	16,026.20	9,709.50	5,841.10	9,899.20	14,426.50	14,383.40	9,447.94	19,092.85	27,018.60
Share of Disbursement in Commitment (%)	152.22	116.21	65.65	20.94	63.81	85.23	233.17	48.91	52.92	130.03
Total Commitment	23,607.53	31,287.00	33,227.70	4,3202.70	23,738.00	38,152.30	20,924.20	37,022.90	49,186.20	43,134.30
Total Disbursement	16,723.33	18,797.40	14,384.80	15,885.50	18,912.40	23,657.30	22,041.80	25,854.37	29,300.60	36,351.70
Share of Bilateral Commitment in Total Commitment (%)										
Share of Bilateral Disbursement	75.10	60.08	43.29	36.77	79.67	62.01	105.34	69.83	59.57	84.28

Source: MOF (2009).

KEY ISSUES

Opportunity Costs

Given the declining exports, decelerating remittances, reduced foreign exchange reserves and sustained balance of payments deficits, Nepal lacks domestic resources to supplement the budget deficit by contributing to development expenditures. In the short-run, available information shows that the external funding supplements domestic resources and their transfers assist in achieving short-run growth targets. Therefore, foreign flow of funds can be expected to contribute to long-term development by releasing hurdles associated with low incomes.

Whatever levels the assistance is received, it has its cost. Shah (2010) states:

1. Aid is often wasted on conditions that the recipient must use overpriced goods and services from donor countries.
2. Most aid does not actually go to the poorest who would need it the most.
3. Aid amounts are dwarfed by rich country protectionism that denies market access for poor country products, while rich nations use aid as a lever to open poor country markets to their products.
4. Large projects or massive grand strategies often fail to help the vulnerable; money can often be embezzled away.

Nepal suffers inexperience in assessing benefit and costs with regard to donors' design in conditionality in the aided projects. Therefore, Nepal has most of the time accepted disparate conditionality even after the execution of FAP in 2002. For example, the conditions that were tied up with aid in Nepal were:

1. All required construction material, equipment, vehicles for the project should be procured from the donor country's market.
2. All consultants and technicians should be from the donor country.
3. Contract should be provided for the firm recommended by the donor (Pyakuryal, Adhikari and Dhakal, 2008).

Partly, as result of principal-agent problem, donors often apply conditions on aid programmes to encourage recipients to act more in accord with the donors' interests (Radelet, 2006). In general, policy conditionality is largely associated with the IMF and World Bank. However, most of other donors also use such instrument.

The practice of enforcing conditionality tied to aid has constrained the use of appropriate and less costly technology, materials and services and has increased opportunity cost. On account of various policy-related and procedural conditionality, which are at times not compatible with the prevailing situation and the needs of the country, aid has had not only a limited beneficial impact but has, at times, run counter to the outcomes expected from some projects.

Debt Burden

The foreign loan, due to low interest rate and long maturity period, can be regarded as the grant in current price. This encourages government to utilize the foreign loan. Nepal received more than 450 per cent loan after restoration of democracy than during the Panchayat regime. But the problem of the loan is that the country has to pay interest and principal regularly at the prevailing exchange rate, not in the exchange rate that prevailed when receiving the loan. The current appreciation of Nepalese Currency should be considered as a temporary phenomenon. The time series data reveals huge loss from currency depreciation (Pyakuryal, Adhikari and Dhakal, 2008).

Principal repayment and interest payment is creating heavy pressure on the recurrent expenditure. Table 8.4 shows the pressure of foreign debt servicing in the economy. The stock of net outstanding external debt of the Nepalese government in 1996–97 was Rs 132,086.8 million and it reached to Rs 249, 965.4 million in the year 2004–05.

Low mobilization of domestic resources, increasing dependence on aid, and failure to increase aid productivity has raised doubts among the development partners about ineffective debt planning and debt management. It is now high time to address the critical issue that in Nepal, aid has failed to address wider inequality in income and mass poverty. Nepal's debt service position, though within sustainable limits, is consuming quite a significant chunk of fresh resources, which could otherwise be used for productive purposes. Its debt service ratio is remaining around one third to one fourth of the annual regular

Table 8.4
Foreign Debt in Nepal (Rs Million)

Year	Borrowing	Repayments	Interest payments	Net outstanding
1996–97	8,963.9	2,102.4	1,247.0	132,086.8
1997–98	13,850.9	2,780.2	1,421.0	161,208.0
1998–99	10,839.5	3,196.5	1,549.0	169,465.9
1999–00	12,362.4	3,681.1	1,640.3	190,691.2
2000–01	11,104.3	4,500.6	1,700.8	200,404.4
2001–02	10,049.5	4,751.4	1,816.1	220,125.6
2002–03	6,192.4	5,497.5	2,021.7	223,433.2
2003–04	9,597.4	5,767.1	2,141.8	232,779.3
2004–05	7,743.7	5,954.5	2,146.8	219,641.9
2005–06	3,732.8	6,987.0	2,163.8	233,968.6
2006–07	11,856.8	7,538.8	2,055.7	216,628.9
2007–08	8,573.9	7,869.4	2,145.3	249,965.4
2008–09	7,764.2	10,120.3	2,373.7	27,7040.4

Source: Pyakuryal, Adhikari and Dhakal (2008); MOF (2009).

expenditure since the very beginning. With the dominance of loan portions in the foreign assistance (except after 2002–03) and the maturity of debts incumbent upon the nation, a cautious approach to proper management of the valuable external resources is deemed a necessity.

Complementing to the discussion on debt, it is necessary to elaborate briefly about the linkages between domestic as well as external borrowing with regard to Nepal's increasing savings-investment gap. When supply is relatively inelastic because of the rising demand for post-war recovery, rehabilitation and reconstruction, an increase in the prices and wages of the skilled workers is a natural phenomenon. Nepal's macroeconomic difficulties have put heavy pressures on high price rise in food and non-food products. Consecutively for last two years, Nepal suffers double digit inflation. Domestic borrowing is constrained by liquidity crunch and declining credit flow to the private sector. Higher side of total public spending is covered by recurrent expenditure because capital expenditure hardly covers 30 per cent of the budget estimate. Secondly, disbursement from development partners is steadily declining as compared to their commitments because current political instability is contributing more to declining aid utilization. This strengthens the case for analyzing impact of foreign aid by diagnosing relationship between political instability and foreign aid regime.

With the dominance of the loan portion, in average, in foreign assistance and the maturity of debt, the stress on the regular expenditure for debt servicing will be further widened. It demonstrates the increasing pressure on the available resources, creating difficulty on adequately financing socio-economic infrastructure building and maintenance, social welfare, and poverty alleviation programmes. The national priority on poverty-focused programme demands additional resources for the vital sectors such as education and health. However, the growing burden of debt, which is estimated to rise exorbitantly, will restrict further increase of financial resources in the social sector.

Conditionality

Conditionality tied up with foreign aid has been under considerable controversy in the developing world. Partly as a result of the principal-agent problem, donors often apply conditions on aid programmes to encourage recipients to act more in accord with the donors' interests (Radelet, 2006). As stated above, enforcing conditionality has increased overhead costs of the projects. On account of various policy-related and procedural conditionality, which are at times not compatible with the prevailing situation and the needs of the country, aid has had not only a limited beneficial impact but has, at times, run counter to the outcomes expected from some projects.

Policy conditionality is most often associated with the IMF and World Bank, but all donors use conditions to some extent (Radelet, 2006). However, the conditions from multilateral agency, leaving some exceptions, are less problematic than that of bilateral donor. Donors may also have their own vested interest for providing aid, such as political benefit, benefit in trade or providing employment for their own citizens. Bilateral aid is often designed at least partially to help support the economic interests of certain firms or sectors in the donor country.

Beside these problems, shortcomings in institutional capacities, the country's geographical location and mountainous terrain, widespread poverty, high rate of population growth and urgent environmental concerns, among others, pose daunting challenges to development and the effective absorption of aid (MOF, 2002–03).

Effectiveness of Foreign Aid

Often foreign aid is criticized for not contributing to economic growth in general and poverty reduction in particular. Foreign aid (development assistance) is regarded as being too much, or wasted on corrupt recipient governments despite any good intentions from donor countries (Shah, 2010). While there are also a number of issues for effectiveness of foreign aid, for example, higher level of democracy, human rights, good governance, liberalization and economic reforms backed by decelerating state of corruption, and mitigating conflict in recipient countries; the central debate is over its overall contribution to national development in a real sense. These issues are important since it is often argued that foreign aid, being supply side driven attributing solely to the motives and objectives of donors, does not contribute much to developmental activities of national priorities.

The Government of Nepal undertook a survey on monitoring the 2005 PD in 2008 largely to judge the effectiveness of foreign aid. The findings reveal discrepancies on the part of donors to comply with their own commitments. The result shows, that it has negatively affected the effectiveness of the aided projects by putting more pressures on the already overburdened Nepal's bureaucracy. The major concern for accepting foreign aid is to reduce cost and also increase its benefits. Therefore, to increase the effectiveness of foreign aid, the PD on Aid Effectiveness was endorsed. The Declaration had five basic principles, that is, *(a)* Ownership, *(b)* Alignment, *(c)* Harmonization, *(d)* Managing for Results, and *(e)* Mutual Accountability, that promotes development.

The survey addressed 12 indicators to measure aid effectiveness. These indicators include: *(a)* partners have operational development strategy, *(b)* reliable country system, *(c)* aid flows are aligned with national priorities, *(d)* strengthen capacity by coordinated support *(e)* use of country public financial management system and use of country procurement systems, *(f)* strengthen capacity by avoiding parallel implementation structure, *(g)* aid is more predictable, *(h)* aid is untied, *(i)* use of common arrangements and procedures, *(j)* encourage shared analysis, *(k)* result oriented frameworks, and *(l)* mutual accountability (http://www.ner.com.np/vol-1/issue-2/54-performance-and-effectiveness-of-foreign-aid-in-nepal.html). The survey shows, out of Rs 100 foreign aid extended to Nepal, only Rs 74 passes through the government budgetary system. The rest Rs 26 is outside government's information, which is anticipated that the donors have probably executed directly.

The review of available literatures reflects, that in development economics, policy reforms occupy a key position in crucial development dialogue both in developed and developing countries. Literatures on aid effectiveness show varying impact under various policy environments with differing quality of governance. As explained above, aid effectiveness study on Nepal shows that the relationship between aid and per capita real GDP is found to be negative in both aggregate and disaggregated forms in the short-run. Aid is effective when it is moderate in volume and counter-productive when it increases in size, i.e., when it exceeds the absorptive capacity (Brynt, 2005). High level of aid erodes institutional quality, increases rent-seeking and corruption, and therefore, negatively affects growth (Knack, 2000).

FUTURE POLICY PRIORITIES

Role of Aid in the Context of Costs and Benefits

Draft FAP, 2009 intends to develop and adopt a National Action Plan (NAP) on Aid Effectiveness both by the Government of Nepal and donors, which is expected to formulate a roadmap on foreign aid management in the spirit of the PD on Aid Effectiveness and Accra Agenda for Action. The FAP will help develop a common aid effectiveness platform as envisaged through the NAP which will lead Nepal's aid regime towards properly identifying key priority areas, contribute to harmonization and bring about sustainable outcomes.

Besides humanitarian interest, the benefit and cost of external assistance largely depends on donor-recipient strategic interests. At times, strategic interest may overlook economic concerns, and aid at whatever level is executed, the benefit may exceed cost. The US has earmarked US$75 billion, US$65 billion, US$3.25 billion and US$3 billion in 2010 annual budget respectively for Afghanistan, Iraq, Pakistan and Israel (http://www.jpost.com/Opinion/Op-EdContributors/Article. aspx? ID=172721). Therefore, it is tricky to precisely define the relative merit of the expenditures in these countries.

Foreign aid has both cost and benefits to the recipient and donors. To some extent, aid has been an investment in maintaining global stability. Globally, about one billion survive on less than US$1 a day. The challenge is to bring about real change in the lives of children and families living in extreme poverty. In the case of Nepal, access to aid has not been a problem. The key obstacle to address people's expectations for better life through aid-oriented priority projects is the inability to utilize aid.

About Rs 48 billion in foreign aid was committed to Nepal by development partners during the FY 2008–09. By 9 July 2010, Nepal has received Rs 97 billion in foreign aid commitment. In relation to the encouragement received by increasing aid commitment, as stated above, aid utilization has been minimal (MOF, 2010).

Box 8.2 offers the efficacy of foreign aid, a case of US aid to developing countries.

There is tons of money in wasteful and ineffective economic development aid and other non-essential accounts. Since the Second World War, the US has spent nearly US$1 trillion (in 1997 dollars) on foreign aid. The impact remained discouraging. Countries, who received assistance experienced debt, dependence and poverty. The USAID admits, in 1993, much of the investment financed by USAID and other donors between 1960 and 1980 has disappeared without a trace and government-to-government transfers could not generate self-sustaining economic growth. Not only this, over US$2 billion investments in Zaire served no purpose (Bandow, 1997).

Box 8.2

What Does US Foreign Aid Buy?

- For just one penny, clean drinking water for a family of six can be provided.
- One child can be immunized for the cost of a piece of bubble gum (16 cents).
- For the cost of a magazine (less than US$5), a treated bed net can be provided to one person to fight malaria.
- For the cost of a movie ticket (US$7.50), a daily dose of HIV/AIDS medicine can be purchased.
- For the cost of a dinner entrée (US$20), prenatal care and a healthy delivery for one woman can be ensured.
- For the monthly cost of cable television (US$40), a child can be educated for one year in the developing world (http://www.care.org/getinvolved/advocacy/pdfs/foreignaid.pdf).

Source: Hockstein (2004).

In the past, many of the biggest recipients of foreign assistance have been among the globe's worst economic performers. A hundred nation's review also shows that long-term aid is not a means to create growth. To complement to the widely acknowledged view that the impact of foreign aid is positive under the better policy, some empirical findings can be illustrated. During the year 1980 to 1994, countries with a rating of A or B, averaged real per capita GDP growth of 2.4 per cent, however, 27 countries whose economy was graded an F actually shrunk (http://www.cato.org/pub_display.php?pub_id=6569). The benefit and cost may therefore, interpreted in terms of policy success and policy failure.

Domestic Policy and the Future of Foreign Aid

The role of ODA in recipient countries is a contentious issue that often evokes emotions. Majority thinks it sustains corrupt governments and works as a disincentive for governments to support domestic resource mobilization. There is another school of thought that presumes foreign aid complements domestic savings and supports growth and poverty reduction in recipient countries (Radelet, 2006).

Nepal's savings-investment gap reveals that the ODA will continue to play a significant role in supporting development expenditure and, therefore, Nepal will remain reliant on ODA in the shortrun. However, FAP documents show that domestic resource mobilization should be the basis for financing long-term sustained growth. The million dollar question is how aid can be designed to enhance capacity for domestic resource mobilization for sustained and inclusive growth.

As foreign aid commitment is in increasing trend, the governments' reluctance to expedite additional venues for revenue collection including the revision of non-tax revenue, has encouraged identifying the resource gap and filling it up with ODA. This is the reason why such approach has been inimical to increase savings and tax collection. The diversion of the bulk of resources to meet Millennium Development Goals (MDGs), reflects a suspicion to undermine the development of productive capacity which is so crucial for dynamic and sustained growth (ESCAP, 2009) The consensus is needed either to justify or falsify the understanding that financing of social sectors is not achieved at the expense of financing of the economic infrastructure and production sectors since these sectors should not be in competition with each other, as financing for economic infrastructure can make a positive contribution to growth and generate more revenue for financing social sectors (ESCAP, 2009).

External assistance has both economic and strategic dimensions. Even the 'food' assistance is linked to security concerns. For example, 'Feed the Future' is the US' new foreign policy initiative because Americans believe global hunger as one of their moral challenges for developmental efforts. Such initiative is taken as a model for development, based on partnership not patronage. The bottom line of food assistance is to monitor national security through such initiatives. Accepting aid blindly as offered by the donors, should not therefore, be the future aid policy. It should rather be integrated strictly into the country's development priorities based on donor-specific packages, where the benefit of accepting aid is higher than the cost of its rejection. The recent policy of the new government of the Federal Democratic Republic of Nepal is in line with this spirit. Inclusive of foreign assistance, the policy states of safeguarding sovereignty, national unity, territorial integrity, independence and self respect, national security, foreign policy, utilization of water resources and mobilization of foreign aid according to the national interests of the country.

Approaching 'New Donors' Such as China and Middle Eastern Countries

Literature shows China wants to test itself how it can be a new international power centre by extending development assistance to Asia and Africa. Many think Africa can be taken as a test case for China to experience its own potential role in the world. Secondly, observers believe that as both China and United States are oil consumers, there is potential for US-China cooperation in the region (Kurlantzick, Shinn and Minxin, 2006). In recent years, as communist parties combined together are larger than democratic parties, China's advantage in Nepal to neutralize political risks is higher compared to even India.

China's policy towards African nations has become more active in recent years. China is concerned about depending on too few energy sources; Africa is a good place for China to expand its sources because it is rich in natural gas and oil, and Chinese companies are sometimes better equipped to deal with the political risks that exist in some African countries than Western multinationals. China is also looking to make friends and project its influence globally in order to isolate Taiwan and appear like a great power. Furthermore, many African nations may find China's development model of state-driven development without political reform attractive, particularly since some of the Washington Consensus reforms have not always reduced poverty in Africa. Also, China has the added benefit that aid and public diplomacy decrease the threat of China as an economic competitor against some African nations and increase access to African markets for Chinese companies.

China being itself a developing country, has additional advantages to understand the failures of Washington Consensus and develop a separate model for development based on their political system and also their eagerness to become a helping hand in trade negotiations. It is realized that after the peace accord of seven party alliances with the Maoists in 2006, the frequency of visits by Chinese diplomats and leaders is in increasing trend to strengthen age-old relations.

Nepal's bilateral deal with China is smooth. As the history of Nepal–China bilateral economic ties is comfortable if not very encouraging, the effort should focus on identifying mutually beneficial areas of cooperation for increased bilateral trade by evaluating the successes and failures from both ends. The authorities in both countries should not be preoccupied with controlling imports than promoting exports.

Information is available, which indicates China's desire to increase trade to Nepal amounting to US$30 billion by 2025. The planned highway to connect Nepal to Tibet and the near completion of the Kathmandu-Rasuwagadhi road is expected to enhance Nepal-China trade relations. China is looking forward to assist Nepal to connect China from the eastern part of Nepal. The repair and widening of the Kathmandu-Syabrubeshi road can also promote religious tourism by encouraging Nepali and Indian pilgrim tourists to go to Mansarovar and Kailash in a day or two (http://www.kantipuronline.com/kolnews. php?&nid=12147).

In 2002, when China became more liberal, her trade-to-GDP ratio reached 75 per cent. It remains at only 33 per cent for South Asia. The problem in Nepal and whole of South Asia is the negligence of pursuing trade facilitation measures by emphasizing on the growth induced trade expansion by linking trade expansion with industrial expansion. This lesson can be learnt from China. If this effort is made, the fundamentals of market economy will be functional and it will be the supply and demand forces operating in the trading countries that determine competitiveness.

China's aid is guided by three major elements to make the most of her limited aid funds. These factors are the preferential loan with interest subsidies by the Chinese government; joint venture and co-operation for China's aid projects; and gratuitous assistance. The first 'Agreement between China and Nepal on Economic Aid' was signed in October 1956 (http://www.fmprc.gov.cn/ce/cenp/eng/ChinaNepal/Economic/t167780.htm).

Since then, different agreements and Protocol have promoted financial and technical assistance to Nepal based on the form of gratuitous assistance. It is an opportunity to pursue economic ties with China which has sustained over the last 25 years, the highest growth rate of income that has ever been achieved by any major economy. Nepal should learn from China to manage and utilize the country's own resources and also the way China has successfully maintained the stability in inflation and growth rate.

Based on Nepal's competitive strength and China's potential, the historical ties between the two countries offers plenty of scope for bilateral economic and trade cooperation. China is concerned about holding negotiations with South Asian nations on how to make trade in the mountainous border region more convenient. Nepal should actively be involved in the development and management of the proposed special trade transit point that links India and China for the convenient and fair border trade among the entire South Asian countries. This initiative can offer Nepal plenty of spin-off benefits.

The combination of Chinese capital and technology with Nepal's untapped resources can no doubt benefit both countries enormously. Nepal can offer good opportunities to China in investing in agro-based and forest-based industries, hydropower, construction materials, banking and financial institutions, the production of cement, electronics, electrical items, medicinal herbs and pharmaceuticals, fertilizers, IT sector, solar and hydropower, training of professionals and the promotion of regional tourism.

To find out who is funding what and where, some 36 bilateral and multilateral development donors have made their aid and loan figures available online. The donors, not members of the DAC, who are non-traditional aid givers, contribute more to their neighbours than DAC donors (http://www.irinnews.org/report.aspx?ReportId=88601). Table 8.5 lists the top 10 non-DAC bilateral and multilateral donors in 2007.

Table 8.5
Top 10 Non-DAC Donors in 2007 (in US$)

Non-DAC bilateral donors		Non-DAC multilateral bank donors	
Kuwait	667,333,097	European Bank for Reconstruction and Development	7,662,974,112
Qatar	95,000,000	Corporación Andina de Fomento	6,606,000,000
South Africa	53,756,417	Arab Fund for Economic and Social Development	1,320,893,178
Thailand	16,121,634	OPEC	723,631,400
Iceland	7,223,328	International Fund for Agricultural Development	548,528,000
Brazil	6,495,261	World Bank Managed Trust Funds	540,617,925
Lithuania	3,167,079	Caribbean Development Bank	189,073,000
Monaco	2,899,963	Arab Bank for Economic Development in Africa	179,600,000
Hungary	2,696,839	World Bank Guarantee	160,000,000
Estonia	2,307,779	World Bank Carbon Offset	102,431,525

Source: http://www.irinnews.org/report.aspx?ReportId=88601

As hunger and malnutrition claim more lives than AIDS, Saudi Arabia's donations especially in these areas is commendable. World Food Programme (WFP) has praised the kingdom for major increases in its support in 2006 to help WFP fight hunger worldwide, inclusive of the assistance in focusing more on tuberculosis and malaria combined among young children. The Government of Saudi Arabia's contribution of nearly US$31 million in 2006 alone was a tenfold increase compared to 2005. In the Middle East, Saudi is by far the biggest donor to WFP's global activities and the 16th largest donor overall to the UN food aid agency (http://www.wfp.org/stories/saudi-arabia-becomes-leading-donor-fighting-hunger-worldwide).

By 2007, Saudi Arabia contributed US$1 billion to the Islamic Solidarity Fund for Development (ISFD). This fund is linked to support achieving UN's MDGs. Saudi is also the largest donor to a US$10 billion poverty-reduction fund, which is set up by the Islamic

Development Bank (IDB). This fund will specifically target fostering sustainable economic growth and job creation, reducing illiteracy, eradicating diseases and epidemics. It is used for developing basic infrastructure as well (ArabianBusiness.com/(http://www.arabianbusiness.com/515679-saudi-largest-donor-to-10bn-poverty-reduction-fund).

Nepal's political environment is fragile, which is suspected to reverse to conflict due to the set-back in development. Although, Nepal has almost a decade long experience in administering aid policy, people allege that the decisions with regard to the quality of grants, loans and aid and criterion to administer, is still dictated by multilateral institutions such as the World Bank and IMF. Turning towards Arabian sources of grants, it is found that although enthusiasm is found to cover broader areas of development, it still is very modest, and is less than that of Sweden alone (Chacra, 2006).

Exit Policy for Aid

Nepal's FAP needs to be re-visited after the country was declared a federal democratic republic. The review is important because of several reasons:

1. Experiences learnt from the implementation of FAP, 2002.
2. There have been efforts to re-design political and economic architecture.
3. Nepal has also endorsed the regional and global effort to improve aid effectiveness and donor harmonization, including the Paris Principles on Aid Effectiveness 2005 and Accra Agenda for Action (AAA), 2008.
4. The need for redesigning FAP and priority in line with the proposed federal structure.

Furthermore, Nepal's FAP emphasizes on the issue of national ownership and leadership as well as the serious treatment in the course of foreign aid management as stated in the Paris Principles. The challenge to make local governments economically a viable unit demands sustained and accelerated economic growth based on government's new federalist economic structure, which is under preparation. To complement such changed policy priority, the foreign aid needs to be increasingly geared towards these new contexts. To make external aid responsive to growth, donors should also be prepared to fit into the changed priority areas.

Despite the heavy flow of foreign aid, especially after the promulgation of FAP 2002, the review of macroeconomic indicators reveals that the country is not able to optimize the gain from aid. Problems visualized were lack of ownership by the government in the development projects, particularly those financed by donors; lack of leadership and direction by the government, particularly in expenditure prioritization and taking more responsibility in designing, preparing, and implementing projects; little involvement of local level institutions, community groups, and beneficiaries in programme preparation and implementation, and so forth (Pyakuryal, Adhikari and Dhakal, 2008). Although these trends may encourage early exit from aid arrangements, the vulnerability of financial position and unacceptable degree of political instability necessitates bringing about adjustments in existing aid operation and management. Without external support, even achieving MDGs goal is not possible. For instance, Nepal will actually need to spend US\$16.4 billion to achieve the eight MDGs by the target date of 2015. But US\$4.8 billion will come from government sources and US\$3.8 billion from households, communities and the private sector, says 'Needs Assessment for Nepal', published by the NPC and the United Nations Development Programme (UNDP), Kathmandu.

There are some positive developments as well, after the execution of FAP, 2002. The grant has exceeded loan and projects have been prioritized; Poverty Reduction Fund has been established and Nepal has also received Poverty Reduction Support Credit. Not only this, both the government and donors agree that aid has started to flow according to recipients' priority. However, it is still questionable whether these priorities are set independently by the government or not?

Although a FAP 2008 (which had yet to be ratified by the Constituent Assembly) emphasized the need for a critical re-look into the non-performance on the part of both the donors and recipient, during this period there has been a growing dependence, increased corruption and short-term unsustainable deliveries. Therefore, the need is to revise the current concept, scope, motive, quality, utility and mobilization instruments for adding value to the revised FAP, 2009.[1]

A draft FAP, 2009 prepared for the Nepal Development Forum Stakeholders' Consultation Meeting realizes the fact that to bail the country out of its low-income status, ODA is needed until the country reaches the middle-income status in the next 10 to 15 years' time with an expectation that development assistance would:

- supplement rather than substitute Nepal's domestic savings so as to mobilize additional resources for high, inclusive and equitable growth;
- channel increased resources toward priority sectors of the economy to accelerate economic growth and development;
- create an enabling environment for attracting Foreign Direct Investment (FDI) and private capital inflow by highlighting the areas of comparative and competitive advantages of the economy; and
- enhance the nation's capability to envision, implement and sustain (MOF, 2009).

The proposed policy is to link foreign aid with trade, investment and private capital inflow with an aim to make donors facilitators than a rescuer of the country's economic pains. Relatively, a higher weight is given to the question of inclusion and equity in Nepal's proposed aid policies. As the vision of 2009 policy is to make Nepal self-sustaining, which can preserve growing social harmony, it is expected to be free from absolute poverty. The foreign aid objectives, policies and strategies will therefore, be channelized in this direction. While considering this policy, Nepal has also guaranteed to fully comply with the PD on Aid Effectiveness and AAA for Action ensuring greater attention to all tenets of international commitments.

CONCLUSIONS

Nepal's FAP is undergoing a major overhaul, since the first FAP, 2002 was promulgated. The revised version appeared in 2008 and again in 2009 for policy endorsement by successive NDFs. Despite these efforts, the review shows that Nepal still needs to bring about comprehensive reform programmes to address the changed global environment to competitive lending procedure and Nepal's proposed model for fiscal decentralization under the federalist characteristics. Nepal's current policy has failed to use the resources productively and maximize the benefits especially for the deprived groups of people. Overemphasis on political restructuring at the cost of economic restructuring by the country's political process is inexcusable with regard to strengthening aid utilization capacity.

At a policy level, as long as foreign aid is not designed to integrate with priority developmental activities, the need for making periodic assessment of the impact of foreign assistance will always be marginalized. This has created a huge gap in collecting information on the impact of aid in inflation, exchange rate and other critical indicators so necessary for public expenditure management and the formulation of appropriate fiscal and monetary policy to contain inflation. The time, therefore, has come to develop domestic aid policy in compatible with the country's priorities and harmonize it with the New Approach to Development endorsed by the G8 Summit.

NOTE

1. As political instability is prolonging and the Parliamentary meetings are not held, the finalization of revised policy may take time.

REFERENCES

Bandow, Doug (1997), *Foreign Aid Costs US More and Gains US Less,* Washington, D.C: Cato Institute.

Beckman, David (2010), *What Real Foreign Aid Reform Means,* The Huffington Post, USA.

Berg, Elliot (ed.) (1988), *Policy Reform & Equity, Extending the Benefits of Development,* San Francisco, International Center for Economic Growth.

Bhattarai, Badri Prasad (2009), 'Foreign Aid and Growth in Nepal: An Empirical Analysis', *The Journal of Developing Areas,* 42(2): 283–302.

Brynt, Judy (2005), 'Assesing Aid Effectiveness', *ADB Review,* Manila, 37(3): 9.

Chacra, S.A. (2006), *Asia and the Middle East: Alternative Priorities,* Reality of Aid, Philippines.

Deutscher, Eckhard and Sara Fyson (2009), *Committing to Effective Aid: Why can't donors walk their talk?* Development Outreach, World Bank Institute, Washington, D.C.

Easterly, William (2006), *The White Man's Burden; Why the West's Efforts to Aid the Rest have Done so Much Ill and so Little Good,* Penguin Press, New York.

ESCAP/African Union (2009), *Enhancing the Effectiveness of Fiscal Policy for Domestic Resource Mobilization,* Issues paper, Twenty-eighth meeting of the Committee of Experts, Bangkok.

ESCAP (2010), *Economic and Social Survey of Asia and the Pacific, 2010, Sustaining Recovery and Dynamism for Inclusive Development,* Bangkok, ESCAP.

Hockstein, Evelyn (2004). Why Foreign Aid Counts, CARE http://www.care.org/getinvolved/advocacy/pdfs/foreignaid.pdf (accessed on 5 July 2010).

Khadka, Narayan (1997), *Foreign Aid and Foreign Policy: Major Powers and Nepal,* New Delhi, Vikas Publishing House.

Knack, Stephen (2000), *Aid Dependence and the Quality of Governance: A Cross-Country Empirical Analysis,* Development Research Group, Washington D.C.

Kurlantzick, Josh, David Shinn, and Minxin (2006), 'China's Africa Strategy: A New Approach to Development and Diplomacy', The Carnegie Endowment for International Peace, Washington, D.C.

MOF (2002), *Foreign Aid Policy,* Ministry of Finance, Kathmandu.

―――― (2002–03), *Economic Survey,* Ministry of Finance, Kathmandu.

―――― (2008), *Foreign Aid Policy,* Ministry of Finance, Kathmandu.

―――― (2008–09), *Economic Survey,* Ministry of Finance, Kathmandu.

―――― (2009), *Foreign Aid Policy,* Ministry of Finance, Kathmandu.

NPC (1975), *Fifth Plan (1975–80),* National Planning Commision, Kathmandu.

―――― (1980), *Sixth Plan : 1980–85,* National Planning Commission, Kathmandu.

―――― (1985), *Seventh Plan* (1985–90), National Planning Commission, Kathmandu.

―――― (1992), *Eighth Plan (1992–97),* National Planning Commission, Kathmandu.

―――― (1997), *Ninth Plan (1997–2002),* National Planning Commission, Kathmandu.

―――― (2002), *Tenth Plan (2002–2007),* National Planning Commission, Kathmandu.

―――― (2008), *Interim Plan (2008–11),* National Planning Commission, Kathmandu.

OECD (2010), *Aid Statistics, Donor Aid Charts.,* OECD, Paris.

Pyakuryal, Bishwambher, Dadhi Adhikari, and Dipendra P. Dhakal (2008), *Is Foreign Aid Working?,* Mandala Book Points, Kathmandu.

Radelet, Steven (2006), *A Premier on Foreign Aid.* Working paper number 92, Center for Global Development, Washington D.C.

Shah, Anup (2010), 'Global Issues', http://www.globalissues.org/article/35/foreign-aid-development-assistance (accessed on5 July 2010).

UNDP (2010), Asia Pacific Human Development Report, New York.

World Bank (1998), *Report from Committee on Development Effectiveness (CODE)* (unpublished), Kathmandu, The World Bank.

―――― (2000), World Bank Policy Research paper, Washington, D.C., The World Bank.

POLICY PRIORITIES AND ROLE OF AID IN LEAST DEVELOPED COUNTRIES

9

Bangladesh

SELIM RAIHAN

INTRODUCTION

The regime of foreign aid in Bangladesh has undergone important changes over the last decades in terms of its focus, scale, composition and operational modalities. There has been an important shift, particularly in the context of a gradual decline in Bangladesh's aid dependence. It appears that Bangladesh has now evolved from an aid to a trade dependent economy. During the 1990s and 2000s, the remarkable performance of the ready-made garment exports in the markets of the EU and the US and large inflow of remittances, shaped Bangladesh's foreign policy than its requirement for foreign aid. However, the picture was different during the 1980s when Bangladesh's foreign policy was meant to ensure an uninterrupted flow of foreign aid.

An analysis of the flows of aid over the last decade suggests that there is a diminishing but significant role of aid in government finances. Over the years, the importance of food aid has declined in Bangladesh and aid can now play an important role in improving human development indicators as part of the Millennium Development Goals (MDGs) as well as in attaining infrastructural development to achieve much of the development objectives of the latest five year plan (2011–15).

There is also an important issue with respect to the effectiveness of aid in Bangladesh. Drawing experiences from Bangladesh and many other countries, it can be argued that the results have been mixed and a consensus has emerged that aid does not automatically benefit its recipients. There are also instances that aid, in the recipient country, is wasted and increases unproductive public consumption. This is because of weak institutions, corruption, inefficiencies and bureaucratic failures in these countries. Also, there are problems of aid-tying practices and conditionality.

Against this backdrop, this chapter provides an analysis of the change in importance, focus, and composition of aid in Bangladesh. This chapter also discusses the issues related to the effectiveness of aid in Bangladesh. Finally, the chapter highlights the critical factors that should be taken into consideration for the effective utilization of aid in Bangladesh.

Trends in Foreign Assistance Receipts

A Snapshot of the Aid Inflow

Bangladesh has been one of the regular receivers of external assistance since her independence. In the early years of liberalization, the country used to largely depend on external assistance or foreign aid in order to implement most of her development projects and mitigate the balance of payments deficit. Though the dependence on foreign assistance has decreased significantly over time, yet after 40 years of liberation the development of the country is to a large extent determined by two corresponding trends: mobilization of concessional foreign aid and effective market access for export. Over the years, a considerable amount of foreign assistance has been received by Bangladesh. Table 9.1 presents a snapshot of the total inflow of the assistance in Bangladesh during 1971–72 and 2007–08.

From 1971–72 to 2007–08, a total of US$59,033.42 million of foreign assistance was committed of which US$48,522.36 million of aid was disbursed which is about 82 per cent of the commitment. In the total disbursement, US$21,305.01 million was disbursed as grant and US$27,217.35 million was as loan. The relative shares are about 44 and 56 per cent, respectively. Table 9.1 also shows the information on the total aid disbursement in terms of purpose. It is evident that during the mentioned time period, Bangladesh received US$6,440.19 million as food aid while the commitment was US$6,576.92 million. Thus, about 98 per cent of the total food aid committed was disbursed where the relative shares of grant and loan were about 88 and 12 per cent,

Table 9.1
A Snapshot of Total Inflow of External Assistance in Bangladesh from 1971–72 to 2007–08

Purpose	Grant	Loan	Total
Food Aid (Million US$)			
Commitment	5,814.36	762.56	6,576.92
Disbursement	5,677.64	762.56	6,440.19
Disbursement as % of Commitment	97.65	100.00	97.92
Grant/Loan as % of Disbursement	88.16	11.84	100
Commodity Aid (Million US$)			
Commitment	5,696.45	5,376.02	11,072.47
Disbursement	5,650.83	5,257.01	10,907.84
Disbursement as % of Commitment	99.20	97.79	98.51
Grant/Loan as % of Disbursement	51.81	48.19	100
Project Aid (Million US$)			
Commitment	13,380.36	28,003.68	41,384.04
Disbursement	9,976.54	21,197.78	31,174.33
Disbursement as % of Commitment	74.56	75.70	75.33
Grant/Loan as % of Disbursement	32.00	68.00	100
Total (Million US$)			
Commitment	24,891.17	34,142.26	59,033.42
Disbursement	21,305.01	27,217.35	48,522.36
Disbursement as % of Commitment	85.59	79.72	82.19
Grant/Loan as % of Disbursement	43.91	56.09	100

Source: ERD (2010).

respectively. A keen look on the inflow of commodity aid reveals the fact that a total of US$11,072.47 million was committed as commodity aid, of which almost 99 per cent (US$1,0907.84) million was disbursed. The grant and loan shares in the commodity aid inflow were 52 and 48 per cent, respectively. The external assistance which used to come under the name 'project aid', is thought to be the biggest contributor to the implementation of development programmes of the recipient country. From 1971–72 to 2007–08, Bangladesh received a total of US$31,174.33 million foreign assistance as project aid while the commitment was US$41,384.04 million. Therefore, 75.33 per cent of the commitment was disbursed. Out of the total disbursement of project aid, 68 per cent was disbursed as loan and 32 per cent was as grant. From the above analysis it can be concluded that the ratio of disbursement to commitment is the lowest (75.33 per cent) for project aid in Bangladesh. At the same time, the relative share of loan in the total project aid disbursement is also the highest (68 per cent) compared to commodity and food aid disbursement. The share of loan is also higher (56 per cent) in the volume of total aid inflow. It is a fact that the loan compared to the grant is attached to more conditionalities, and also the recipient country has to pay a substantial amount as interest of that loan every year.

Bangladesh and Aid Dependence

Figure 9.1 presents the historical trend of the amount of export, remittance and aid disbursement and their shares in the Gross Domestic Product (GDP) of Bangladesh. Figure 9.1a suggests that in the years immediately after independence, the amounts of exports and remittance were very low and the country was almost entirely dependent on aid. Thus, in the early years of liberation, the country's one of the largest sources of foreign exchange was aid. However, as the economy maintained a handsome growth over the years and other sources of income have been consolidated, the dependence on aid declined significantly. The spectacular performance of two factors i.e., exports and remittance actually helped Bangladesh to curb her dependence on aid. The integration of the economy with the rest of the world increased over the years as the economy became more and more open. Secured quota facility under the Multi Fibre Arrangement (MFA) and duty free quota market access in some of the developed countries, helped the exports of ready-made garments flourish from Bangladesh, which resulted in a large and robust inflow of foreign exchange into the country. Moreover, the export of manpower from Bangladesh consistently increased which also caused a huge amount of foreign exchange inflow into the country as remittance. From Figure 9.1a it is evident that the amounts of exports and remittances

Figure 9.1
Export, Remittance and Aid

9.1a. Trend of Export, Remittance and Aid

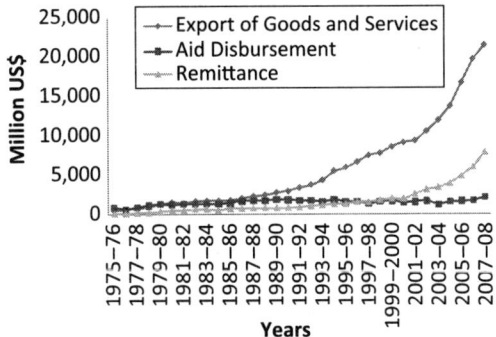

9.1b. Annual Average Share of Aid, Export
and Remittance in GDP in Different Decades

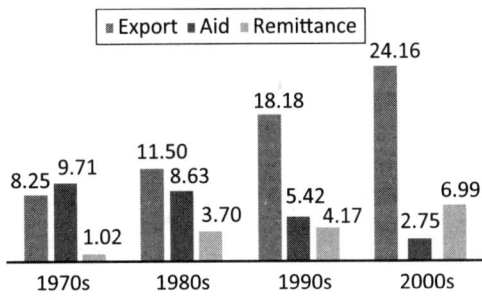

Source: ERD (2010).

have been ever increasing. However, the amount of aid disbursement
has been downward since 1980. The amount of export also exceeded
that of aid in 1980. Since then, the former has always been higher
than the latter one and Bangladesh has turned into a trade dependent
economy from an aid dependent one. Also, since the late 1990s, the
remittance has been higher than the aid. Figure 9.1b shows the annual
average contribution of aid, export and remittance to the GDP in
different decades. During 1970s, the average aid dependence was 9.7
per cent of GDP, which came down to only 2.75 per cent during the
2000s. The annual average export GDP ratio increased from 8.25 per
cent during the 1970s to 24.16 per cent during the 2000s. In the case

of the remittance–GDP ratio, the annual average rose from only 1 per cent in the 1970s to 7 per cent in the 2000s.

Figure 9.2 presents the trend of aid disbursement in Bangladesh as percentage of the country's Annual Development Programme (ADP) and annual budget. From 1972–73 to 1990–91 for almost each year, 80 per cent of ADP was financed by external assistance. Dependence of ADP on foreign assistance had started declining from early 1990s. It continued to fall until 2004–05 when the ratio became 45 per cent. However, since then it started picking up again and in 2007–08 the ratio stood at 63 per cent. It thus implies that till now there is much reliance on external assistance for the implementation of the country's development programme. The trend of aid as percentage of budget has however been consistently declining. During 1975–76 it was as high as 78 per cent which came down to 16 per cent in 2007–08.

Figure 9.2
Aid as Percentage of Bangladesh's ADP and Annual Budget

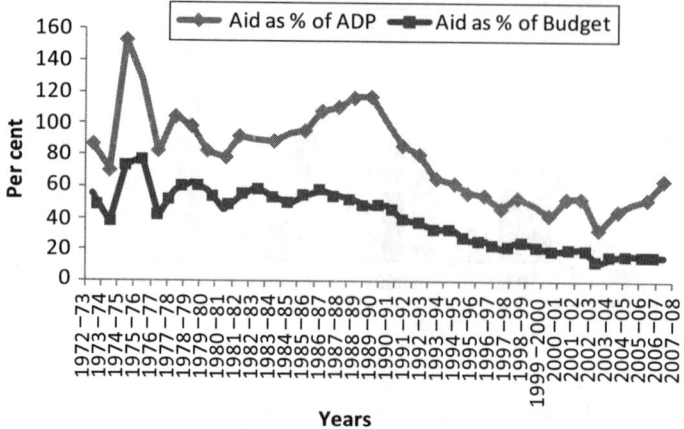

Source: ERD (2010).

Despite some dependence on aid for the development programmes, overall, Bangladesh has reduced its dependence on foreign aid. This has been due to government's relative success in the mobilization of domestic resources and the increasing dynamism of the private sector. It should also be mentioned that in recent years, Bangladesh has received less foreign aid as a percentage of the GDP than either heavily indebted poor countries (HIPCs) or other low income countries (LICs) (Figure 9.3).

Figure 9.3
Net ODA: Bangladesh, HIPCs and LICs (Percentage of GDP)

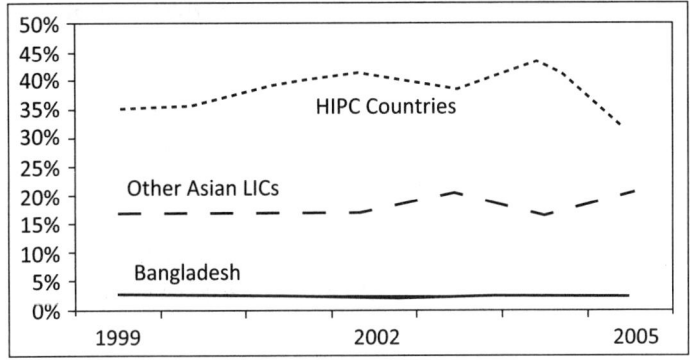

Source: IMF (2007).

Aid Inflow Scenario of Bangladesh

There is no denying the fact that spectacular changes have taken place over the years in the composition of aid inflow with respect to type, source and purpose to Bangladesh. A number of features of this change can be noted, a few of which have been summarized.

Commitment vs Disbursement

Except for a few exceptions, there has always been a difference between aid commitment and disbursement. Disbursement has remained persistently below the commitment. Figure 9.4a shows the trend of aid commitment and disbursement in Bangladesh from 1971–72 to 2007–08. During 1971–72, out of US$611 million commitment only US$271 million was disbursed which was only 44 per cent of the commitment. In 2007–08, a total of US$2,061 million was disbursed against a commitment of US$2,842 million implying that almost 73 per cent of the aid committed was disbursed in 2007–08. From Figure 9.4b, it is evident that the annual average aid disbursement as percentage of aid commitment was only 73 per cent during the 1970s which increased by almost 22 percentage points to reach at a level of 95 per cent during 1990s. During 2000s the average declined to almost 86 per cent.

Figure 9.4
Aid Commitment and Disbursement

9.4a: Trend of Aid Commitment and Disbursement

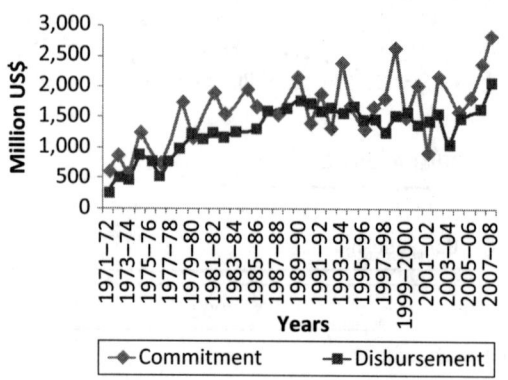

9.4b: Annual Average Disbursement as Percentage of Commitment in Different Decades

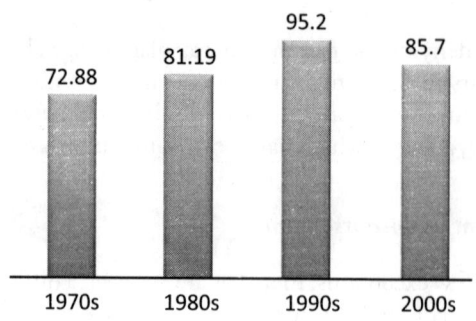

Source: ERD (2010).

Grants and Loans

Bangladesh's aid basket is comprised of both grants and loans. Figure 9.5a presents the trend of grants and loans in the total aid basket from 1971–72 to 2007–08. Over the years, the grant has been declining while loan has been increasing. However, since 2004–05, there has been some rise in the amount of grants. Figure 9.5b shows that during the 1970s the share of grant was as high as 55 per cent which came down to an annual average of 31.4 per cent during the 2000s. In contrast, the share of loan increased from 45 per cent during the 1970s to around 69 per cent

Figure 9.5
Grants and Loans in Aid

9.5a: Trend in the Grants and Loans

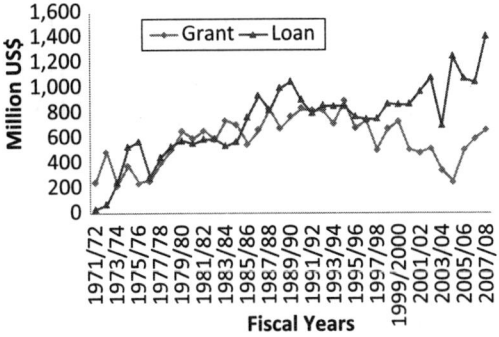

9.5b: Decade-wise Dynamics of Aid Composition
(share in aid)

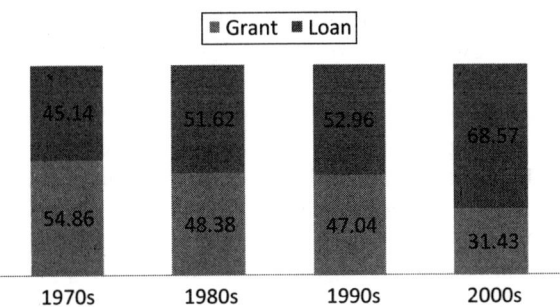

	1970s	1980s	1990s	2000s
Grant (top)	45.14	51.62	52.96	68.57
Loan (bottom)	54.86	48.38	47.04	31.43

Source: ERD (2010).

during the 2000s. Thus, it is evident that Bangladesh's aid basket has become loan dependent over time. Loan always comes with much more stringent conditionalities compared to grant and it also throws an almost unavoidable burden on the recipient country in the form of debt. In Bangladesh, the amount of loan is rising and so is the amount of outstanding debt.

Figure 9.6 presents the trend of outstanding debt and its ratio with respect to GDP from 1974–75 to 2007–08. It appears that the amount of outstanding debt is ever increasing for Bangladesh. In 1974–75, the total amount of outstanding debt was US$973.8 million, which by 2007–08 increased by US$2,0320.4 million to reach at US$2,1294.2 million. Until mid-1990s, the outstanding debt as percentage of the

Figure 9.6
Trend of Debt–GDP Ratio for Bangladesh

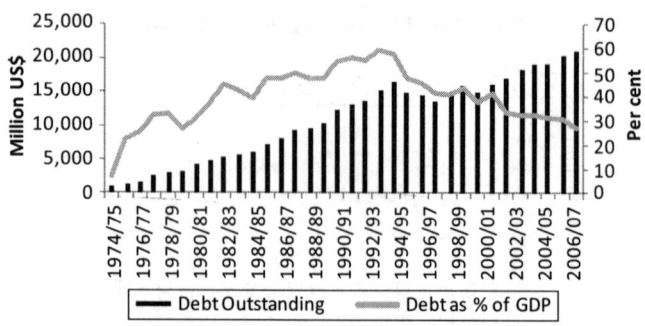

Source: ERD (2010).

GDP had been increasing. Since late 1990s, the debt–GDP ratio has been decreasing due to a higher GDP growth rate. However, debt–GDP ratio has increased from 7 per cent in 1974–75 to 27 per cent in 2007–08. In 1993–94, the ratio became as high as 59 per cent.

Despite improvements in recent years, debt service remains a concern for Bangladesh. A significant amount of national budget is owed for debt servicing in Bangladesh every year. Figure 9.7a shows the yearly debt service by Bangladesh from 1973–74 to 2007–08. Amount of interest paid by Bangladesh on debt is mounting day by day. Interest payment which was US$10 million during 1973–74 increased to US$226.2 million by 2007–08. Figure 9.7b shows the trend of debt service from 1974–75 to 2007–08 as percentage of GDP and as percentage of export of goods and services. During 1973–74 and 2007–08, the ratio of debt service to the GDP increased from 0.73 per cent to 2.79 per cent while that with respect to export of goods and services decreased from 20.76 per cent to 9.18 per cent. The debt repayment by Bangladesh always absorbs the precious funds that are exigently required for ensuring the supply of basic needs of its poor people.

Food, Commodity and Project Aid

External assistance received by Bangladesh for different purposes can be divided into three major types: food aid, commodity aid and project aid. Increasing number of population and frequent natural disasters such as floods and cyclones always put an upward pressure on the net requirement of food in Bangladesh. However, because of the sustained

Figure 9.7
Debt Service by Bangladesh

9.7a: Yearly Debt Service by Bangladesh

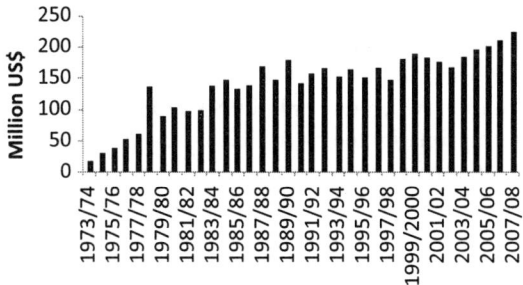

9.7b: Debt Service as Percentage of GDP and
Exports of Goods and Services

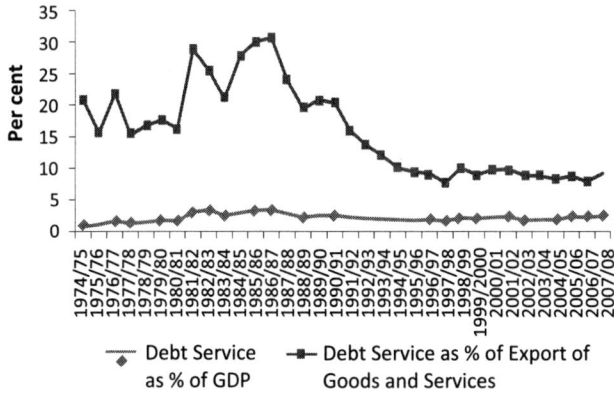

Source: ERD (2010).

growth in agricultural productivity, the economy is becoming near
self-sufficient and the importance of food aid is also lessening.
Figure 9.8a suggests that in 1971–72 the total food aid disbursement
was US$129.6 million which decreased to US$59.9 million in 2006–07.
However, in 2007–08 food aid disbursement was increased to US$111
million as a result of number of economic and environmental shocks
faced by Bangladesh during that year. However, in Bangladesh there
will be a need for food aid to support several food-based social safety
net programmes.

In order to meet the balance of payments deficit and to generate local
currency to fund development projects, commodity aid has been used

by the country. However, commodity aid which was quite significant in the past, even during the 1990s, has fallen down to zero in recent years. From 1971–72 to 2007–08 with some obvious fluctuations, commodity aid sharply decreased from US$137.7 million to zero. The largest share of foreign aid since 1980 comprises project aid. It has been ever increasing. In 2007–08 the amount of project aid stood at US$1,950.5 million which was only US$3.5 million in 1971–72. Project aid has been primarily meant to finance the ADP, and Bangladesh has been heavily relying on project aid for the programmes related to human resource development, social, health, education and family welfare, infrastructural development, and development of the power sector.

Figure 9.8b shows the decade-wise annual shares of the above three types of aid in the total aid disbursement from 1971–72 to 2007–08. In the early years after liberation during the 1970s, the shares of food and commodity aid were higher than that of project aid. However, during the later decades the relative significance of the former two types of aid has shrunk. It is the project aid which has been dominating the aid composition since 1980s. During the 1980s, the annual average share of project aid was 51 per cent which increased to 70.2 per cent during the 1990s and to almost 92 per cent during the 2000s.

Bilateral Aid and Multilateral Aid

Bangladesh receives aid both from bilateral and multilateral sources. While the bilateral source includes individual countries, the multilateral source includes several international development organizations. From 1971–72 to 2007–08, a total of US$4,8521.8 million of foreign aid is disbursed in Bangladesh, of which US$2,4967.6 million (51.45 per cent) and US$2,3554.2 million (48.55 per cent) are disbursed through bilateral sources and multilateral sources, respectively. Therefore, the gross aid bundle is dominated by the contribution from bilateral sources. However, the conclusion is not the same for all the years. Figure 9.9a presents the trends of bilateral and multilateral aid during 1971–72 and 2007–08. It is evident that until 1989–90, bilateral aid was higher than multilateral aid. However, during the 1990s and 2000s, the amount of bilateral aid declined and that of multilateral aid increased. Figure 9.9b shows that during the 1970s, the annual average share of bilateral aid was as high as 74.5 per cent and the share of multilateral aid was only 24.5 per cent. However, during 2000s, the annual share

Figure 9.8
Aid in Terms of Purpose

9.8a: Trend of Aid in Terms of Purpose

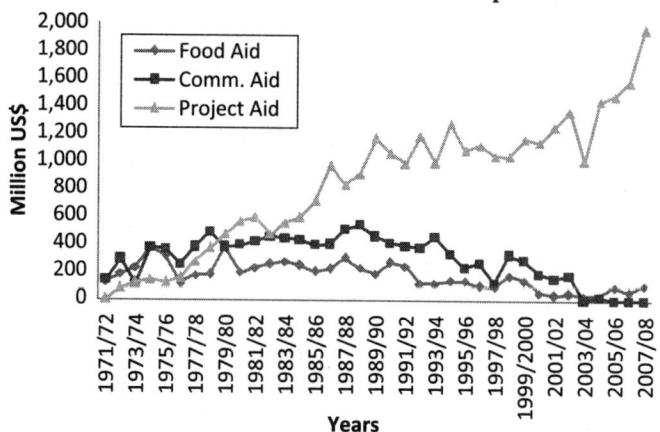

9.8b: Decade-wise Dynamics of Aid Composition with respect to Purpose (Percentage of Total Aid)

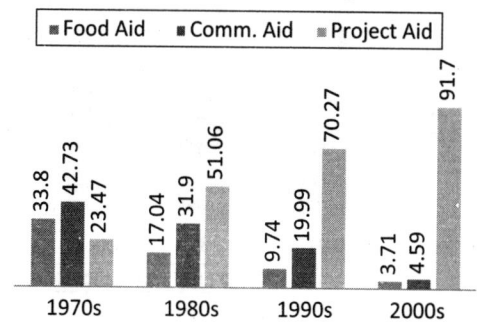

Source: ERD (2010).

of bilateral aid came down to 26.86 per cent and that of multilateral aid increased to 63.14 per cent.

Table 9.2 contains the information on the amount of aid disbursed by major bilateral sources and multilateral agencies from 1990–91 to 2006–07 in Bangladesh. It is found that Japan is the biggest donor amongst bilateral sources in terms of cumulative disbursement followed by the US. Japan is the major source of commodity aid in Bangladesh. Other countries that contribute to Bangladesh's aid basket significantly

Figure 9.9
Aid in Terms of Source

9.9a: Trend of Aid in Terms of Source

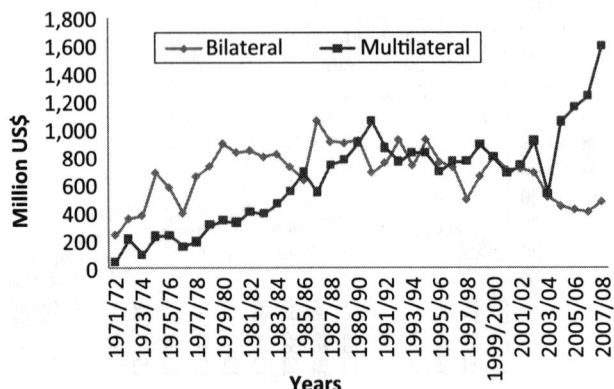

9.9b: Decade-wise Dynamics of Aid Composition with respect to Source (Percentage of Total Aid)

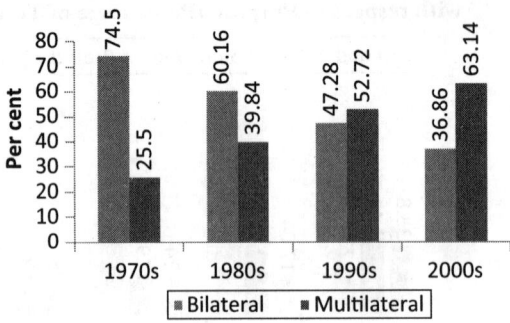

Source: ERD (2010).

and consistently are Netherlands, USA, Germany, Canada, Sweden, Norway, Denmark and the UK.

International Development Organization (IDA) is the largest contributor to the aid basket of Bangladesh amongst the available multilateral sources. It has also got the largest share among all sources (whether bilateral or multilateral). The other large multilateral contributor to Bangladesh's aid basket is Asian Development Bank (ADB). It appears that Japan, which used to be the highest aid provider to Bangladesh, had been contributing a declining share in the total aid basket during 1990–91 and 2006–07 when its share sharply declined from

Table 9.2
Aid Disbursement by Major Sources from 1990–91 to 2006–07

Country/Agency	1990–91	1991–92	1992–93	1993–94	1994–95	1995–96	1996–97	1997–98	1998–99	1999–2000	2000–01	2001–02	2002–03	2003–04	2004–05	2005–06	2006–07
Canada	6.6	3.8	5.6	2.1	2.7	1.7	2.0	1.1	1.8	1.8	1.4	1.3	1.5	2.0	0.6	4.0	1.1
Denmark	1.9	2.5	0.6	1.4	1.8	1.0	1.6	1.5	2.1	1.8	0.4	2.0	2.9	1.9	0.3	0.9	3.1
Germany	3.2	5.3	3.6	2.1	6.4	4.4	2.3	3.9	2.4	1.3	3.1	1.5	0.4	2.5	1.7	1.0	1.2
Japan	20.0	9.5	15.8	18.9	20.5	22.9	24.9	13.7	15.3	24.6	22.7	20.2	15.3	7.7	3.1	2.0	2.0
Netherlands	1.6	1.6	2.9	2.6	1.0	2.3	4.9	1.7	2.8	1.8	3.3	0.1	0.6	4.0	0.3	0.8	1.5
Norway	1.2	1.7	2.1	2.2	2.0	2.1	1.1	1.5	0.7	1.2	1.2	0.6	3.2	0.6	0.3	0.7	2.9
Saudi Arabia	1.6	2.9	3.6	1.6	1.1	2.1	0.7	1.1	0.3	0.4	0.0	0.5	0.0	0.7	0.0	0.0	0.0
Sweden	1.3	1.6	2.6	1.2	0.7	0.3	1.5	2.2	1.4	1.3	1.1	0.5	0.9	1.1	0.0	0.1	3.5
UK	3.2	3.7	3.1	2.5	3.0	2.3	1.4	2.8	3.4	3.8	3.8	1.2	2.5	9.1	5.9	10.0	4.2
USA	6.0	8.6	4.1	6.9	6.6	3.5	2.4	2.1	4.5	5.8	2.8	1.4	2.2	1.2	0.6	0.3	3.8

(continued table 9.2)

(continued table 9.2)

Country/ Agency	1990–91	1991–92	1992–93	1993–94	1994–95	1995–96	1996–97	1997–98	1998–99	1999–2000	2000–01	2001–02	2002–03	2003–04	2004–05	2005–06	2006–07
Bilateral	**46.5**	**41.0**	**44.0**	**41.4**	**45.9**	**42.7**	**42.7**	**31.6**	**34.6**	**43.8**	**39.7**	**29.2**	**29.5**	**30.7**	**12.7**	**19.7**	**23.2**
A.D.B	16.5	26.2	16.4	19.8	19.4	19.3	17.2	19.2	14.1	17.8	16.9	12.8	13.1	16.7	14.3	16.9	21.0
E.E.C/E.U	3.1	1.7	2.8	3.5	3.7	6.3	4.2	4.6	2.5	0.3	2.3	5.6	1.2	2.0	0.6	4.7	4.0
I.D.A	19.4	14.9	19.6	24.3	16.4	15.6	21.2	26.5	31.1	22.3	21.4	22.7	35.4	21.8	47.9	40.5	41.7
UNICEF	0.5	2.1	0.9	0.8	2.9	1.5	4.1	1.8	1.2	1.7	3.5	3.2	2.5	2.9	1.7	1.1	1.8
UN System	5.7	6.7	4.2	3.4	3.7	2.6	1.8	5.9	7.7	5.1	1.6	3.7	2.4	3.5	2.3	7.1	5.2
Multilateral	**45.2**	**51.6**	**44.0**	**51.7**	**46.1**	**45.3**	**48.5**	**57.9**	**56.6**	**47.2**	**45.8**	**48.0**	**54.5**	**46.9**	**66.9**	**70.3**	**73.8**
Others	8.3	7.3	12.0	6.9	8.0	12.0	8.8	10.5	8.7	8.9	14.5	22.8	16.0	22.4	20.5	10.0	3.0
Total	**100**	**100**	**100**	**100**	**100**	**100**	**100**	**100**	**100**	**100**	**100**	**100**	**100**	**100**	**100**	**100**	**100**

Sources: Various Issues of *Statistical Yearbook* of Bangladesh. Others include Australia, Belgium, China, France, Ford Foundation, Finland, IDB/ISDB, IFAD, India, Italy, Kuwait, OPEC, Pakistan, Switzerland, Suppliers Credit, NDE, South Korea, Spain and the UAE.

20 per cent to only 2 per cent. In the same time period, the share of UK has increased by 1 percentage point while that for Canada curbed by 5.5 percentage points. For the US, the share fell from 6 per cent to 3.8 per cent during the same period. Since 2003–04, the UK has been the largest bilateral donor to Bangladesh. On the other hand, a keen look at the trend in the share of other bilateral aid partners who used to have very small but consistent contributions in the aid basket will establish the fact that without few exceptions, majority of them accounted for declining shares. The trends in the share of two major multilateral aid partners suggest that both the IDA and ADB accounted for an increasing trend, with the IDA having the lion share. The share of the IDA increased from 19.4 in 1990–91 to 41.7 per cent in 2006–07, while that for the ADB rose from 16.5 per cent to 21 per cent during the same period. A bird's eye view on the other multilateral aid sources will reveal that their shares didn't increase considerably. Therefore, the dominancy of multilateral aid sources in Bangladesh's total aid basket is actually driven by the two large multilateral sources namely, the IDA and ADB.

FOREIGN ASSISTANCE AND DEVELOPMENT IN BANGLADESH

Development Perspectives in Bangladesh and Aid

In recognition of the substantial development challenges, recently the Government has embarked on a perspective plan covering 2010 to 2021 aimed at implementing Vision 2021. The key message of Vision 2021 (Outline Perspective Plan of Bangladesh) and the associated Perspective Plan can be summarized as follows:

> The development perspective envisages to achieving, in the coming days, a prosperous progressive nation in which food and energy security shall prevail with drastic reduction of poverty and a low level of unemployment. The perspective also includes great strides in human development including health and nutrition, effective population control, progress in all levels of education, primary, secondary and tertiary in addition to commendable improvement in science and technology, along with great achievement in ICT. Infrastructure development will improve integrated multi-modal transport encompassing, railways, roads and inland water transport having connectivity with our neighbours. In other words, the

development perspective implies the simultaneous fulfilment of economic and social rights of the people alongside civil and political rights. For this to happen, strong links between economic growth on the one hand, and expansion of employment opportunities, reduction of poverty, expansion of democracy and empowerment, consolidation of cultural identity and protection of environment with its freshness for the next generation on the other will be established. (Planning Commission 2010)

Furthermore, the envisioned policy and institutional environment of the Perspective Plan to attain the desired development goals constitutes a set of structural, social, human and physical conditions for which the thrusts for action are:

- building a secular tolerant liberal progressive democratic state;
- promoting good governance and curbing corruption;
- promoting sustainable human development;
- instituting a prudent macroeconomic policy mix;
- promoting a favourable industrialization and trade policy regime;
- addressing globalization and regional cooperation challenges;
- ensuring adequate supply of electricity and fuel;
- achieving food security;
- making available adequate infrastructure;
- pursuing environmental friendly development; and
- building a digital Bangladesh.

The Perspective Plan sets the strategic directions and provides a broad outline for the course of actions for making the Vision 2021 a reality. This broad framework leaves considerable latitude for the Sixth Five Year Plan (2011–15) and the Seventh Five Year Plan (2016–20) to work out operational details of how the country should move forward. It is important to note that foreign aid is likely to have an important role in meeting part of the resource requirement for realizing these objectives.

Raihan and Khondker (2010) estimated the resource requirement for attaining the MDG goals. Two scenarios are considered for the MDG financing assessment. These are: *(a)* baseline, and *(b)* high growth scenario. Bangladesh needs foreign assistance of US$5 and US$3 billion per year under the baseline and high growth scenario respectively, if the entire additional deficits are to be covered from the foreign source. Ideally these resources should come in the form of grants. However, realities suggest that raising US$3 to 5 billion per year as grants may be an implausible option. Under this circumstance, following proposals are made:

1. In the case of baseline scenario, development partners may raise foreign grants by about US$1.5 billion and provide the remaining resource in the form of loans. In particular, government may seek foreign grants in the range of US$1.4 billion to US$1.7 billion and foreign loans in the range of US$2.3 billion to US$3.2 billion over the next five-year period.

2. Under the high growth scenario, development partners may provide foreign grants by about a billion and give the remaining resource in the form of loans. In particular, government may seek foreign grants in the range of US$1 billion and foreign loans in the range of US$1.9 billion to US$2.4 billion over the next five year period. It appears that reliance on external source for MDG financing declined significantly in the high growth scenario compared to the base line situation, due to expanded fiscal space and household income as a result of higher economic growth. In this case, only around 3 per cent of resources may need to be sought from the external source. Remaining 97 per cent of total resources for MDGs would come from domestic sources made of government budget (i.e., 82 per cent) and household (i.e., 15 per cent).

Sectoral Share in Foreign Aid

Though the dependence of Bangladesh on foreign aid has condensed spectacularly over the years, there is still need for external assistance for the development programmes within the country. More than 95 per cent of the aid now comes as project aid and a good number of projects in the ADP of the national budget are funded through this assistance. Besides this, requirement of external assistance is important for the implementation of the projects related to social sectors such as health and education. Figure 9.10 shows the trend in the share of aid disbursement by broad economic sectors during 1972–73 and 2007–08. It can be concluded that services and infrastructure always got the priority in case of sector-wise aid disbursement. Agriculture and industry experienced declining shares in the total aid disbursement during period under consideration.

Figure 9.10
Trend in Shares of Aid Disbursement
by Sector from 1972–73 to 2007–08

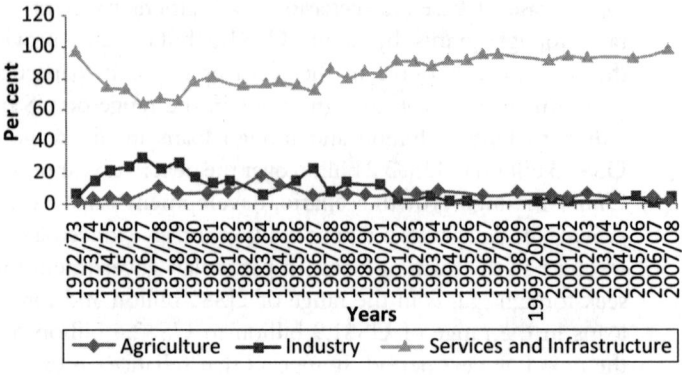

Source: ERD (2010).

Figures 9.11 and 9.12 show the trend in the shares of sub-sectors in total aid. It appears from Figure 9.11 that the aid disbursement in the sectors namely, education, health and rural development amplified and so their shares in the total aid disbursement. However, the share of sector containing social welfare, women's affairs and youth development remained very low and declined over time. Figure 9.12 indicates that the shares of the transport sector and water resources in total aid declined during the time period under consideration. The power sector experienced some rise in the share during the 2000s.

Effectiveness of Foreign Aid in Bangladesh

Quibria and Shafi (2007) summarize donors' perspectives on foreign aid in Bangladesh. There are several 'independent' reviews of the programmes by the donors. These reviews are based on a set of predetermined broad criteria such as relevance, efficiency, efficacy, impact, etc., and they provide the donors with evaluations of their own programmes and performance. From donors' perspective, aid effectiveness has been mixed in Bangladesh. In donors' view, the investment projects have been more successful than their policy loans. It is concluded that Bangladesh has not been successful in implementing many policy loans. However, it should be mentioned that the

Figure 9.11
Trend in Share of Aid Disbursement
by Social Sectors from 1972–73 to 2007–08

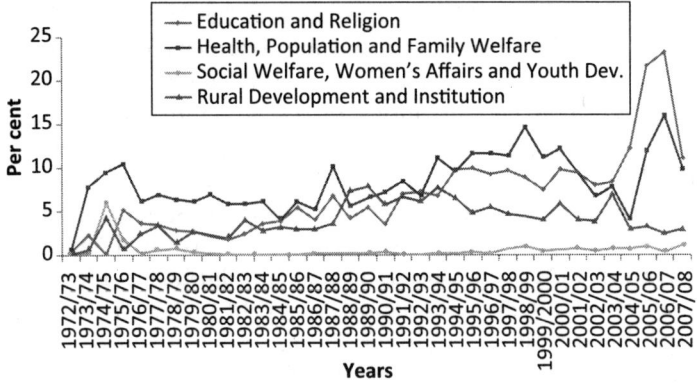

Source: ERD (2010).

Figure 9.12
Trend in Share of Aid Disbursement
by Infrastructural Sectors, 1972–73 to 2007–08

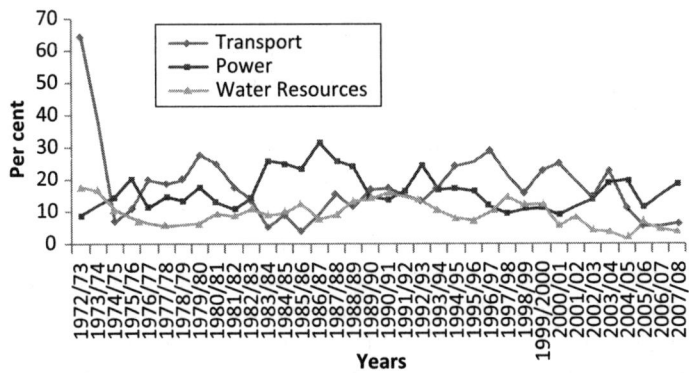

Source: ERD (2010).

country's failure to implement policy reforms, as prescribed by the donors, is not unique to Bangladesh and there are many instances of such failures across the developing world. There are also arguments that though poor project implementation performance no doubt reflects the country's insufficient capacity, this is not exclusively a domestic problem, but also due to the fact that the multiplicity of donors with diverse reporting and accounting requirements exerts heavy demands on scarce domestic managerial capacity.

As mentioned earlier, before 1990, most of the aid came in the form of food aid and commodity aid and the conditionality of those aids were to induce the government to adopt overall reforms like privatization, deregulation, etc. But during 1990 and onwards, the amount of sector-specific project aid increased significantly with increasing conditionality. This created space for more policy influence by donors to the government. Since the mid-1980s and early 1990s, aid came through a wide range of policy reform agenda under the Structural Adjustment Programme (SAP), Enhanced Structural Adjustment Programme (ESAP), Poverty Reduction Strategy Paper (PRSP), Poverty Reduction Growth Fund (PRGF) and so on. But the problem with the reform packages is that these are the predetermined path of reform agenda of the donors and were replicated in different African, Latin American and Asian countries including Bangladesh without considering the ground realities and real problem of these countries.

There are few studies on the macroeconomic effects of foreign aid in Bangladesh. Islam (1972) and Alamgir (1974) used data for East Pakistan to explore the impact of foreign aid on domestic savings and came to the conclusion that foreign aid was not conducive for either growth in savings or growth in the GDP per capita. Sobhan (1982) was of the view that aid regime in Bangladesh during 1970s grossly failed in promoting its development agenda. Aid led to substantial concentration of wealth among the urban and rural elite. Also, aid hindered mobilization of domestic resources and the effective use of production capabilities. Islam (1992), using time series econometrics, concluded that foreign loans have stimulated growth in Bangladesh, while grants have not. Taslim and Weliwita (2000) investigated the aid-savings relationship in Bangladesh during 1960–95 and found that the long run relationship between aid and savings has been strongly negative. Similar results are also found in Razzaque and Ahmed (2000). It thus appears that most of the studies indicated negative effects of aid on savings and economic growth in Bangladesh.

The current study, using an updated database for the period of 1973–2006, runs an error correction model of the following type to examine the relationships between per capita savings and per capita real foreign aid in Bangladesh:

$$\Delta PCS = C + \beta \Delta PCY + \gamma \Delta PAID + \Gamma_1 PCS(-1) + \Gamma_2 PCY(-1)$$
$$+ \Gamma_3 PAID(-1) + error$$

Where,

PCS = per capita savings

PCY = per capita real GDP

PAID = per capita real foreign aid

Data are taken for the period of 1973–2006. All three variables (PCS, PCY and PAID) are non-stationary on their levels, but stationary on first differences. Thus, PCS, PCY and PAID are integrated of order one.

The regression results of the unrestricted error correction model are reported in Table 9.3. It appears that both the short run and long run coefficients on per capita real foreign aid are negative and statistically significant.

The long run coefficients are derived from Table 9.3 and the long run relationship between per capita savings and per capita aid is shown below:

$$PCS = 1.86 + 0.12\ PCY - 1.23\ PAID$$

The negative relationship between foreign aid and domestic savings can be explained in two ways:

1. It is possible that foreign aid is being substituted for domestic savings and a significant proportion of foreign aid is used to

Table 9.3
Regression Results of the Unrestricted Error Correction Model

Variables	Estimated coefficients (t-ratio)
Intercept	–1.43 (–0.64)
$\Delta.43$ (–0)	0.095 (1.21)
$\Delta.095$	–0.98 (–6.54)
PCS(–1)	–0.77 (–5.48)
PCY(–1)	0.09 (2.86)
PAID(–1)	–0.95 (–3.33)
Adjusted R2	0.86

Source: Results of econometric regression carried out by the author.

increase consumption—the issue of 'fungibility of aid'. In Bangladesh, ADP projects, which are largely financed by aid money, involve substantial current expenditures which are likely to increase consumption propensity.

2. Domestic resource mobilization efforts by the government. Since, the late 1980s, a sharp decline in the PAID has been accompanied by a rise in PCS.

CONCLUSION

Despite the declining importance of aid in Bangladesh, it can safely be argued that the dependence on aid will continue for quite some time to meet some of the critical human development objectives and infrastructural development which are vital for economic growth. However, for aid to be effective in meeting the development goals there is a need to bring in some reforms in the aid regime. These reforms should include aid conditionalities originating within the country, sustained commitment of the country, and the active participation of the functionaries in the design of the projects and programmes. It is also important to note that, the government should not consider aid as a means of solving the fiscal deficits, but it should be seen more as a source for enhancing investments.

Institutional reforms are very important, and long-term commitment is necessary for such reforms. Poor design, lack of ownership, multiple controls, ad hoc procedures, the divergence between development and revenue budgets, and the poor coordination between the ministries are the major factors contributing to the weak implementation of aid financed development programmes in Bangladesh. Only institutional and procedural reforms can enhance Bangladesh's aid absorptive capacity.

REFERENCES

Alamgir, M. (1974), 'Foreign Capital Inflows, Saving and Economic Growth: A Case Study of Bangladesh', *The Bangladesh Economic Review*, 11(2), April: 577–98.

ERD (2010), 'Flow of External Resources', Economic Relations Division (ERD), Ministry of Finance, Government of the People's Republic of Bangladesh.

IMF (2007), *Bangladesh: Selected Issues*. IMF, Washington, D.C.

Islam, A. (1992), 'Foreign Aid and Economic Growth: An Econometric Study of Bangladesh', *Applied Economics*, 24(5): 541–44.

Islam, N. (1972), 'Foreign Assistance and Economic Development: The Case of Pakistan', *Economic Journal*, 82(325), March: 502–30.

Planning Commission (2010), 'Outline Perspective Plan of Bangladesh 2010–2021: Making Vision 2021 a Reality', General Economics Division, Planning, Commission, Government of Bangladesh.

Quibria, M.G., and A. Shafi (2007), 'Aid Effectiveness in Bangladesh', MPRA Paper No. 10299, posted 30. September 2008.

Raihan S. and B. H. Khondker (2010), 'MDG Financing Strategy for Bangladesh', Report prepared for UNDP, Bangladesh.

Razzaque, A. and N. Ahmed (2000), 'A Re-examination of Domestic Saving-Foreign Aid Relationship in the Context of Bangladesh', *The Bangladesh Development Studies*, XXVI(4).

Sobhan, R. (1982), *The Crisis of External Dependence*, ZED Press, London.

Taslim, M.A., and A. Weliwita (2000), 'The Inverse Relation between Saving and Aid: An Alternative Explanation', *Journal of Economic Development*, 25(1): 75–95.

10

Bhutan

Thinley Namgyel

Country Profile

Bhutan is a landlocked country in the eastern Himalayas, bordering China to the north and India to the east, south and west. Bhutan has a geographical area of 38,394 km² and a population of 634,982 (Royal Government of Bhutan, 2005).

Over the last five decades, since planned development started in 1961, Bhutan has made impressive socio-economic development progress. The high levels of investment in the social sector, averaging more than 20 per cent of the annual budget, thereby exceeding the global 20:20 compact agreed on at the World Summit for Social Development in 1995, has brought about significant improvements in the social conditions of the people, as reflected in the Table 10.1.

In terms of economic performance, the Gross Domestic Product (GDP) growth rate has been growing at around 7–8 per cent per annum, inflation averages around 3–4 per cent annually and the overall balance of payments situation positive, averaging around 5 per cent of the GDP mainly on account of the inflow of foreign aid. The sustained economic growth has resulted in GDP per capita increasing from US$835 in 2002 to about US$1,980 in 2008 (National Statistical Bureau of Bhutan, 2008). The contribution of the major sectors to the GDP in 2008 was primary sector 21.2 per cent, secondary sector 39.1 per cent

Table 10.1
Selected Social Indicators

S. No.	Indicators	2008
1.	Net primary enrolment rate	88.00%
2.	National literacy rate	59.50%
3.	Adult literacy rate	53.00%
4.	Population growth rate	1.33%
5.	Infant mortality rate (per 1,000)	40.13%
6.	Under 5 mortality rate (per 1,000)	61.53%
7.	Maternal mortality rate (per 100,000)	150–200
8.	Access to improved sanitation	89%
9.	Access to improved drinking water	84%

Source: Royal Government of Bhutan (2008).

Note: The indicators are grouped on sector basis. The first three are education indicators and remaining health.

and tertiary sector 39.7 per cent (National Statistical Bureau of Bhutan, 2008).

As a result of these developments in the social and economic sectors, the Human Development Index for Bhutan has climbed steadily from 0.583 in 2003 to 0.613 in 2006, moving Bhutan from low human development countries to medium human development countries. Bhutan currently ranks 131 among all countries.

In spite of the remarkable socio-economic progress, around one-fourth of the population, mostly living in rural areas, continue to live below the national poverty line (Ngultrum 1,096 per month or US$0.80 per day). As per the Poverty Analysis Report 2007, about 23.2 per cent of the population lives in poverty. Therefore, poverty reduction still remains a challenge and to address it, the continued support and cooperation of our development partners/foreign aid is important.

Further, as per Bhutan Millennium Development Goals (MDGs) Needs Assessment and Costing Report (2006–15),[1] Bhutan will need to invest around US$2.5 billion in 2005 prices between 2006 and 2015 to achieve the MDGs or US$3,937 per capita for the next 10 years from 2006 to 2015. With Bhutan yet to realize self-reliance in financing its development activities, aid would be critical if Bhutan is to achieve the MDGs.

SOCIO-ECONOMIC DEVELOPMENT FRAMEWORK

Bhutan's socio-economic development is guided by the philosophy of maximizing and attaining Gross National Happiness (GNH). The GNH essentially attempts to secure a harmonious balance between material well-being (Gross National Product or GNP), and spiritual, emotional and cultural needs of an individual and society. The four pillars of GNH which sets the broad framework for socio-economic development in Bhutan include sustainable economic growth and development, preservation and promotion of cultural heritage, preservation and sustainable use of environment, and good governance.

Within this broad socio-economic development framework, Bhutan has prepared a 20-year perspective strategy, entitled 'Bhutan 2020: A Vision for Peace, Prosperity and Happiness', which sets the preferred direction where Bhutan wants to be twenty years from base year of 2000.

On a medium-term basis, the vision articulated in the 20-year perspective strategy, is translated into five-year development plans. Bhutan currently is in its 10th Five Year Plan which started in July 2008 and will conclude in June 2013. The main objective of the 10th Plan is Poverty Reduction with the target of reducing poverty from 23.2 per cent[2] in 2007 to below 15 per cent by 2013.

The Five Year Plans are then further translated into annual plans through the annual budgets.

FINANCING OF SOCIO-ECONOMIC DEVELOPMENT PLANS

The Five Year Plans are financed through domestic revenues, external development assistance, external concessionary borrowings and domestic borrowings.

The 10th Plan outlay projected in Table 10.2 illustrates the contribution of various financing sources to the Plan outlay.

Table 10.2
10th Five Year Plan Outlay

	US$ (million)	Percentage of outlay
Total Expenditure	3,363	
(i) Recurrent Exp	1,650	49
(ii) Capital Exp	1,672	49
(iii) Net Lending	41	2
Total Resources	2,804	83
(i) Domestic Revenue	1,713	51
(ii) External Grants	1,091	32
Overall Fiscal Position	(–)559	
Financing	559	
Net Borrowings	215	
External Borrowings	259	8
Repayment	44	
Resource Gap	344	10
Annual Average Fiscal Deficit (% of GDP)	6.76%	
Annual Average Resource Gap (% of GDP)	4.15%	

Source: Royal Government of Bhutan (2008).

Domestic revenue finances 51 per cent of the total outlay, external grants 32 per cent, external borrowings 8 per cent, and domestic borrowings 9 per cent. Foreign aid, including both grants and borrowings, account for about 40 per cent of the total financing.

Aid received by Bhutan comprises the following:

1. Grants
2. Borrowings
3. Technical assistance (TA)
4. Food aid (World Food Programme or WFP)

The government's fiscal policy towards achieving self-reliance and sustainable development has been to finance all recurrent costs through domestic revenues and capital costs through foreign aid. Dependence on foreign aid is going to continue till such time the government is able to meet all development costs through its internal revenue.

RECENT AID TRENDS

Trends in Levels of Foreign Aid and Donors

In terms of absolute value, foreign grants to Bhutan have increased from Ngultrum 16 billion in the 8th Plan to Ngultrum 48 billion in the 10th Plan. However, in terms of the overall outlay, the share of foreign grants has decreased from 39 per cent of outlay in the 8th Plan to about 32 per cent in the 10th Plan (Table 10.3).

Trends in the Role of Traditional Donors and New Donors

India is the oldest and the largest development partner to Bhutan and it continues to remain so. The first two Five Year Plans, starting in 1961, were financed entirely by the Government of India. Besides India, some assistance was provided by Switzerland and Austria in the 1960s. Following Bhutan's membership in the UN in 1971, Bhutan started receiving assistance from UN agencies. Many of Bhutan's bilateral partners used to channel their assistance through the UN system, and it was only in the early 1980s that they started providing assistance directly. The other major bilateral development partners include Austria, Australia, Canada, Denmark, Dutch, the EU, Japan, Switzerland, Norway, Thailand, etc. Among the UN agencies, the major partners include United Nations Development Programme (UNDP), United Nations Children's Fund (UNICEF), United Nations Population Fund (UNFPA), United Nations Capital Development Fund (UNCDF), WFP, World Health Organization (WHO), etc.

International Financial Institutes providing soft term loans include the World Bank, Asian Development Bank (ADB) and International Fund for Agriculture Development. Bhutan also receives concessional bilateral loan financing from the Government of India (mainly for hydropower projects), Denmark (mixed credit), Japan (JBIC loan) and Austria (export promotion scheme) (see Figure 10.1).

Table 10.3

Expenditure, Revenue and Foreign Grants

	Eighth Plan (Ngultrum in million)	Percentage of expenditure	Ninth Plan (Ngultrum in million)	Percentage of expenditure	10th Plan (Ngultrum in million)	Percentage of expenditure
Total expenditure	41,000	100	85,000	100	148,000	100
Percentage change			107		74	
Domestic revenue	21,000	51	46,000	54	75,000	51
Percentage change			119		63	
External assistance	16,000	39	30,000	35	48,000	32
Percentage change			88		60	

Source: Royal Government of Bhutan (various years).

Figure 10.1

Contribution of Bilateral, Multilateral and IFIs to Development Assistance in 9th and 10th Plans

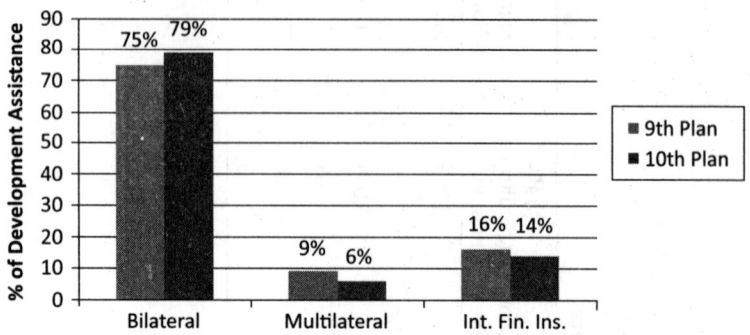

Source: Royal Government of Bhutan (various years).

In terms of foreign aid composition, on an average, grant aid constitutes about 85 per cent of total foreign aid and concessionary loans about 15 per cent. Bilateral development partners contribute about 79 per cent of total grants and multilateral partners 11 per cent. Among the bilateral development partners, India's contribution to aid constitutes about 75 per cent of total bilateral grants.

Bhutan receives foreign aid in the form of both budgetary grants and project-tied grants. India, Denmark, Austria, Dutch and the European Commission (EC) provide part of their assistance in the form of sector budgetary grants.

Significance of Foreign Aid in National Budgets and Fiscal Policy

Foreign aid plays an important role in the national budget as foreign aid finances a large part of the budget. Foreign aid finances capital investment while domestic revenues finance recurrent expenditures.

Over the years, composition of foreign aid to budget has been declining from about more than 50 per cent in Seventh and Eighth Plan to about 35 per cent in 2009–10 financial year (see Figure 10.2).

In terms of foreign aid as per centage of GDP, it has reduced from 50 per cent in the early 1980s to about 14 per cent in 2009–10 (see Figure 10.3).

Figure 10.2
Grants as a Percentage of Expenditure

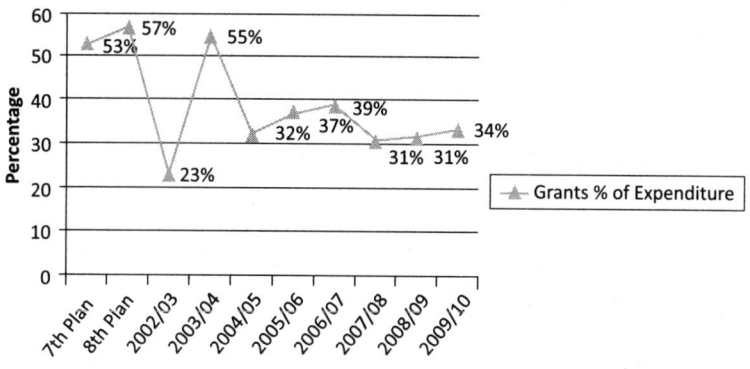

Source: Royal Government of Bhutan (various years).

ROLE OF DEVELOPMENT ASSISTANCE

Which Sectors Have Foreign Assistance been Financing

The main areas financed by development assistance are capacity building, institutional strengthening and infrastructure investments. The

Figure 10.3
Grants as a Percentage of GDP

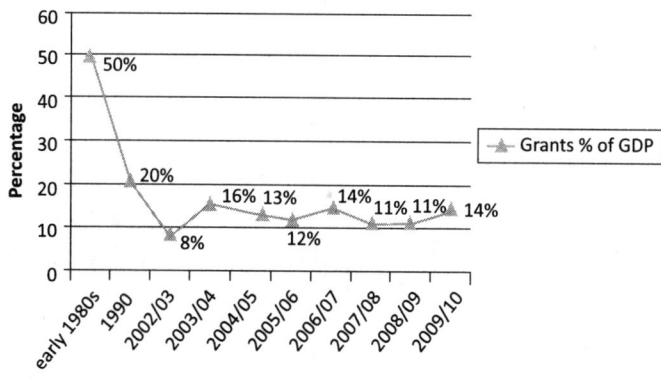

Source: Royal Government of Bhutan (various years).

education sector received the largest share of external grants followed by agriculture, transport and communications, health, etc. (see Figure 10.4). The share of electricity is only about 5 per cent of the total as mega hydropower projects are not included as these are implemented under non-plan programme.

Are These in Line with Development Priorities in Bhutan

With the primary objective of reducing poverty from 23.2 per cent in 2007 to below 15 per cent by 2013, the sectoral allocation of development assistance is in line with the development priorities. The Bhutan Poverty Analysis Report, 2004, indicates a strong link between educational attainment and poverty incidence. The findings from the report indicate that mid-secondary level education was generally adequate to raise an individual out of poverty. Accordingly, the education sector receives the highest share of foreign aid.

The second largest recipient of foreign aid is the agriculture sector. Some of the causes of poverty in rural areas, which is largely dependent on agriculture, are low productivity, subsistence farming and lack of market access. Therefore, investments in increasing productivity, commercial farming, promotion of horticulture/cash crops, creation of rural infrastructure (farm roads, storage, etc.), are some of the major strategies in the current plan for which large portion of foreign aid is allocated.

Figure 10.4
Share of External Grants for 2008–09

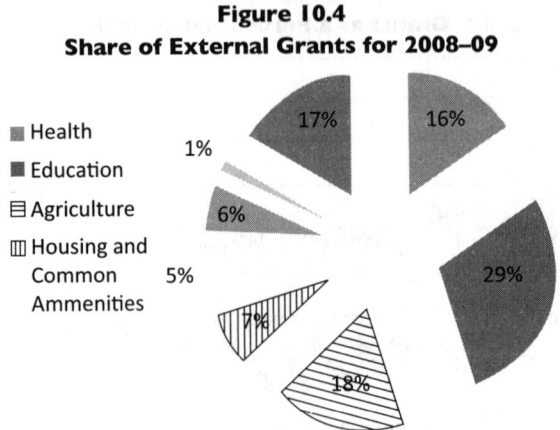

- Health
- Education
- Agriculture
- Housing and Common Ammenities

Source: Royal Government of Bhutan (various years).

Roads, bridges, telecommunication continue to be of high priority and a healthy population is essential for a healthy economy. Therefore, sectors financed by foreign aid are in line with the development priorities.

CONTEMPORARY ROLE OF DEVELOPMENT ASSISTANCE

Need for Foreign Assistance in Medium- and Long-term Development

Development assistance has played an important role in Bhutan's socio-economic development over the last five decades and it will continue to do so in the medium- and long-term development.

While domestic revenues have grown significantly over the years, it has not been able to keep pace with the expenditure growth, as a result of which it will not be possible to cover all development costs through domestic revenues. The cost of maintaining infrastructure such as schools, roads, hospitals, etc., constructed in the past is increasing every year. In the 10th Plan, expenditures are projected to grow annually by 6 per cent while revenue growth is projected at 4 per cent per annum. This trend is expected to continue until some of the hydropower projects, the main source of revenue, come on stream.

Bhutan has hydropower potential of about 30,000 MW, but as of now only 1,489 MW has been harnessed. In spite of having harnessed only 5 per cent of the total potential, it still continues to drive the economy, and contributes close to a quarter of the GDP and 40 per cent of total national revenue. Recognizing the potential of hydro-power's contribution to the economy, in the medium term the target is to increase hydropower generation from the present levels to 1,602 MW[3] by 2013, and 10,000 MW by 2020 by accelerating development of hydropower plants. Construction of 1,200 MW Punatsangchhu HEP I (2008–15) is under way and preparation for construction of 1,000 MW Punatsangchhu HEP II and 720 MW Mangdechhu HEP is ongoing.

Development Assistance and National Development Strategies/Poverty Reduction Strategy Paper (PRSP)

The national development strategies/PRSP, in the case of Bhutan—the Five Year Plans, is the basis for seeking development assistance. The

Round Table Meeting (RTM) between the development partners and the government is held twice during the plan period. The first RTM, which is a resource mobilization exercise, is held prior to the launch of the new Five Year Plan and this is where the development partners are sensitized of the government's policies, priorities and programmes for the next five years based on which the support of development partners are sought. The second RTM is held mid-way through the plan period to take stock of the progress achieved over the last two and half years and to realign strategies if necessary.

The last RTM was held in February 2008 and the next RTM is scheduled to be held in May 2011.

National Development Strategies/PRSP, drive the level and areas of foreign assistance required over the plan period.

AID EFFECTIVENESS

Although not a signatory to the Paris Declaration (PD), Bhutan has been following the principles of the PD on aid effectiveness:

1. Strengthening country's ownership of the development process: Bhutan's socio-economic development process is guided by the 20-year vision document which is then translated into Five Year Plans, and currently Bhutan is in the 10th Five Year Plan. The Five Year Plans articulate what the country wants to achieve over the next five years. The main objective of the Plan, major policies and programmes are clearly highlighted along with resource requirements and monitoring and evaluation mechanism. The Five Year Plans dictate the country's development process and forms the basis for foreign aid mobilization.

    While the central government plans are based on national priorities, the local government plans are based on local priorities, prioritized by the local governments.

2. Ensuring alignment of development partner support to national priorities: The development cooperation between Bhutan and its development partners are based on the country programme document, country partnership document, Country Assistance Strategy (CAS), United Nations Development

Assistance Framework (UNDAF), etc. These documents are prepared by the development partners in close consultation with the government as a result of which the development partner's support is closely aligned to national priorities. Review of cooperation between the government and development partners are held to re-prioritize and realign development cooperation.

The preparation of these documents, are timed to ensure that its implementation, as far as possible, coincides with the implementation of the Five Year Plans.

3. Ensuring harmonization of donor procedures and country systems: The emphasis of the government has been on national execution of projects and programmes, whereby country systems are followed and to a large extent this has been the modality of execution of most donor assisted projects and programmes in Bhutan.

   The government continues to strengthen its financial and procurement management system, auditing systems, budgeting and accounting system, monitoring systems, etc. These efforts on the part of the government have provided greater confidence to donors to adopt the country's systems. However, there are some donors who continue to use their systems mainly because of the modality of assistance provided, for example, assistance from Japan that is largely generous.

   Efforts are also being made to harmonize procedures not only between the government and development partners but also among development partners to reduce the administrative burden and transaction cost. These include the UN's Common Country Action Plan (cCAP), joint annual work plans, joint government–UN country programme board, etc. aimed at harmonizing procedures among different agencies in the UN systems.

4. Management of resources on the basis of agreed results and use of information to improve decision-making: Bhutan's 10th Five Year Plan is based on the Results Based Management (RBM) framework whereby allocation of resources is tied to achievement of results (output/outcome). The Planning and Monitoring System (PLaMS), online monitoring system is used to monitor the programmes. This monitoring system

will be integrated with the Multi Year Rolling Budget (MYRB) and Public Expenditure Management System (PEMS) to further improve information flow and comprehensive monitoring of programmes both in terms of physical and financial progress.

The 10th Plan mid-term review, scheduled to start in November 2010, will be focusing on results (output/outcome) rather than the budget utilization, as was the case in the past. These are some of the initiatives government is taking to move towards RBM.

5. Ensuring mutual accountability in relation to resource flow and results achieved through implementation of national strategies.

FUTURE POLICY PRIORITIES

Bhutan has been receiving high quality foreign aid in terms of the following:

1. Foreign aid Bhutan receives is aligned to its national priorities and Five Year Plans.
2. The CAS, UNDAF, partnership documents, etc. between government and development partners clearly indicate the areas of support and indicative financial support over a period of 3–5 years making aid more predictable.
3. Part of the aid received is in the form of budgetary support from selected development partners. This allows greater flexibility in terms of prioritization, allocation and utilization of resources.
4. Large numbers of donor funded programmes/projects are executed through national execution modality. This has facilitated in further strengthening country systems and capacity building.

However, both the development partners and the government could do more to make aid even more effective.

Role of Development Partners

1. Provide more untied aid in the form of budgetary support, programme support, sector budget support. This would not only provide greater flexibility to the government but also make aid more effective in terms of where to use, when to use and how to use foreign aid.
2. National execution of programmes/projects. Many development partners prefer to use their systems as the country systems may not be adequate. This does not really help the country in the long run. Development partners could help improve the country systems and capacity building by moving towards national execution of programmes and projects and helping countries strengthen their systems.
3. Greater transparency of information from development partners, particularly on direct disbursements for procurements and technical assistance.
4. Towards greater harmonization and alignment, development partners could consider government-led common arrangements/procedures for reviewing, reporting, monitoring, etc. This would reduce administrative burdens and transaction cost of multiple reviewing, reporting and monitoring.

Role of Governments

1. Clearly articulated national development strategies. Governments need to put in place clearly articulated national development strategies that include well defined objectives, strategies, targets and resource requirements.
2. Strengthen country systems for procurement, financial management, monitoring and evaluation, etc., and enhance governance by improving transparency and accountability and reducing corruption.
3. Enhance efforts to increase domestic resource mobilization through accelerated socio-economic development. In Bhutan, some of the recent initiatives to address poverty and to accelerate economic development include:
   a. Rehabilitation strategy attempts to address poverty at individual or household level by granting of land to the

landless, functionally landless and the socio-economically disadvantaged/marginalized communities. Landlessness is a major cause and effect of poverty in developing countries, particularly in rural areas. In Bhutan, majority of the rural people depend on agriculture and agriculture-related activities to sustain their livelihoods. In some areas, the poor are more vulnerable to chronic poverty due to their dependence on sharecropping and inadequate land. Recognizing strong linkages between poverty and land, the landless, near landless and those practising shifting cultivation are granted land by His Majesty, the King. Together with granting of land, adequate socio-economic facilities are provided to create and enhance income generation opportunities to the people.

b. Rural Economy Advancement Programme (REAP) attempts to address poverty at village level by focusing on development of village level plans. The REAP focuses on the reduction of extreme poverty and as such, targets the poorest villages in the country. The AP endeavours to take into consideration the special needs of the rural poor who have not benefited much from broad-based poverty reduction interventions and economic growth, and to address them specifically through targeted interventions that supplement, in a synergistic way, mainstream development efforts.

c. Accelerating Bhutan's Socio-economic Development (ABSD) programme[4]—The programme was initiated in 2009 with three key objectives, *(a)* improving efficiency and effectiveness of public service, *(b)* generate substantial portion of jobs required during the current Five Year Plan, and *(c)* enabling and managing change to ensure real and sustained impact.

The initiative focuses on 10 key sectors/agencies with potential to contribute towards achieving the above objectives. A detailed diagnostics of the sector is carried out and critical initiatives to be implemented over the next three years (till June 2013) prioritized. This is followed by signing of a Performance Compact between the prime minister and the sector minister, whereby the sector minister commits to the prime minister to deliver the initiatives included in the Performance Compact within the agreed time frame. The prime minister, on his part, commits to provide all resources, cooperation and support required for the sector minister to deliver the initiatives.

To facilitate the implementation of the initiatives, a special unit called 'Performance Facilitation Unit' (PFU) within the Gross National Happiness Commission Secretariat is created. The PFU is responsible for facilitating smooth implementation by addressing de-bottlenecking issues, inter-ministerial coordination, participating in weekly review meetings, facilitating quarterly review meetings between cabinet and the sectors and keeping the prime minister informed on the progress of the programme.

The programme is being implemented with McKinsey and Co., an international management consulting firm.

CONCLUSION

Bhutan has made significant progress in its socio-economic development efforts and foreign aid has played an important role. While significant progress has been made, Bhutan continues to face the challenges of delivering socio-economic facilities/services to all sections of the population due to its rugged terrain, scattered population and harsh geographical conditions as a result of which poverty remains a concern.

In terms of financing of socio-economic development activities, while the dependence on foreign aid has been declining gradually over the years it is still yet to achieve 100 per cent self-reliance in financing. Therefore, foreign aid will be necessary and will continue to play an important role in Bhutan's socio-economic development effort and achieving MDGs.

Foreign aid received by Bhutan is of high quality and includes both grants and soft loans, budgetary and project-tied assistance and is aligned with the national development strategies. Many of the programmes and projects are implemented on national execution basis, whereby country systems are used in the implementation of programmes and projects. However, Bhutan believes that there is still room for further improvements, both on the part of the government and its development partners, to make foreign aid more effective.

NOTES

1. Planning Commission, Royal Government of Bhutan, November 2007.
2. Poverty Analysis Report 2007.
3. 10th Five Year Plan.
4. www.gnhc.gov.bt/absd/ (accessed on September 2009).

REFERENCES

National Statistical Bureau of Bhutan (2008), 'National Accounts Statistics (2000–2008),' National Statistical Bureau, Bhutan. Royal Government of Bhutan.

Rehabilitation Strategy Framework (draft), Royal Government of Bhutan.

Royal Government of Bhutan (2005), 'Population and Housing Census of Bhutan', Royal Government of Bhutan.

——— (2007a), 'Poverty Analysis Report', National Statistical Bureau, Royal Government of Bhutan.

——— (2007b), 'Bhutan Millennium Development Goals, Needs Assessment and Costing Report (2006–15)', Planning Commission, November, Royal Government of Bhutan.

——— (2008), 'Tenth Year Plan (2008–2013), Volume I and II', Gross National Happiness Commission, Royal Government of Bhutan.

——— (2010), 'National Budget Financial Year 2010–11', Ministry of Finance, Royal Government of Bhutan, June.

——— (various years,) 'Annual Financial Statements of the Royal Government of Bhutan', Department of Public Accounts, Ministry of Finance for the years 2002–03, 2003–04, 2004–05, 2005–06, 2006–07 and 2008–09.

ROLE OF AID IN SMALL AND VULNERABLE ECONOMY

11

Maldives[1]

HUSSAIN NIYAAZ

INTRODUCTION

Since the Maldives emerged as an independent nation in 1965 and joined the international family of nations by becoming a member of the UN in 1968, it has transformed both economically, as well as, socially during the decades that followed. From a virtually unknown group of isolated islands in the Indian Ocean, largely dependent on two primary industries of fisheries and agriculture, it has rapidly changed to a world renowned holiday destination, with tourism, since its introduction to the country in 1972, now its economic backbone.

Parallel to the growth of the tourism industry, the Maldives fishing industry also underwent a major modernization programme with its entire fishing fleet getting overhauled from a solely sail-based one to a fully mechanized fleet. This has vastly improved the fish catch and hence the livelihoods of the island fishing communities. These two economic sectors have jointly contributed to the rapid economic development experienced by the country during the past decades. Per capita Gross Domestic Product (GDP) estimated at 1995 constant prices was US$404 in 1977. The corresponding estimate for 2008 was US$2,912 (Department of National Planning, 2010). However, serious issues relating to the distribution of income exist in the country. Compared to regional countries, income distribution is relatively unequal in the Maldives with marked increases in inequality between Male' the capital and the rest of the country.

During the past 40 odd years, the Maldives have benefited from its membership in the UN and other International Multilateral Organizations, and from its close bilateral political relationships with donor countries across the world. Against extreme human resource constraints and geographical challenges, the Maldives has always maintained high rates of aid utilization focusing on key social sectors such as health and education. As a result, indicators such as Under Five Mortality Rates, Childhood Immunization Rates and Gross Enrolment Rates, particularly in the primary school ages, rose rapidly. These achievements have been reflected in the performance of the Maldives in the United Nations Human Development Index since it was first published in 1990. In 1991, the first assessment where the Maldives was reported, its Human Development Index was 0.503 and in the medium category. The latest report, released in the Maldives on 30 November 2010, showed that, at present, the Human Development Index for the Maldives stands at 0.602.

Rapid developments in the socio-economic conditions have brought immense benefits to the Maldivian people. However, it has also resulted in several fallouts. Inadequate consideration of the population dynamics in national development planning in the past has led to mounting social issues such as housing congestion, congestion in schools, inadequate services for the growing youth population, which in turn have created daunting social challenges for the country today. Lack of sufficient space within their crowded homes have led youth to spend more time outside their homes, thus leading to a growth in gang culture in the Maldives during the recent decades. Without appropriate attention and mentoring from adults both in the schools, as well as homes, a large component of the youth population do not have the skills nor the attitude to participate actively and productively in the job opportunities that exist in the job market, leaving them vulnerable to drugs, exploitation and crime.

All the above problems have been compounded with the 2004 Asian tsunami, which physically washed away 60 per cent of its GDP. According to the World Bank, ADB and UN (2005) reports,of the 198 inhabited islands in the archipelago, 53 per cent suffered severe damage, 10 per cent of the islands were totally destroyed and 7 per cent of the entire population was displaced. Schools, clinics and pharmacies were destroyed in some 50 islands. According to the National Disaster Management Centre, 64 schools, 30 health centres and 60 island administrative facilities need to be reconstructed or rehabilitated. In total, more than 5,000 buildings were damaged, 79 islands had no safe drinking water and 15 per cent of the water systems are destroyed or contaminated. In the tourism sector, out of the 87 resorts, 19 were severely damaged and had to be closed down, while 14 others suffered major partial damage.

With the unprecedented levels of external humanitarian assistance received following the tsunami, the Maldives was making a recovery when again the triple shocks of the Food, Fuel and Financial crises swept the world with drastic effects on the already weakened economic and social structures of the country. Ironically, the United Nations decided to graduate the Maldives from being on the list of Least Developed Countries (LDCs) just a week before the tsunami wreaked havoc. Subsequently, it decided to give only a three-year extension to the period of smooth transition, at the end of which the Maldives would graduate. The new smooth transition period ended on 31 December 2010.

It could not have coincided with a worse timing for the Maldives. The world is still recovering from the worst economic downturn in living memory, hugely impacting tourist arrivals and worsening the fiscal situation in the country; fish catch records are at an all time low; the country is compelled to enter into a Standby Credit Facility with the International Monetary Fund (IMF) for the first time, undergo severe budget cuts and slash down the salaries of the public service employees, expenditure on health and education and introduce other cost-cutting measures.

Amidst such extreme social and economic difficulties, the country is also going through a phase of rapid political transformation. Within a short space of about five years or so, the country has changed from an autocratic rule without any freedom of expression to a democratic multi-party system of governance with full freedom of speech. With a Parliament under the control of the opposition coalition, this makes adoption of alternative development financing options such as privatization of public infrastructure, attraction of Foreign Direct Investment (FDI), introduction of legislation to facilitate taxation, civil service reform and governance reform extremely difficult to implement.

While in the middle of these mounting challenges, the Maldives will graduate at the end of 2010. It is likely that this will have several undesirable effects on the levels and amounts of concessionary development financing it can receive from traditional development partners, both bilateral and multilateral and, thus, impose further pressures on sustainable social and economic development of the country.

RECENT TRENDS IN FOREIGN ASSISTANCE RECEIPTS IN THE MALDIVES

Trends in Levels of Foreign Aid

The development achievements that the Maldives has witnessed during the past four decades would not have been possible without the much needed support of the international community. As seen in Figure 11.1, foreign grant receipts to the Maldives have been decreasing since the 1990s. The decline roughly coincides with the period when the question of the Maldives' graduation was debated in the UN. Many of the traditional development partners of the Maldives that were closely observing these developments were already giving indications that they will not be able to continue assistance under their regular grant aid windows as the Maldives graduates from the UN's list of LDCs. On 20 December 2004, the decision was finally made to graduate the Maldives.

Shortly after, on 26 December 2004, the Indian Ocean tsunami struck and wreaked havoc on the entire length and breadth of the archipelago, wiping out several years of development and leaving psycho-social marks on the population that would last decades, if not generations, to overcome. The fragility and vulnerability of this Small Island nation

Figure 11.1
Foreign Grant Receipts, 1994–2009

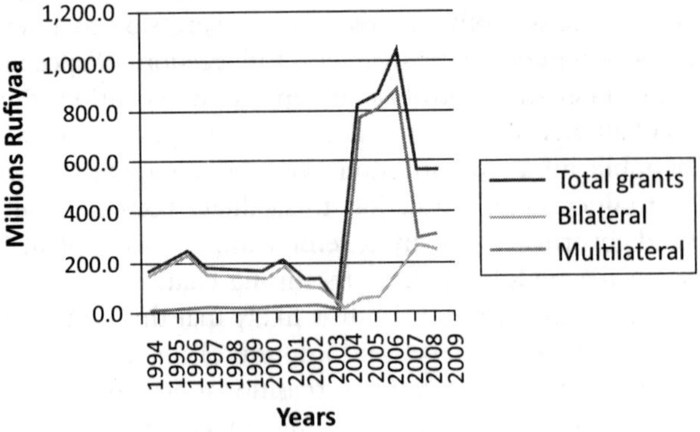

Source: Department of National Planning (2010).

became fully apparent with the profoundness of the impact of this one disaster on the entire nation.

As was the case with all other tsunami affected countries, unprecedented levels of aid flowed in to the country following the devastation. Local capacities were tested and criticisms about the inability of the local authorities to absorb foreign assistance were levelled at the government. Despite such problems, all sorts of aid were dispatched to the affected islands and their people. While many of the infrastructure and equipment provided by donors have helped the people to reclaim their lives and livelihoods, some of it still lay unutilized, either because of high recurrent costs of maintenance or some even due to their incompatibility with the local environment.

As the reconstruction period ended, most of the donors gradually pulled out as planned but several reconstruction projects still remain to be completed. Figure 11.1 clearly shows the dynamics of grant aid flows immediately following the tsunami and during the last couple of years. Many of the donor financed tsunami reconstruction projects took painfully long to deliver on the ground results, and the steep rise in the cost of construction materials in the international market, that coincided with the tsunami reconstruction period, meant that many of the reconstruction projects had to be scaled down to fit the available budgets of specific donors. As a result, tensions between the government and the already stressed local populations worsened, compelling the government to look for alternative means of financing the gaps. The only alternative for the cash pressed government appeared to be to borrow. A significant portion of the borrowings came from the commercial banks at significantly high interest rates with more stringent repayment terms. Figure 11.2 shows the steep rise in foreign loan disbursements between 2004 and 2008. It can be seen that while borrowings from multilateral sources and bilateral development or export-import banks declined, commercial borrowings increased up to 2008.

Figure 11.3 shows the trends in overall inflow of foreign aid to the Maldives and the proportionate distribution of types of foreign aid between 2000 and 2008. While bilateral grants comprised the major share of foreign resource flows to the Maldives at the beginning of the decade, the following years up to 2004 (tsunami) saw the increasing prominence of bilateral loans in the flow. By 2003, loans—bilateral, multilateral and commercial—have become the major external source of development financing in the country. The tsunami changed it abruptly for a while, with multilateral grants contributing more than

Figure 11.2
Foreign Loan Disbursements, 1994–2008

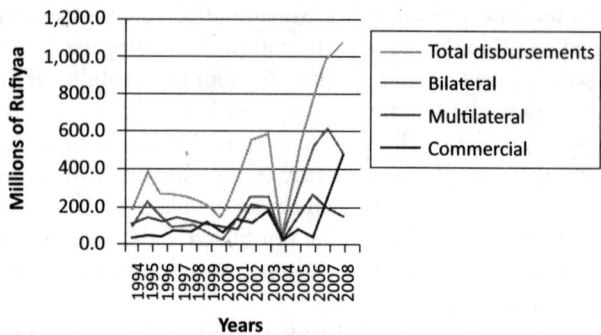

Source: Department of National Planning (2010).

Figure 11.3
External Resources by Type, 2000–08

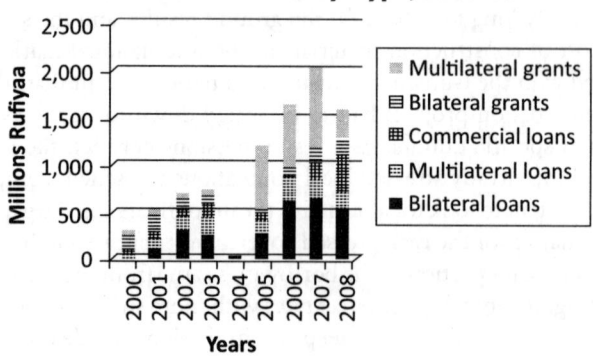

Source: Department of National Planning (2010).

half of all external resource flows in 2005. Recent data indicates that this was only a temporary effect resulting from the tsunami.

Trends in the Role of Traditional Donors and New Donors

Since the Maldives first started receiving Overseas Development Assistance (ODA) at a significant scale, up to the end of the last century, bilateral grant assistance from Japan contributed significantly to the development projects in the Maldives. Most of these were high cost

infrastructure projects such as school buildings, social service buildings and coastal protection infrastructure. Throughout the 1990s and up to the year 2003, Japan contributed the largest share of all grant assistance that came into the country.

However, as the Maldives approached graduation from LDC status, Japan scaled down its grant assistance programme to the Maldives and encouraged the country to seek the Yen loan option instead. The first such loan was sanctioned for harbour and sewerage rehabilitation projects following the tsunami of 2004.

Despite this shift in policy, Japan contributed significant levels of grant assistance towards the rehabilitation of infrastructure and livelihoods lost during the tsunami, and Japan continues to provide food aid to the Maldives. In addition to this, Japan has also recently made indirect contribution towards budgetary support in the form of Non-project Grant Assistance to purchase petroleum for local consumption.

With the declining annual grant contribution of Japan, except for the growing importance of grant assistance from China, and to a certain extent, from India, new donor assistance has not been as forthcoming as currently needed for the sustainable socio-economic development of the Maldives (see Figure 11.4).

With the declining annual grant contribution of Japan, except for the growing importance of grant assistance from China, and to a certain extent, from India, new donor assistance has not been as forthcoming as currently needed for the sustainable socio-economic development of the Maldives.

Maldives is, in this sense, at a development paradox where, due to its human development indicators and the impending LDC graduation, donors are reluctant to extend grant assistance, while, given the current fiscal woes of the country, the extent to which it can avail itself of the various concessionary loan financing options to finance critical sectors such as health care and education, is strictly limited.

Significance of Foreign Aid in National Budget and Fiscal Policy

With a narrow economic base, dependent on two key economic sectors, fishing and tourism, that are highly vulnerable to exogenous shocks, the Maldives has, and will continue to, depend on external sources of funding for a significant proportion of its development budget. The types and levels of assistance required may vary from time to time.

Figure 11.4
Bilateral Grant Inflows by Source Country, 1994–2009

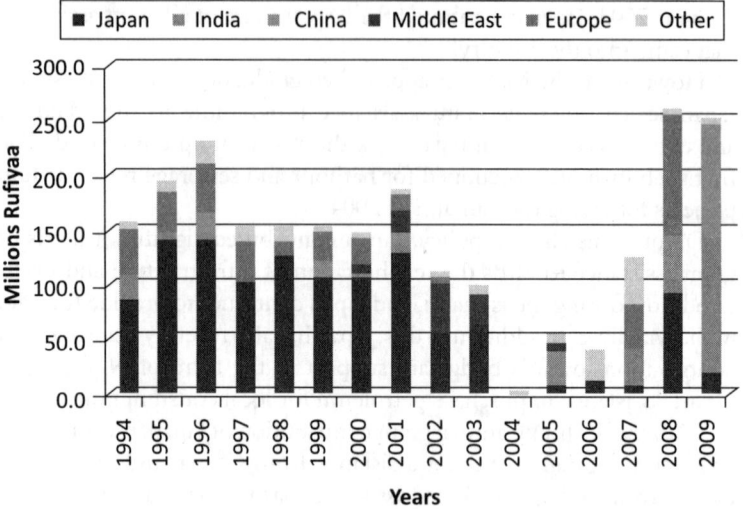

Source: Department of National Planning (2010).

At present, grants comprise a significant component of the national budget, particularly for non-recurrent capital expenditure. It is not only grant assistance but the growing importance of concessionary loan financing for the establishment of essential infrastructure, must be highlighted. Grant assistance also plays an important and indispensable role in the development of human resources. Without the existence of adequate higher education institutions in the country, the Maldives relies heavily on bilateral and multilateral scholarships for Maldivian students to study in overseas universities and other training centres. Several countries, including Australia, India and Egypt, among others, provide considerable numbers of full scholarships to Maldivian students to study at their universities.

The Maldives has also received direct budgetary support from friendly countries during times of extreme budgetary difficulties.

Aid Effectiveness

The most visible indicators of effectiveness of aid to the Maldives are its high levels of educational enrolment, childhood immunization, life expectancy at birth, low prevalence of communicable diseases, low infant and childhood mortality rates and birth rates, all achieved within a relative short space of time. The success of these achievements has been instrumental in leading to graduation of the Maldives from the list of LDCs.

CONTEMPORARY ROLE OF FOREIGN ASSISTANCE IN THE MALDIVES

Maldives is at development crossroads.It is undergoing an age-structural transition from having the majority of its population under the age of 14 to the majority of its population in the youthful ages; it is transitioning from an autocratic, one party system of government to a muliparty democracy with full separation of powers, and it is graduating from the category of an LDC to a developing country. Each of these transitions presents their peculiar challenges and opportunities. It is imperative that the international community provides its fullest support to the Maldives at this important juncture in its development. Inadequate attention to any of these issues have the potential to lead to long lasting negative consequences for the country's long-term goals of becoming a well-functioning democratic state and a productive member of the international community that is less dependent on international aid for its own development.

Relevance of Foreign Aid for Medium- and Long-term Development

For reasons described above, the Maldives needs, at present, perhaps more than any other time in its history, the fullest cooperation of the international community in achieving its set developmental targets. With the inherent difficulties of being a Small Island developing state, raising sufficient resources on its own would be extremely difficult to achieve and perhaps more difficult to sustain.

Under the leadership of the first democratically elected president, the government is committed to install alternative revenue generation mechanisms such as the introduction of a Tourism Tax and Business Profit Tax over a period of time. The FDI is being vigorously pursued to fund major infrastructure projects and, to the extent possible, in the efficient running of social services. However, with the smallness of the domestic market and with a highly vocal political opposition, these policies are proving to be challenging to implement.

Key Opportunity Costs of Foreign Aid

The Maldives received unprecedented levels of grant assistance following the tsunami of 2004. In addition to the large inflows of funds that entered into the national economy through contract payments for the rehabilitation projects, cash handouts were also given to affected families. These led to increasing costs of construction materials and essential food items in the domestic market.

Much of the foreign aid still comes as tied aid. This means that for the most part of a project, contractors and construction materials are procured overseas, with little involvement of the beneficiary communities. This often leads to a lack of community participation in the project in the construction or development stages and therefore a lack of ownership. Traditionally, community projects are implemented with the full participation of the beneficiary communities and without this vital link between the projects and the beneficiaries, the traditional spirit of community volunteerism and participation is lost. Capacities of the local people are not developed in the process and people's expectations from the government are increased.

It must also be noted that often, due to increasing cost of project inputs, projects initially promised to communities are scaled down and people and the government are left with the extra burden of completing the projects and in many instances, with huge recurrent costs.

Government Structure for the Prioritization and Decision on Projects Requiring External Assistance

Foreign aid mobilization is coordinated by the government through an established aid-coordination mechanism that has been agreed with development partners through interactions such as the annual Maldives Partnership Forum and the Donor Conference. The National Planning Council, chaired by the president and represented by key ministers (finance, economic development, housing and environment) and representatives of the private sector and social sector, decides and prioritizes on the projects to be submitted for donor financing.

Decisions are based on the government manifesto and the Strategic Action Plan of the manifesto document, with considerations for duplication and recurrent cost to the budget.

Despite the existence of such a mechanism, in practice, specific sectors are often dictated by donor preference. For example, environment and climate change is a priority area for most donors at present, and the success of securing donor funding depends to a great extent on how well the project addresses the donor priority area. While this is the case, climate adaptation projects for island communities which are often too costly for funding from the national budget, are easily brushed off by donors, as they categorize such projects as commercial infrastructure projects.

Although health and education continue to be important areas requiring urgent donor intervention for the Maldives, donors do not accord priority to such projects at present. Much emphasis is made on providing only soft interventions such as training and technical assistance (TA), whereas, the ground reality is that the high capital investments required, particularly in the health sector, is at the moment beyond the means of local resources.

EFFECTIVENESS OF AID

National Ownership, Alignment, Harmonization and Managing for Results

To ensure *national ownership*, the Maldives exercise effective leadership over development policies and ODA projects and programmes. The president himself dedicates considerable time to ensure that requests for assistance are streamlined and prioritized and that ongoing development projects, particularly those that are donor funded are implemented efficiently and effectively. However, real issues of capacities exist in the line ministries that are responsible to deliver on the ground implementation of projects, thus, leading to inevitable delays at all stages of the project cycle. The government has acknowledged this shortfall and is trying to address it through the establishment of a central project implementation unit under the Ministry of Finance and Treasury.

To ensure *alignment and harmonization*, the Maldives works with development partners to base their overall support to national development plans and strategies. Examples of such efforts are the Maldives Partnership Forum convened in the Maldives on an annual basis, and the recent Donor Conference held in the Maldives. This has become a key feature of the Government of Maldives and the international donor community interactions.

For the first time in the Maldives, the government budget was prepared under the principles of Managing for Development Results (MfDR). While this proved to be an arduous task and tough learning experience for most of the government ministries and departments, the unwavering commitment from the Executive was instrumental in driving all departments, to align the budget to deliver the outputs and outcomes stated in the Strategic Action Plan of the government.

Role of Domestic Governance in Aid Effectiveness

Typical of Small Island states, the Maldives suffers from severe shortages of skilled personnel, particularly in the public service. This imposes constraints on the efficiency with which aid is utilized in some instances. However, when sufficient planning and consultation precedes the actual project implementation, the results have been more positive and when there is a close match between the needs of the recipient population (in the present case, the particular island population) and the donor priorities, effectiveness of aid has been greater. The National Planning Council ensures that aid is properly streamlined and donor complementarity is maintained in the allocation of donor funded projects. The National Planning Council further ensures that donor funded projects are both sustainable in the longer term as well as has minimal impact on the government's recurrent expenditure budget.

The existing division of responsibility between the Ministry of Foreign Affairs, Ministry of Finance and Treasury and the External Resources Coordinating Committee, chaired by the vice-president is, at times, ambiguous. This has resulted in a clear lack of ownership in the coordination of ongoing aid funded projects and hence unnecessary delays in implementation. A clearer division of responsibility and closer coordination needs to be worked out in order to ensure that aid is more effectively utilized in the future.

FUTURE POLICY PRIORITIES

Future policy priorities must be based on more streamlined foreign aid to address the implications of Maldives' graduation from LDC status, by negotiating with key donors on continuing support for critical projects that would assist the country to achieve its internationally agreed development targets, and to extend the existing concessional arrangements, open up new markets for the export of fisheries products to the international markets after graduation and beyond. It should also include preparing effective and high quality development projects that would continue to be financed by either grants or through concessional loans to ensure smooth transition to a developing country status.

In order to facilitate this, continuous engagement and dialogue should be maintained by the government between the civil society, private sector and development partners in order to effectively implement the national development strategies and achieve the MDGs and other internationally agreed developmental goals, including those on the environment front.

The government should work with the international community on the wider interests of other Small Island Developing States (SIDS) that are graduating from LDC status and ensure that SIDS, as a group is well represented in all international negotiations regarding environment, development and sustainable growth.

Approaching New Donors

The Maldives is in the process of donor mapping exercise to identify the right kind of aid. This exercise includes the traditional donors as well as new players to the donor landscape such as China and India. Maldives is implementing the following five-point approach:

1. develop a long-term international cooperation strategy to identify the role of development partners as donors, investment partners, etc;
2. enhance and streamline and clearly define the roles of key aid coordination institutions in the country;
3. revisit External Resources Coordinating Committee (ERCC) mandate;
4. make ERCC to be more active;
5. encourage donor presence in the country.

Towards a Longer Term Exit Strategy for Aid

The government is keen to see that most of the social services such as health care, education, utilities provision and housing are outsourced to the private sector, and encourage FDI initiatives to fund these. Several incentives are being established. However, these incentive packages that have been announced by the government in the past two years and many expected ventures have not progressed much due to the lack of appropriate legislation. Once proper legislation is in place, it is expected that these modes of development financing will be more successful in the longer run.

It must, however, be noted that the typical 'island paradox' would remain a reality, no matter how much the country is able to diversify its resource base. Similar to all other Small Island states, the Maldives would have to depend on the international community for certain types of aid, although the types of aid required may change over time.

CONCLUSION

Starting from very basic levels of development, the Maldives has managed to make considerable headway in the path of socio-economic development during the decades following its independence in 1965. Its economic conditions have improved several fold, with the introduction of the tourism industry and the modernization of the fishing industry. Thanks to the assistance of the international community, remarkable progress has also been made in social development. Most indicators of social development are now at levels comparable to many of the more advanced Small Island states of the world. These indicators are testament to the high levels of aid effectiveness in the Maldives. As a result of these successes, the Maldives will graduate from the list of LDCs at the end of 2010.

With graduation, the Maldives stands to lose many of the grant aid and concessions that it has enjoyed in the past. More specific bilateral arrangements with donors must be entered into in order to sustain, to the extent possible, concessionary financing during a mutually agreed smooth transition period. Furthermore, innovative modes of financing will be required to fund its development projects in the longer term. The government is already introducing appropriate legislation to enable the generation of domestic financing through taxation and other revenue generation methods.

While the existing aid prioritization mechanism has been commended by the donor community, the government needs to pay closer attention to improve the efficiency of aid coordination in the country. A greater donor presence in the country is being encouraged, in addition to measures that can be taken locally, such as making the External Resources Coordinating Committee more effective.

In spite of such measures, being a Small Island state, the Maldives will continue to be highly susceptible to exogenous shocks. Such shocks can only be overcome with the cooperation and assistance from the international community during such times.

NOTE

1. The chapter was written before Maldives graduated from an LDC to that of a Middle Income Country on 1 January 2011.

REFERENCES

Department of National Planning (2010), http://www.planning.gov.mv/statistics_ archive/statistical_tables.html (accessed on 21 December 2011). Department of National Planning (2010).

The World Bank, ADB and UN (2005), 'The Republic of Maldives, Tsunami: Impact and Recovery', http://www.adb.org/Documents/Reports/Tsunami/joint-needs-assessment.pdf (accessed on 21 December 2011).

About the Editor and Contributors

THE EDITOR

Saman Kelegama, D.Phil. (oxon), is the Executive Director of the Institute of Policy Studies of Sri Lanka (IPS), Colombo. He is a Fellow of the National Academy of Sciences of Sri Lanka, Colombo, and was also the President of Sri Lanka Economic Association (SLEA), Colombo, during 1999–2003.

An alumni of Indian Institute of Technology, Kanpur, India, where he received his Masters degree, Dr Kelegama has published extensively on economic issues of South Asia, and especially on Sri Lanka, in both local and international journals. His latest books are: *Trade Liberalization and Poverty in South Asia* (2011) and *Economic and Social Development under a Market Economy Regime in Sri Lanka* (2011). *Migration, Remittances, and Development in South Asia* (2011), *Promoting Economic Cooperation in South Asia: Beyond SAFTA* (2010), *Trade in Services in South Asia: Opportunities and Risks of Liberalization* (2009), *South Asia in the WTO* (2007), *Development under Stress: Sri Lankan Economy in Transition* (2006), *Contemporary Economic Issues: Sri Lanka in the Global Context* (2006), *South Asia After the Quota System: The Impact of the MFA Phase-Out* (2005), *Economic Policy in Sri Lanka: Issues and Debates* (2004) and *Ready-Made Garment Industry in Sri Lanka: Facing the Global Challenge* (2004) among many others.

He is the editor of the *South Asia Economic Journal* and serves as a referee for a number of international journals. He serves and had served in a number of government and private sector Boards as an independent member. He was a member of the National Economic Council under the President of Sri Lanka and the Presidential Taxation Commission of Sri Lanka.

THE CONTRIBUTORS

Vaqar Ahmed has worked as a Senior Economist with the United Nations Development Programme (UNDP) and the ministries of finance, planning and commerce in Pakistan. He is a faculty member at National University of Ireland, Dublin, Ireland, where he teaches public sector economics. He is currently an Advisor at the Planning Commission of Pakistan, where he coordinates the overall work on under formulation economic growth strategy and 10th Five Year Plan.

Indrajit Coomaraswamy was an official in the Central Bank of Sri Lanka, Colombo, from 1974 to 1989. He worked in the Economic Research, Statistics and Bank Supervision Divisions. During this time he was also seconded to the Ministry of Finance and Planning (1981–89).

He was employed by the Commonwealth Secretariat from 1990–2008. During this time, he held the positions, inter alia, of Director, Economic Affairs Division and Deputy-Director, Secretary-General's Office. He was subsequently Interim Director, Social Transformation Programme Division, Commonwealth Secretariat (January–July 2010).

He completed his undergraduate degree at University of Cambridge, UK, and obtained his Doctorate at the University of Sussex, UK.

Deshal de Mel is Research Economist at the Institute of Policy Studies of Sri Lanka (IPS), Colombo. His primary research areas include international trade, regionalism, international aid, trade in services and macroeconomics. He completed his undergraduate degree at the University of Oxford, UK, where he read philosophy, political science and economics. He completed his Masters Degree in International Political Economy from the London School of Economics, UK. Along with academic research, Deshal has been involved in international trade negotiations representing Sri Lanka. He has been active in consultative and collaborative work with USAID, UNIDO, UNESCAP, ADB and World Bank, among others.

Anneka De Silva is a researcher at GHK Consulting Limited, London, UK. She completed her MSc from the University of Manchester, UK, in 2009, before undertaking research at the Institute of Policy Studies of Sri Lanka (IPS), Colombo. Her main research areas are: aid effectiveness, international trade, climate change, mitigation and labour economics in South and South East Asia. She has co-authored articles on aid effectiveness and international trade for the IPS annual publication, *State of the Economy,* and *Trade Insight* magazine.

Michael Dickerson is currently working on his PhD at Brown University, Rhode Island, USA. He has published articles on inequality, basic education and India as an emerging donor of development assistance, while serving as a research associate and consultant at the Indian Council for Research on International Economic Relations (ICRIER), New Delhi.

Rajiv Kumar, a well-known economist and the author of several books, joined the Federation of Indian Chambers of Commerce and Industry (FICCI) as Director General in October 2010. Prior to FICCI, he was Director & Chief Executive of the Indian Council for Research on International Economic Relations (ICRIER), one of India's leading independent economic policy thinktanks. He is a non-executive member of the Central Board of Directors of the State Bank of India; a member of the G-20 Advisory Group, Ministry of Finance, Government of India; Member of India Brand Equity Foundation (IBEF) Board of Trustees; and has a seat on the Board of Directors for the United States–India Educational Foundation (USIEF). He is also a member of the Expert Committee of the National Small Savings Fund (NSSF) of the Ministry of Finance, Government of India. He was a member of the National Security Advisory Board during 2006–2008.

From 1987 to 1989, Dr Kumar taught at the Indian Institute of Foreign Trade, New Delhi, India. Subsequently, he worked for the Government of India from 1989 to 1995, first in the Bureau of Industrial Costs and Prices, Ministry of Industry, and then as Economic Adviser in the Department of Economic Affairs, Ministry of Finance. In 1995, Dr Kumar joined the Asian Development Bank (ADB) in Manila, Philippines, and assumed several positions during his 10-year term. In 2004, he returned to India to join the Confederation of Indian Industries, New Delhi, as Chief Economist.

A PhD from University of Lucknow, India, Dr Kumar also has a D.Phil. in Economics from University of Oxford, UK. His latest book, *Many Futures of India*, published in April 2011, is a compilation of his columns in some of India's leading dailies. He contributes a regular column to *Business Line*, a leading business daily. His views on matters relating to the economy are widely sought.

George Mavrotas, D.Phil. from the University of Oxford, UK, is the Chief Economist of the Global Development Network (GDN), New Delhi. He is also a Visiting Professor at Center for Studies and Research on International Development (CERDI), University of Auvergne, Clermont-Ferrand, France; a Non-Resident Associate Fellow at the Centre of Regional Integration Studies of the United Nations University (UNU-CRIS), Bruges, USA; and an Adjunct Professor of Economics in the Faculty of Economics and Business at the University of the South Pacific, Fiji. He was formerly a Senior Fellow and Project Director at the World Institute for Development Economics Research of the United Nations University (UNU-WIDER) and, prior to that, at the Economics Faculties of the Universities of Oxford and Manchester. He has published more than 120 papers in leading journals and 9 books on a broad range of development issues.

Thinley Namgyel is Chief Programme Officer at the Gross National Happiness Commission in Bhutan.

Hussain Niyaaz has a PhD from the University of Waikato, New Zealand, and an MA from The Australilan National University, Canberra, Australia. He is a demographer by training and has vast experience in the areas of population surveys and censuses, analysis of demographic data, population and development policy and teaching and supervision for tertiary students. Currently, he is involved in mobilizing external resources for the national development projects in the Maldives. In his personal capacity, he continues to be engaged in population research and teaching activities.

Bishwambher Pyakuryal is Professor of Economics at the Tribhuvan University, Nepal; a Professional Associate of the East-West Center, Hawaii; a Senior Fulbright Scholar in the United States and Scholar-in-Residence of the Rockefeller Foundation in Italy. Professor Pyakuryal was a member of Independent South Asian Commission on Poverty Alleviation (ISACPA). He has been on the Management Committee of South Asian Network for Development and Environmental Economics (SANDEE), Kathmandu, Nepal. Professor Pyakuryal is the President of Nepal Economic Association. He is also a member of the Policy Analysis and Advisory Network for South Asia (PAANSA), of the International Food Policy Research Institute (IFPRI), Washington, D.C., USA. Professor Pyakuryal has been on various missions in Bangladesh, India, Nepal, Pakistan and Sri Lanka as Chairman of

South Asia Regional Programme Committee of the International Planned Parenthood Federation (IPPF), London, UK, and has worked as a consultant and resource person for several international organizations.

Selim Raihan is Associate Professor in the Department of Economics at University of Dhaka, Bangladesh. He holds a PhD from the University of Manchester, UK, and his research has focused on international trade, macroeconomic policies and poverty. Some of his recently published books are: *Trade Development Poverty Linkages: Experiences from Selected Asian and Sub-Saharan African Countries—Vol. I and II* (2008); *Domestic Preparedness for Services Trade Liberalization: Are South Asian Countries Prepared for Further Liberalization?* (2008); *Dynamics of Trade Liberalization in Bangladesh: Analyses of Policies and Practices* (2007); *WTO and Regional Trade Negotiations Outcomes: Potential Implications on Bangladesh* (2007); *Trade and Industrial Policy Environment in Bangladesh* (2007) and *Export Diversification for Human Development in the Post-ATC Era* (2007). Dr Raihan has collaborated with several organizations including ADB, UNDP, World Bank, IFPRI, DFID, Commonwealth Secretariat, ILO, IDRC and CUTS International.

Surabhi Tandon graduated in 2009, with an MSc in Development Studies, from the London School of Economics, UK, where she also received the Rajiv Gandhi Scholarship for her Master's thesis. In 2009, Surabhi worked as a consultant with the Indian Council for Research on International Economic Relations (ICRIER), New Delhi, India, where she co-authored a paper with Dr Rajiv Kumar, the then Director of ICRIER and Michael Dickerson. They also presented their paper at the high-level forum in Bogota, Columbia, organized by the OECD on South–South Cooperation in Aid-Effectiveness. Since early 2010, Surabhi has been working with the Global Development Network (GDN), New Delhi, as a Research Associate. Surabhi also has a BA Honours (distinction) in History from Lady Shri Ram College, University of Delhi, New Delhi.

Muhammad Abdul Wahab is currently working as an Economist with the Planning Commission of Pakistan. He has also worked as an economic and financial analyst for National Highway Authority (NHA), Long Term Engineering Pvt Ltd (LTE), National Logistic Cell (NLC) and Wi-tribe, all in Pakistan. He has published in areas such as aid policy, human resource development and small and medium enterprises.

Index